LEWIS & CLARK

THE·JOURNEY·WEST

LEWIS & CLARK

THE·JOURNEY·WEST

by ALBERT and JANE SALISBURY

Drawings by CARTER LUCAS

PROMONTORY PRESS

New York

Published in 1993 by

Promontory Press
A division of Budget Book Service, Inc.
386 Park Avenue South
New York, NY 10016

Promontory Press is a registered trademark of
Budget Book Service, Inc.

Published by arrangement with Howell North-Darwin-Superior.

Library of Congress Catalog Card Number: 90-60115
ISBN: 0-88394-080-9 *30167414* *3/04*

Printed in the United States of America.

To those Young Travelers of Old Trails
BERT, LIL and JOE SALISBURY

FOREWORD

THE LEWIS AND CLARK EXPEDITION was a live and real experience to me when I was a small boy in Montana. Then as now there were a few men and women who studied each detail of the great adventure, who pondered over the location of the expedition's campsites, and who loved to tell of the journey as much as I loved to listen.

It was surprising to me, when I grew up, to find that many people knew very little about this first venture into the unknown west. It is for these readers, who wish a full rounded story of the Lewis and Clark Expedition, that we have written LEWIS AND CLARK: *The Journey West.*

We hope that our research in locating Lewis and Clark landmarks, the maps we prepared and the directions we give on how to reach the spots will be of use to future students, and that the photographs of these places will be helpful and interesting to present-day historians. But our text, although accurate throughout, is intended to present the expedition as a moving story rather than the finely-detailed study which would interest the deep student.

The person wishing to go into the almost endless minutiae of the Lewis and Clark journey will find source books in most libraries. These books are out of print although they can occasionally be found in used-book stores, at a high price. They were our reference material: *"Original Journals of the Lewis and Clark Expedition,"* edited by Reuben Gold Thwaites; *"The Journals of Lewis and Ordway,"* edited by Milo M. Quaiffe; *"The Trail of Lewis and Clark,"* by Olin D. Wheeler; *"The Expedition of Lewis and Clark"* and *"Gass's Journal"* edited by James Hosmer; and Elliott Coues' *"History of the Expedition Under the Command of Lewis and Clark."* A fine, detailed biography of the two captains, *"Lewis and Clark, Partners in Discovery,"* by John Bakeless, was first printed in 1947 and is available in most bookstores.

We have quoted freely not only from the journals of Lewis and Clark, but from those of Floyd, Whitehouse, Ordway and Gass. These quotations are from the sourcebooks mentioned above although they are not so indicated. We have made no attempt to footnote the book. The layman doesn't care from what books the quotations were obtained as long as they are authentic. And the student usually prefers to use original sources.

Our plan to take the reader on a tour, either actual or imaginary, of the Lewis and Clark trail presented various problems. What were we going to call the men of the expedition? There is so much confusion on the spelling of their names that we had to arbitrarily make a choice. We adopted the spelling as used by Hosmer, except in the case of Warvington, which is written as it appears on the government list of personnel, and Charbonneau and Sacajawea, which are written according to popular usage. Clark's commission was that of lieutenant, but we call him Captain Clark because Lewis and the others of the expedition did so, and because even President Jefferson did not know that Clark had not been given the requested captain's commission.

We have used the modern geographical names rather than those which Lewis and Clark gave to rivers, valleys and mountains, to make it easier for the reader to place himself throughout the story.

There seem to be many conceptions of Sacajawea. Some think of her as a glamorous Indian princess who led Lewis and Clark to the Pacific. We decided we must present her as the captains did in their journals — the wife of Charbonneau, permitted to accompany the explorers because she might be helpful when they contacted her people, the Shoshones.

Every stream, rock and old tree on the route is a Lewis and Clark landmark. When photographing the trail we sometimes selected interesting scenes described in the journals rather than known campsites. These places, which we feel carry more of the flavor of the expedition than would a constant repetition of campsites, are indicated on the maps.

Most of the photographs were taken with a Super Ikonta B. The journals describe in great detail the wild life of the west. We have substituted for these descriptions pictures of the animals. Good wild animal photographs are difficult to get. In several places we have used pictures taken by others, which are listed in the acknowledgments. Instead of the descriptions of Indian tools and weapons which are so plentiful in the journals, we have run pictures of the artifacts we unearthed along the trail.

Jane has written of our own experiences when we covered the trail from St. Louis to the Pacific, in a section following each chapter. In almost every area there is at least one enthusiastic Lewis-and-Clarkite. These people were most helpful to us. Several are listed in the acknowledgements.

It is literally impossible to list all those who helped us bring this book into being. But we are grateful to them all, from Dr. George Savage, whose criticism class kept us on our toes, to Robert Freeman, M.D., who gave us the formula for Rushes Pills.

SEATTLE, WASHINGTON   ALBERT P. SALISBURY

CONTENTS

PAGE

FOREWORD ix

MAPS . . . . xv to xix

JEFFERSON'S DREAM 3

    LEWIS AND CLARK, PARTNERS 5

    WINTER OF 1803-04 AT WOOD RIVER 6

        Travelogue 13

        How to Get There 13

WOOD RIVER TO FLOYD'S CREEK 15

    PAINTING ST. CHARLES RED 18

    THE DEVIL'S RACEGROUND 20

    THE FRENCH VOYAGEURS 21

    FOURTH OF JULY ON THE MISSOURI 23

    SUMMER HEAT AND STORMS 25

    DEATH AND DESERTION 27

    THE SINKING ISLAND 34

    OUTFACING THE TETON SIOUX 38

    YORK A CELEBRITY 40

        Travelogue 43

        How to Get There 46

FORT MANDAN TO YELLOWSTONE 47

    INTO THE UNKNOWN 55

        Travelogue 57

        How to Get There 58

PAGE

YELLOWSTONE TO GREAT FALLS 59

    MISADVENTURES OF THE WHITE PIROGUE 60

    WHICH WAY? 63

    THE GREAT FALLS OF THE MISSOURI 64

    SACAJAWEA ILL 70

    NATURAL PHENOMENON AND THE PORTAGE OF GREAT FALLS 73

    THE EXPERIMENT AT WHITE BEAR CAMP 78

        Travelogue 79

        How to Get There 80

THREE FORKS TO THE GREAT DIVIDE 81

    THE WRONG RIVER 86

    FRUSTRATION 90

    SHOSHONES AND HORSES 95

    SHOSHONE INDIANS 100

    SACAJAWEA'S BROTHER 104

    CLARK ON THE LEMHI RIVER 106

    LEWIS AND PARTY TO LEMHI 108

    OLD TOBY LOSES THE TRAIL 110

        Travelogue 112

        How to Get There 114

THE BITTER ROOTS TO THE PACIFIC 115

    WEIPPE PRAIRIE 118

    CANOE BUILDING CAMP 120

    DOWN THE CLEARWATER 124

    DOWN THE SNAKE RIVER 124

PAGE

CAMP ON THE COLUMBIA RIVER 127

DOWN THE COLUMBIA 129

THE STORMY PACIFIC OCEAN 133

    Travelogue 137

    How to Get There 140

WINTER ON THE PACIFIC OCEAN 141

    Travelogue 153

    How to Get There 154

PACIFIC TO THE BITTER ROOT VALLEY 155

    OVER THE CASCADES 158

    OVERLAND TO THE CLEARWATER 162

    PRACTICING AT MEDICINE 165

    A MONTH'S DELAY 166

    FIRST ATTEMPT TO CROSS LOLO 170

    UP AND OVER LOLO PASS 172

    PLAN MADE AT TRAVELERS REST 174

        Travelogue 176

        How to Get There 177

CLARK'S RETURN TO THREE FORKS 179

    THE GALLATIN VALLEY 183

    DOWN THE YELLOWSTONE 185

    TANDEM CANOES 187

    WHERE IS LEWIS? 188

        Travelogue 190

        How to Get There 192

LEWIS TO THE MOUTH OF THE YELLOWSTONE 193

    THE CACHE REOPENED 195

    LEWIS UP MARIAS RIVER 197

    LEWIS'S FIGHT WITH THE BLACKFOOT INDIANS 199

    LEWIS'S FLIGHT FROM THE BLACKFEET 202

    LEWIS GETS SHOT 203

DOWN THE MISSOURI TO ST. LOUIS 205

    DOWN THE MISSOURI 209

    THEY MEET THE YANKTON SIOUX 213

    NEWS OF THE WORLD 213

    THE LAST LONG MILES 216

ACKNOWLEDGMENTS 231

INDEX 233

MAPS OF THE LEWIS AND CLARK TRAIL

Eₐᴄʜ of the maps on the following pages covers a section of about 500 miles of the Lewis and Clark trail. Campsites or landmarks are indicated as Clark indicated them on his maps with a dot, a flag and the date. Most of the course was in the river. Where it was not, it is indicated by dotted lines, dot and dash lines, or dashes. Modern highways paralleling the route are shown with heavy black lines. The northwestern states covered by the route, shown below, are blocked off in sections numbered to correspond with the detail maps which follow.

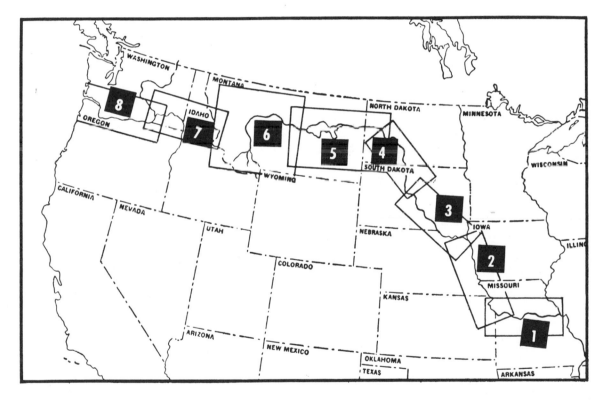

KEY TO MAPS
Route of Lewis and Clark showing area covered by detail maps 1 to 8.

THE LEWIS AND CLARK TRAIL

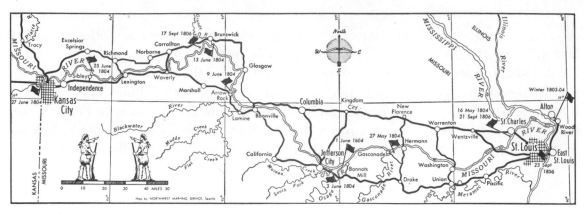

MAP 1. St. Louis to Kansas City, Missouri. The course May 21 to June 27, 1804, on the way west; and September 15 to September 23, 1806, on the return.

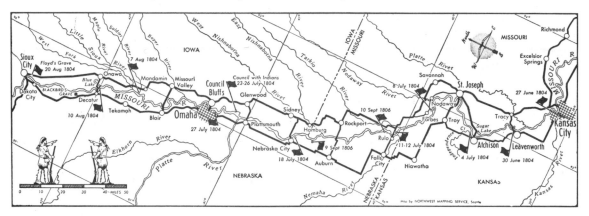

MAP 2. Kansas City, Missouri, to Sioux City, Iowa. The course June 27 to August 20, 1804, on the way west; and September 4 to September 5, 1806, on the return.

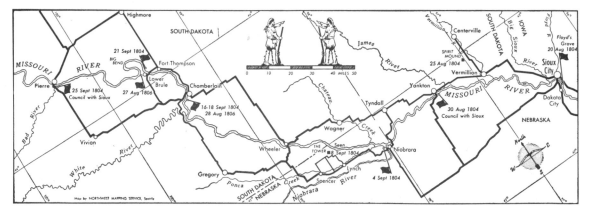

MAP 3. Sioux City, Iowa, to Pierre, South Dakota. The course August 20 to September 25, 1804, on the way west; and August 26 to September 4, 1806, on the return.

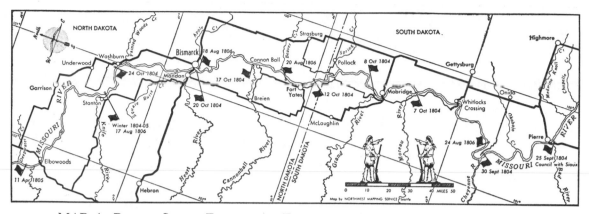

MAP 4. PIERRE, SOUTH DAKOTA, TO ELBOWOODS, NORTH DAKOTA. The course September 25, 1804 — including the winter camp at Fort Mandan — to April 11, 1805, on the way west; and August 13 to August 26, 1806, on the return.

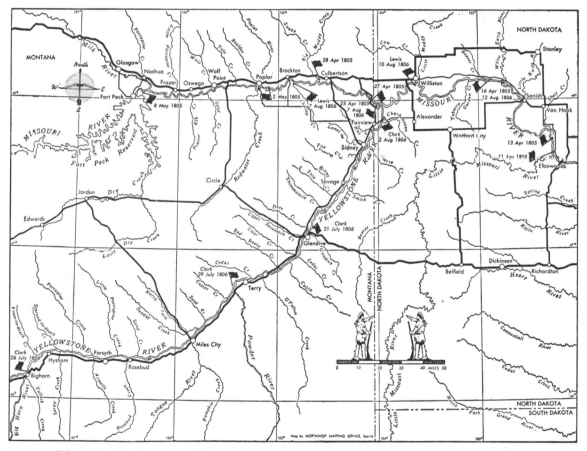

MAP 5. ELBOWOODS, NORTH DAKOTA, TO FORT PECK, MONTANA. The course April 11 to May 8, 1805, on the way west; and Clark's route down the Yellowstone July 26 to August 7, 1806, on the return.

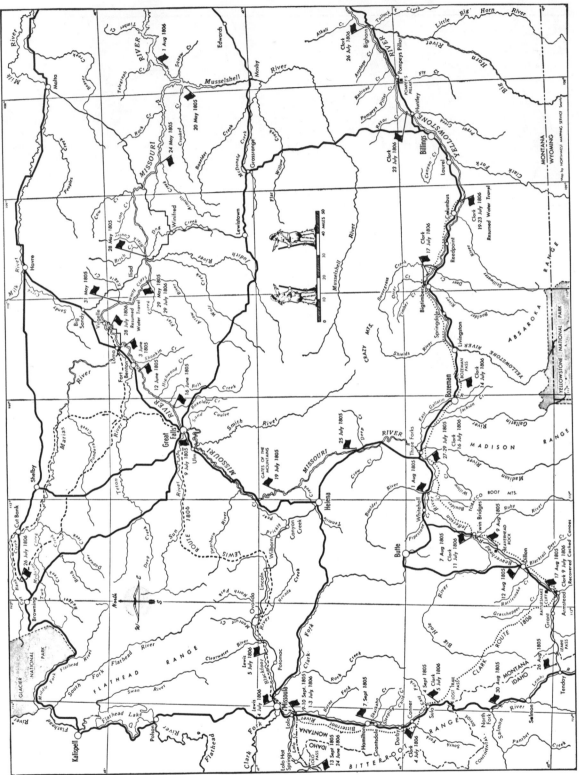

MAP 6. CENTRAL AND WESTERN MONTANA. The course May 8 to September 10, 1805, on the way west; and Clark's return (dotted line) in 1806, and Lewis's return (broken line) in 1806.

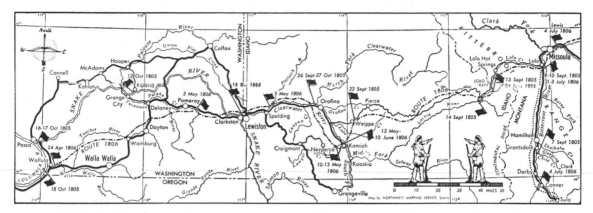

MAP 7. MISSOULA, MONTANA, TO PASCO, WASHINGTON. The course September 10 to October 18, 1805, on the way west; and April 24 to July 4, 1806, on the return, showing overland route from Wallula, Washington, to Lewiston, Idaho.

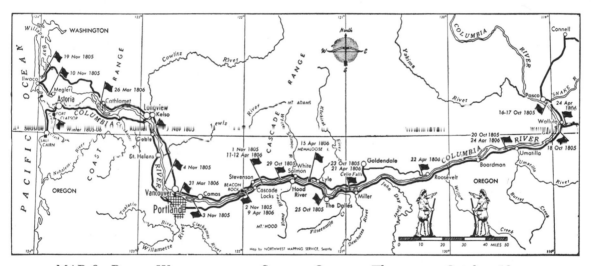

MAP 8. PASCO, WASHINGTON, TO SEASIDE, OREGON. The course October 18 to November 19, 1805, on the way west; the winter camp at Fort Clatsop; and March 23 to April 24, 1806, on the return.

LEWIS & CLARK

THE·JOURNEY·WEST

JEFFERSON'S DREAM

For two centuries men had dreamed of probing into the mysterious lands beyond the Mississippi. Baron La Hontan, a seventeenth-century adventurer, traveled the west extensively. Because his imagination at times traveled faster and farther than his feet, little credence was placed in the records of his journeys. His story of a trip in 1688 up a "long river" appears to be a tall tale but there is one part which interests historians.

He met Indians, he said, who showed him a deerskin map revealing a river behind a mighty range of mountains. The river emptied into a great salt lake near which lived Indians who wore pointed hats. It is the first suggestion of the Rocky Mountains, and the coast Indians of the Pacific Northwest did wear pointed hats.

In the 1740's an old Indian who hung around Fort Factory, a British trading post on the Great Lakes, told of a war party he joined in his youth. Once they fought a tribe of people with flat heads. The warriors reached the coast and saw "a large black fish spouting up water." Some of the coastal Indians flattened their heads, and certainly the "large black fish" could be nothing but a whale.

When Indian Moncacht-Ape claimed he had journeyed up "Long River" and crossed the Shining Mountains to the "Great River of the West," early map makers included the river as he described it.

Energetic and able Thomas Jefferson as early as 1782 was concerned about British exploration in the West. British traders and trappers had explored the upper Missouri and established trade with the Indians of this region. Americans had other things to think about in those days of the Revolutionary War, and the west seemed remote and obscure. Jefferson persisted, however, and in 1783 he wrote George Rogers Clark to interest him in a plan to prevent British exploration toward California.

In 1786 Jefferson engaged John Ledyard, a Connecticut adventurer who had been to the Pacific with Captain Cook, to cross Russia, enter North America by way of Alaska, and explore eastward across the continent. Ledyard enthusiastically conditioned himself by walking from Stockholm, Sweden, to St. Petersburg, Russia, in the dead of winter. He made the 1400 miles in seven weeks.

Queen Catherine of Russia let him go as far as Irkutsk, Siberia. She began wondering about this man from the young democracy. Would he corrupt her imperialism in Russian Alaska? Protesting her concern that the journey might be too hard on him, she had him escorted " in a closed carriage traveling day and night" back to Poland, warning him not to enter Russia again.

In 1790 under the secret sponsorship of the young United States Army, Captain John Armstrong, entirely alone, went up the "Great River of the North" for some distance above St. Louis.

But to the British went the honor of having the first white man to cross the continent north of Mexico. In October, 1792, Alexander Mackenzie left Fort Chipewyan in Northern Alberta, Canada, with several voyageurs in a 25-foot birch-bark canoe. Making their way up the Peace River to the forks, they then went up the Parsnip and overland to the headwaters of the Fraser.

Harried by Indians and battered by the treacherous Fraser River current the voyageurs became so discouraged they sat on the riverbank and wept in despair. Mackenzie prodded them on. They portaged to the Bella Coola River, borrowed canoes from the Indians and took to the water again. When they reached salt water the little party explored Dean Channel, about 100 miles north of Vancouver Island. The Indians became increasingly unfriendly. Mackenzie inscribed his name and the date — July 22, 1793 — on a ledge of rock and turned back. It was a month before he and his voyageurs reached the fort.

The tireless Jefferson, backed by the American Philosophical Society, tried to get Andre Michaux, a French botanist, to make a trip to the Pacific Coast in 1793. The plan failed when it was learned Michaux was a French spy attempting to stir

4

up trouble between the Americans and Spaniards. President George Washington recalled him after he had started.

When Jefferson became President of the United States in 1801 he found himself in a better position to promote his plan. If the Louisiana Purchase fell through, the British probably would claim all the territory north of the Missouri and Columbia rivers, and perhaps some in the south. Thanks to Captain Robert Gray's exploration by sea, during which he discovered the Columbia, America had some claim to this land.

In a secret message to Congress, Jefferson recommended that a move be made to establish trade with the Indians and encourage the natives to raise livestock, engage in agriculture and manufacturing, and better their mode of living. With a straight face he pointed out that ". . . other civilized nations have encountered great expense to enlarge the boundary of knowledge by undertaking voyages of discovery and for other literary purposes." Not much impressed, Congress voted an appropriation of $2,500 to execute the President's scheme for an expedition to the Pacific Ocean.

At last his twenty-year dream could be made a reality. Jefferson wasted no time. He appointed a young army officer who was his private secretary to lead the expedition: Captain Meriwether Lewis.

LEWIS AND CLARK, PARTNERS

THE LIGHT-HAIRED, blue-eyed, rather tall Lewis may have been somewhat less than the ideal secretary for the President of the United States. His grammar was very dubious, his spelling poor and his manners, although polite, stiff and awkward. But the President knew he possessed courage, wisdom and good health and habits, besides having a sound knowledge of botany, mineralogy and astronomy. This observing and thorough man, Jefferson believed, was the ideal leader to fulfill his dream of a westward expedition.

Jefferson wisely let Lewis select his own companion for the trip. The captain's thoughts immediately turned to Lieutenant William Clark, the flame-thatched young officer he had known when serving in the Indian wars under General Anthony Wayne. Clark had learned woodcraft and Indian lore from his older brother, Revolutionary War General George Rogers Clark. While doing frontier soldiering under General Wayne, he learned to draw. Lewis remembered that Clark had illustrated his own intelligence reports to Wayne, and that he was an accurate map maker.

Lewis knew his man well. He was a respected friend whose disposition would not clash with his own. Clark was 33 years old, four years older than Lewis, and had held a higher rank in the Indian wars.

Writing Clark of the plan for an expedition to the Pacific coast by way of the Missouri and Columbia rivers, Lewis coaxed, "If therefore there is anything . . . in this enterprise which would induce you to participate with me in its fatigues, its

5

dangers and its honors, believe me there is no man on earth with whom I should feel equal pleasure in sharing them as with yourself."

President Jefferson had planned a second-lieutenant's commission for Lewis's companion. The captain would have none of that. He insisted Clark share his command with equal rank. ". . . he will grant you a captains commission," Lewis wrote Clark, "which will entitle you to the pay and emoluments attached to that office . . . your situation if joined with me in this mission will in all respects be precisely such as my own." A captain's pay was $60.00 a month.

"I will cheerfully join you," Clark immediately answered, "in an 'official character' as mentioned in your letter and partake of all the Dangers Difficulties & fatigues . . . This is an imense undertaking fraited with numerous dificulties but my friend I can assure you that no man lives with whom I would prefer to undertake and share the Dificulties of such a trip than yourself . . My friend I join you with my hand and Heart."

The Commander in Chief of the army requested the captain's commission for Clark. Although there were only 700 men in the army in 1803, it had its usual quota of petty sticklers for the rules. The manual permitted only a second-lieutenant's commission for Clark. That was the way it was sent through.

The mortified Lewis knew time did not permit a change. "You will observe," he wrote Clark, "that the grade has no effect on the compensation which by G-d shall be equal to my own."

"My feelings on this occasion," Clark remarked dryly, "was as might be expected."

The lower rank was kept secret from the men of the expedition and even from President Jefferson. Clark swallowed his disappointment and Lewis soon made good his promise of sharing everything, including the honor, with his partner.

Meanwhile the President's appetite for territorial expansion was whetted when the size of the United States was doubled by the signing of the Louisiana Purchase. Preparations for the expedition progressed rapidly.

Yet the ostensible purposes of the expedition were to study the lives and customs of the Indians; to make observations about the animals, climate, soil and general geography; and to explore the upper Missouri, past its headwaters, and on to the Pacific Ocean. In a letter to a Spanish commandant whom Lewis was to visit, Jefferson said, "His journey being purely literary . . . for an object as innocent and useful as this I am sure you will not be scrupulous as to the authorities on which this journey is undertaken."

WINTER OF 1803-04 AT WOOD RIVER

SPRING AND EARLY SUMMER of 1803 found Lewis traveling back and forth between Philadelphia, Lancaster and Harpers Ferry to pick up arms, ammunition, medical supplies and scientific instruments and also trade goods for the Indians. The captain had the idea that an iron boat frame which could be put

SITE OF THE TAYON HOME IN OLD ST. LOUIS. Here Charles Tayon entertained Meriwether Lewis on several occasions during Lewis's stay in St. Louis while the expedition was camped at River Dubois. Clark's estate where he lived and died after his trip to the Pacific is now occupied by the tall buildings in the background. The old courthouse, left background, was commenced in 1839, a few years after the expedition.

together easily and covered with bark or skins would save considerable work on the journey. At Harpers Ferry he had an iron skeleton forged, 30 feet long, 4½ feet wide and 2 feet deep. He included the dismantled frame among the supplies.

In August Meriwether Lewis, his great Newfoundland dog Scannon for which he paid $20, seven soldiers, three young men he was taking on trial and a river pilot left Pittsburgh and set off down the Ohio River in a heavily-laden keelboat. The Voyage of Discovery was officially under way.

Here and there along the river the party stopped to recruit additional men. Clark joined them at Louisville on October 26. It was easy work floating down the Ohio to its junction with the Mississippi. The weather was pleasant and the trip leisurely. Scannon amused himself and the men by jumping overboard after swimming squirrels, catching them and bringing them to his master. But going up the Mississippi called for rowing and sailing the keelboat. On November 28 Lewis, leaving Clark in charge of the boat, cut overland to St. Louis where they planned to spend the winter.

Clark and his men toiled up the river in the heavy boat, arriving at St. Louis on the rainy, windy morning of December 10.

Since St. Louis had not yet been formally transferred to the United States, Clark decided it would be wise to move up the Mississippi to Wood River, on the American side. Here they not only could avoid international complications but also could husband their meager congressional appropriation by drawing winter supplies from the U.S. War Department. They camped just opposite the mouth of the mighty Missouri River which soon would swallow them for over two years.

Lewis, staying in town to learn all he could about the country they were to explore, found no one knew much about the west. Information was not the only attraction in St. Louis. The tall, handsome young captain-adventurer was popular with the ladies, so he found reasons to spend much of the winter of 1803-04 in the village.

On March 8, 1804, a few soldiers of Lewis's own regiment, the First U.S. Infantry, under the command of Lieutenant Stephen Worrell crossed the Missouri and marched to Government House in St. Louis. Meriwether Lewis was with them and watched the formal transfer of upper Louisiana to the United States.

Meanwhile Clark, having established the winter camp at Wood River, began to drill and condition the men. Trained in the stern military school of Mad Anthony Wayne, Clark at times literally whipped them into shape.

The group that Clark called the "robust helthy hardy young men" were selected by the captains for their strong physiques, courage and special skills. The oldest probably was Clark himself at 33; the youngest, George Shannon, a boy of 17. The privates pay was $5.00 per month; the sergeants got $8.00.

The partner-captains wanted no "Gentlemens Sons" for their expedition, choosing instead men whom a background of hard knocks had made resourceful and

THE OLD ROCK HOUSE. Built by Manuel Lisa in 1810, this stone building is typical of the St. Louis of Lewis and Clark's time. Near here a riverfront ceremony was held just before the Lewis and Clark expedition set out.

SITE OF SPANISH GOVERNMENT HOUSE, ST. LOUIS. Down this street the troops of the Spanish king paraded on May 10, 1804, when the territory of upper Louisiana was transferred to France. The transfer from France to the United States took place the next day. Lewis was an official witness to the ceremony.

"A LEAVEL RICH BOTTOM," Clark said. "The lands are generally fine . . . and well calculated for farming." There is good farm land farther back from the river, but the river bottoms overrun annually by floods and torn up occasionally by tornadoes as shown here are not good farm land.

"WINTERED AT THE ENTERANCE OF A SMALL RIVER opposit the Mouth of the Missouri," Clark said. This spot at Wood River, Illinois, was the site of Lewis and Clark's camp the winter of 1803-04.

enterprising. Lewis and Clark were searching for tough men, not submissive lackeys. Clark, the drillmaster, knew he would soon teach them all they needed to know of discipline. If a man had a talent such as blacksmithing, carpentry or gunsmithing it was a special point in his favor. He had to be unmarried.

It was a wild and rough bunch at first, giving Top Sergeant Ordway plenty of trouble. Whiskey was barred from the camp except for the "legal ration" which sometimes was supplemented by an extra gill for special duty. To Lewis's disgust the men used "hunting or some other business as a pretext to cover their design of visiting a neighboring whiskey shop."

The captains dealt out discipline like stern, determined parents. When Reuben Fields was insubordinate he was publicly reprimanded on the parade grounds. Colter, Boleye, Wiser and Robertson were refused permission to leave camp for 10 days for being absent without leave.

By the first of April the men, although still a bit unruly, had been trained and drilled until the Corps of Discovery had taken on a semblance of a military group. In the first squad under Sergeant Nathaniel Pryor were George Gibson, Thomas P. Howard, Joseph Whitehouse, George Shannon, John Shields, John Collins, Peter Wiser and Hugh Hall. Sergeant Charles Floyd led the second squad consisting of Hugh McNeal, Patrick Gass, Reuben Fields, Joseph Fields, John B. Thompson, Richard Windsor, Richard Warvington and Robert Frazier. Sergeant John Ordway's third squad comprised William Bratton, John Colter, Alexander Willard, William Werner, Silas Goodrich, John Potts, John Robertson and John Boleye.

In addition there were George Drewyer, the interpreter; Moses B. Reed and John Newman, unattached; Clark's negro slave, the giant York; 12 boatmen; and Lewis's dog, Scannon, the best behaved of the lot.

MULE DEER. These deer, much larger than the Whitetailed Deer of Eastern United States and the Columbian Blacktails of the Pacific Coast greatly impressed the captains. They sent specimens of hide and horns to Jefferson.

TRAVELOGUE . . . When we went to St. Louis to start our journey along the Lewis and Clark trail, we were equipped with the Lewis and Clark journals, three children and two cameras. The children — Bert, 14, Lillian, 10 and Joe, 2 — belong to both of us. The cameras — a Super Ikonta B and an Argus C3 — are Al's and Al's alone. Was a time when the Argus belonged to me. Al bought it as a Christmas gift, then couldn't stand to see me botching up pictures with it. By some neat, forgotten *coup d'etat* it suddenly became his.

Walking along the cobblestone street just east of St. Louis' business district it was easy to reconstruct mentally the village as it was when the expedition set out. In those days it was a little fur-trading post on the banks of the Mississippi, just a few miles below its junction with the Missouri.

Manuel Lisa's rock house — the oldest building in St. Louis — is in this section. When Al started to get a picture of it several men were sleeping off a bad night. They didn't add to the historic quality of the place and Al kept wishing they'd go quietly. Although one wanted his picture taken "just to remind me how I look when I'm drunk," and another stood in front of the camera combing his hair as a prelude to asking for a dime, Al finally got views of the building from all sides.

Surely LaClede, who with the two Chouteau brothers founded what was then called LaClede's village, would be surprised to see this modern city of nearly a million people. The little old section nestles down by the river with great buildings pressing toward it from all sides. Here Old Cathedral stands on the site of the first church built in St. Louis in 1764. Along the cobblestone streets are signs indicating where historic homes and buildings once stood. At the corner of Walnut and Main, Lewis participated in the Louisiana Purchase ceremony, whereby the United States took over 1,172,000 square miles of territory. After the expedition, Clark lived and died here in a house where the Chamber of Commerce building now stands. He is buried in huge Bellefontaine Cemetery.

We could have spent a month in St. Louis, with its fascinating historic spots, its fabulous zoo, its crammed-tight shopping section and sprawling leisurely outskirts, but after all we were on an expedition.

One of Al's favorite projects was to get a picture of the meeting of the two mighty rivers the Mississippi and the Missouri. After crossing the Chain of Rocks bridge we drove along merrily until we came to the turn-off. Here the road toward the Mississippi seemed to be made of bacon grease. Great clouds of mosquitoes roared their welcome as we slid along the ruts in the clay. We finally parked and walked the last quarter mile. With each step a little spray of tiny frogs swished out from under our feet. Bert and Al went ahead to catch the sunlight, leaving Lil and Joe and me to skid along the best we could. Lil kept pleading, "Don't step on the frogs, mother, don't step on the frogs." "Frogs!" I yelped back, "Right now I FEEL like stepping on frogs." We all got our view of the mouth of that great river that challenged Lewis and Clark. As we drove away I said, "That is a tremendous sight. Too bad there's a conspiracy to keep people away from it." "Yeah," Al answered, "there oughta be a road."

We drove on to Wood River, Illinois, wanting to stand right on the spot where the expedition spent the winter of 1804. Wood River now has a large Standard Oil refinery. Within a half mile of the campsite there is a gate and a watchman. "You have to have a permit," he said. "But this is where Lewis and Clark spent the winter. We just want to mosey around a little." "Permit," he said, indicating the office building where we might get one. No one was in the building. We growled and stood across the river where Al could look at and photograph, if not stand on, the River Dubois campsite.

HOW TO GET THERE NOW . . . See map 1.

RIVER DUBOIS CAMP — WINTER 1803-04. From St. Louis take U.S. Highway north to Chain of Rocks bridge. Cross bridge. At St. Thomas junction turn north on Highway alternate 67 to the town of Wood River. Turn left (west) just before the highway turns right past the railroad depot.

Go .8 mile on gravel road to an oak tree on levee. Leave car and walk over levee about .3 mile to the old channel of Wood River. The River Dubois camp was on the point of land between Wood River and the Missouri.

JUNCTION OF THE MISSOURI AND MISSISSIPPI. From St. Louis take U.S. Highway 66 north to Chain of Rocks bridge. Cross bridge. At St. Thomas junction turn north on U.S. alternate 67, 3.2 miles to where highway crosses canal. Take gravel road on north bank of canal, going west. Be sure to take the lower road, not the one on the dike. It is 1 mile to river. The road is narrow, rough, impassable when wet.

14

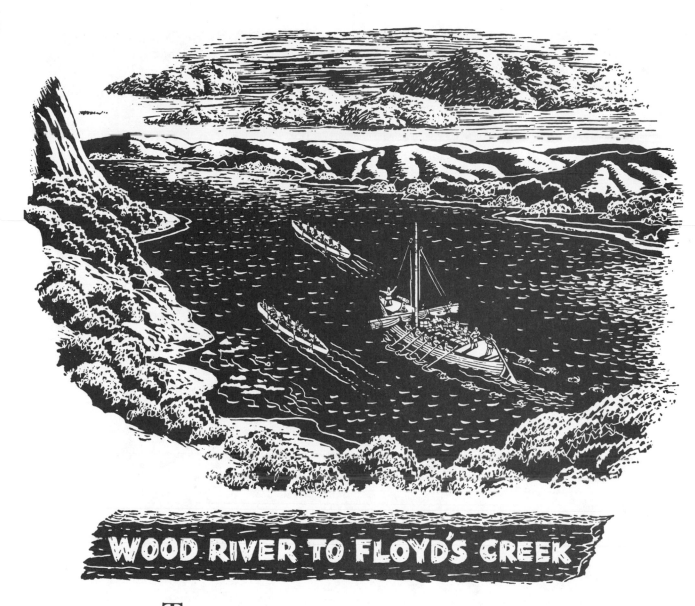

WOOD RIVER TO FLOYD'S CREEK

THERE WERE BOATS to be built, supplies to be packed — and probably many quick trips were made to town by youths who wondered if they really would be back in two years.

Little, barrel-chested Patrick Gass, the carpenter-soldier, showed them how to build a 55-foot keel boat. Under his direction the husky young men soon had their boat complete with square sail, 10-foot decks at bow and stern, 22 oars and a cabin. Lockers built in the middle could be adjusted to make a breast-work if the boat were attacked.

They needed pirogues, too: boats with a light draft which could carry heavy loads of men and cargo. The huge, skilled hands of Gass made two, one of six oars and the other seven. These craft, 40 to 50 feet long and 12 feet wide, were pointed at both ends and had a hold between three and four feet deep. The largest was painted red and the other white.

15

"I SET OUT AT 4 O'CLOCK P.M.," Clark said on May 14, "in the presence of the neighbouring inhabitents and proceeded under a jentle brease up the Missourie." This is a view of the mouth of the Missouri from the east side of the Mississippi. The Missouri has changed its course many times during the years, and is now 4 miles south of where it was in 1804.

16

Most of the week of May 6-12 the men worked like beavers. They packed into seven bales clothing for all climates, tools, medical supplies, guns, ammunition and 12,000 pounds of food — including flour, hulled corn, parch meal, salt pork, coffee, sugar, salt, lard and whiskey. Just in case something happened to the larger bales, they put a small portion of each supply in an emergency box.

Their supplies aboard, they turned to the trade goods and presents which would be their money in dealing with the Indians. They stowed on the boats fourteen bales of richly-laced coats, medals, flags, ribbons, scalping knives, beads, tomahawks, mirrors, brilliant paints and other gadgetry "best calculated for the taste of the Indians."

Clark viewed the 43 men and the loaded boats with satisfaction. "All in health and readiness to set out. Boats and everything complete with necessary stores of provisions." Twelve of the party were boatmen who would be sent back when no longer needed.

Several of the men sent farewell messages to friends and relatives. John Ordway, who was at best only an itinerant correspondent, wrote:

Honored Parents:

> I now embrace this opportunity . . . to let you know where I am and where I am going . . . I am now on an expedition westward, with Capt Lewis and Capt Clark, who are appointed by the President of the united States to go on an Expedition thru the interior parts of North America . . . will write you next winter if I have a chance.

Yours &c

John Ordway Segt.

Lewis was still in town but Clark decided to set out anyway, thinking that there would be delays as they went along while he experimented to find the best arrangement of the loads in the boats. Lewis, he knew, could overtake them easily coming overland.

On the morning of May 14, 1804, the hunters crossed the Mississippi, picked up two horses for carrying game and started working their way along the Missouri River shore to provide meat for the expedition. At noon a few "neighboring inhabitants" gathered in the rain to watch the final preparations.

The last of the boats swung into the river current at 4 p.m. The men fired their ". . . swivel on the bow, hoisted sail and set out in high spirits for the Western Expedition," Whitehouse said.

The watching group on the drizzly shore answered with a faint "huzzah," bolstering their unenthusiastic send-off with a single rifle shot as the Lewis and Clark Expedition passed from sight up the wide channel of the Missouri River.

17

Pʟᴇɴᴛʏ ᴏғ ɢᴏssɪᴘ had been passed around in the men's bunkhouses during the winter camp at Wood River. Each had his own idea about the dangers ahead of them. "We were to pass through a country possessed of numerous powerful and warlike nations of savages of gigantic stature," Patrick Gass believed, "fierce, treacherous and cruel; and particularly hostile to white men."

As the party moved up the river to St. Charles on May 15 Clark was less inclined to worry about the "savages" ahead than about the wild young men under his command. How would they act when they had their last fling at civilization? He hoped, he told them, that each would ". . . have a true respect for their own Dignity and not make it necessary for him to leave St. Charles for a more retired situation."

As the boats of the Corps of Discovery nudged into shore a number of Indians and French Canadians flocked around, "come to see the boat &c."

Scattered along each side of a mile-long street on the north shore of the river were about 100 frame houses; back of them was a row of little hills. Most of the 450 people affectionately called their village "Peetiete Coete." Clark found that the townspeople, who had retained much of the gaiety of their native France, were poor but cordial. The men of the expedition looked around and decided it was a good place for their last fling.

Mr. Duquette who, with his charming wife, lived in "an elegent Situation on the hill Serounded by orchards & a excellent gardain," invited Clark to dinner.

The hospitable Frenchmen gave a gay ball for the members of the party. Private Whitehouse said the men "passed the evening with a great deal of Satisfaction all chearful and in good spirits." Actually they painted the town red. William Warner and Hugh Hall were absent without leave and contrary to orders. John Collins, also A.W.O.L., had a few drinks too many and behaved in an "unbecoming manner" at the ball. Returning to camp late and drunk he sounded off his opinion of the expedition's commanders to all who would listen.

On May 17 Clark selected a detail for court martial, including Reuben Fields, Richard Windsor, Joe Whitehouse and John Potts. With Sergeant Ordway presiding, court martial convened and found all three guilty. Hall and Warner were sentenced to 25 lashes on the bare back; Collins, the most serious offender, to 50 lashes. The punishment was meted out at sunset with the entire party as witnesses.

The townspeople didn't take a serious view of the men's behavior. They gave another ball on the 18th. Clark, still concerned about discipline, said, "It is not in my power to go." His stern attention to duty was rewarded when seven ladies visited him at camp during the day. Whitehouse, however, "Passed the evening verry agreeable dancing with the french ladies &c."

By Sunday, May 19, Clark had his wild bunch well enough in hand to permit them to go to a sermon "delivered by a roman Carthlick Priest." Several of the men

18

"THE VILAGE CONTAINS A CHAPPEL," said Lewis describing St. Charles, Missouri. ". . . one principal street running nearly paralell to the river, the plain on which it stands is narrow tho sufficiently elivated . . . against the annual inundations of the river . . . one hundred dwelling house and about 450 inhabitants." This view is from the south bank of the Missouri near the big bridge.

"GENERALLY SMALL and but illy constructed" was Lewis's opinion of the buildings of St. Charles. ". . . inhabitants are miserably pour illiterate and when home excessively lazy." Clark felt more kindly: "people appear Pore, polite & harmonious." Along this street the men of the expedition celebrated their last night in civilization. This building was constructed three or four years later but is typical of the period.

were interested in the church "which the french call Mass," Whitehouse commented, "and saw their way of performing &c."

When Lewis arrived on Sunday afternoon he and Clark were invited to the home of Charles Tayon, former Spanish commander at St. Charles, for their last supper in civilization.

THE DEVIL'S RACEGROUND

Aₗₜₕₒᵤᴄₕ ᴛₕₑ ₕₒₛₚᵢₜₐₗᵢₜy of St. Charles was tempting, the two captains knew it was time to get on with the expedition. They carefully looked over the canoes Monday, May 21, making minor adjustments here and there. After dining with the Duquettes again, they ordered the men to launch the boats and were off "under three cheers from the gentlemen on the bank" at 3:30 in the afternoon.

The weather, which was going to dictate to them for the next two years, gave them a hint of its authority as soon as they started. A violent wind and rain which blew up from the south forced them to camp on an island only three miles from St. Charles.

Moving on next day they came to a camp of Kickapoo Indians who traded them four deer for two quarts of whiskey. As they floated along the river small groups of settlers on the American side watched them from shore.

The men noticed a cave on the river which Sergeant Floyd said was "a noted place 120 ft long 20 feet in Depth 40 feet purpendickler on the South Side of the River high Cliftes . . ." It was a rendezvous for travelers called by French voyageurs The Tavern, where many names and figures were painted on the rocks.

Lewis put ashore to examine the 300-foot cliffs. His explorations nearly ended for good when he fell from the very top. Fortunately he was caught on a projection only 20 feet below.

The next night Clark, still working hard to weld his group of men into an efficient unit, held arms inspection in camp and found some of the guns in bad condition.

On May 24 they came to the rapids known as the Devil's Raceground. Passing them with difficulty, they found worse dalles just above. When they attempted to cross to the other side of the river they were caught on a sandbar "which is constantly moving and banking with the violence of the current."

The strong pull broke the tow rope. As the current wheeled the craft sidewise, nearly upsetting it, the men jumped overboard. They held on to the boat but it bumped on down the river as the quicksand washed out from under it. It keeled dangerously as it struck another bar. Struggling in the torrent the men fitted new tow ropes. They swam, tugged, and finally landed the boat two miles below the first sandbar. This place "I call the retragrade bend," Clark said.

Sergeant Floyd observed "nothin remarkable. Nothing ocord this day encamped on South Side."

20

On May 25 the party camped near LaCharrette, a little village of seven houses. Although most of the townspeople were poor French Canadians who traded with the Indians upriver, one citizen was a celebrity. The aging Daniel Boone, who lived in the little village on his land grant, must have felt a strong nostalgia as he watched the westward expedition swing up the river.

Two nights later they reached a willow island at the mouth of the Gasconade River. The black night was made bright with a furious thunderstorm. Next morning Clark checked the baggage. The men had been careless, and many of the articles were soaked. It took the full day to dry them. If Clark was discouraged he felt better that evening when he had arms inspection and found "all in order."

Private Whitehouse, while hunting, stopped to explore a cave. Probing underground for a hundred yards, he would have gone farther but had no light. He stayed so long at the fascinating cave that when he returned to camp he found all the boats had gone but one. Eight men had been left to search for him. It was June 2 before they overtook the main party.

On June 4 Sergeant Ordway steered the kneelboat too near shore. The mast caught in a sycamore tree and snapped. It "Broke verry Easy," said Ordway ruefully.

As they moved on, the weather was fine and the men admired the luxuriant growth of cottonwood, sycamore, hickory, black and white walnut, oak and basswood that crowded the river bank. "This is a very handsome place," approved Patrick Gass. "A rich soil and a pleasant country."

That evening the hunters brought in seven deer to their camp at the foot of a little hill on the south side of the river. A nightingale sang all through the night.

Two Frenchmen came down the river on June 5, their fur-laden pirogues lashed together to make one boat. They had been 80 leagues up the Kansas River, they told the captains, trapping and trading with the Indians for beaver pelts.

Next morning, after mending the broken mast, the expedition was off to an early start. On June 7, attracted by a curious limestone rock ashore they landed to look it over. The place was alive with rattlesnakes. They killed three before investigating the rock which was brilliant with pieces of red, white and blue flint. Indian arrowhead makers apparently had used this cliff as a source of supply for many years. Clark said the Indians had "embellished" — Lewis, being no flatterer, changed it to "cover" — the cliff with pictures.

The next day they met another party of Frenchmen coming down on two rafts. Clark noticed one raft held "furs and Pelteries" and the other was loaded "with Greece." Among the Frenchmen was old Mr. Dorion, who spoke several Indian languages. The captains persuaded him to go up the river with the Corps of Discovery "as fur as the Soux nation with a view to get some of their Chiefs to visit the President of the United S."

"A FAIR MORNING," Clark said as the expedition sailed past here. ". . . Several Small Chanels running out of the River below a Bluff & Prarie (called the Prarie of Arrows) where the river is confined within the width of 300 yds." French voyageurs called the bluff Arrow Rock Point because Indians came here to secure stone for their arrow points. The river here is viewed from the park in the town of Arrow Rock, on the south side of the Missouri.

It was beginning to be rough going. Sunken snags and shifting bars of quicksand nearly overturned the boats several times. The sails helped only when the wind was right. Most of the time the men sweat over the oars, or, where the water was swifter, towed the boats with ropes from shore.

Their spirit of adventure was further dampened by the heavy morning fogs that often delayed them, the violent downriver winds that forced them ashore at times, and the muddy drinking water of the river that gave them boils and dysentery. The work and hardship made these young men tougher but it also made them more unruly. About the only members of the party who could be counted on to do as told were Clark's servant York and Lewis's big dog, Scannon.

John Collins, on sentry duty guarding the whiskey, was seduced by Hugh Hall's suggestion that he relax his guard so Hall could steal the whiskey and they would both get drunk. Sergeant Floyd preferred charges against them. The members of the court martial, John Colter, John Newman, Patrick Gass and J. B. Thompson, with Sergeant Pryor presiding and John Potts acting as judge advocate, found the two men guilty. Hall was sentenced to 50 lashes on the bare back. Collins drew a double portion of lashes because he had been on duty. Punishment was inflicted at 3:30 p.m. as the entire company stood on parade for inspection.

Mosquitoes and ticks plagued them as they moved on through country which was "open and beautifully Diversified with hills & vallies presenting themselves to the river." Sometimes a lone wolf loped to the bank above the river and watched curiously as the men toiled upstream. There was plenty of good food. Drewyer, the hunter, brought in three bears. Turkeys, too, were a welcome change from the venison diet. The powerful York at times swam to river islands to get watercress.

Tall tales went around the campfire after the men warmed themselves with the daily whiskey ration. Drewyer related he had seen on a swampy lake a snake that made "goubleing noises like a turkey," spitefully increasing the sound when the hunter fired his gun. One of the Frenchmen nodded gravely and declared he had once seen the same thing.

The Fourth of July was ushered in by a shot from the boat's bow gun. The captains thought it was enough celebration for the moment, and kept the men moving. By noon, "the day being hot the men becom verry feeble," Clark said. The leaders allowed them to pull ashore to rest.

They were tired. The sand was blistering as they rushed over it to reach the shade. Joe Fields was bitten on the side of his foot by a snake. "Not dangerously," Patrick Gass belittled; but the foot swelled and Fields was very sick. Lewis doctored it with a poultice of gunpowder and bark.

When the intense heat subsided, the party continued. The captains commemorated the day by naming one creek they passed Fourth of July Creek and another Independence Creek.

"GOSLIN LAKE" so called by Clark because of "the great quantity of those fowl in this lake." Now called Sugar Lake, it is in Lewis and Clark Park in Missouri on the east side of the river, directly opposite Atchison, Kansas.

"EXTENSIVE VIEW," observed Clark from this place in Atchison. "the Prarie had a most butifull appearance Hills & Valies interspsd with coops of Timber gave pleasing deversity to the Senery." Joe Fields was bitten by a snake, probably a copperhead, near the point of land on the right.

Probably more heartwarming to the men was the extra gill of whiskey they had that night, when they "closed the day by a Descharge from our bow piece."

SUMMER HEAT AND STORMS

Tᴴᴇ ᴡᴇᴀᴛʜᴇʀ is verry warm . . . the Sweet pores off the men in Streams," Sergeant Ordway said on July 6. "The water was So strong," added Charles Floyd, "that we could Hardley Steem it."

The fiery rays of the sun were intensified by their reflection on the river. As the party labored along, a wolf, lying asleep on a ledge, awakened to the sound of the oars and stood up bewildered. "Capt Lewis shot at him and wounded the animal Colter likewise killed him," said Whitehouse, himself confused.

When the current grew heavier, the men started trudging along shore, pulling the boats with tow lines. The white-hot sand burned their moccasined feet. Frazier had a sunstroke. Lewis bled him and gave him nitre to revive him. Whitehouse had a narrow escape when a rattlesnake four feet long and five inches around sunk its fangs in his "leggins."

Five men were sick with violent headaches on July 8. Three days later the captains decided to let the party rest since they were only making 10 or 12 miles a day. They camped opposite the mouth of the Nemaha River. "The men is all sick," Sergeant Floyd explained. But at least Joe Fields had recovered from his snake bite.

They rested and washed and repaired their clothes during the afternoon. That night the exhausted Alexander Willard, on sentry duty, fell asleep at his post. Lewis and Clark, knowing they must persist in shaping their group into a tough fighting unit, conducted the court martial themselves. At 1 o'clock Willard was sentenced to 25 lashes on his bare back to be administered at sunset on each of four successive nights.

Arms were inspected on the evening of July 12 and found in good order.

Next day the hunters with the two horses, supplemented now by a couple of Indian horses they had picked up along the way, swam across the creek. The main party took to the oars again. The rest had done them good. They made 20 miles that day.

25

"NEAR THE BANK WHERE OLD VILLAGE STOOD," said Clark. ". . . passed Some bad sand bars." These sand bars so clogged the river that it changed its course. The old channel is viewed from the site of the second "Kanzas" village just north of Atchison, Kansas. Lewis and Clark were here on the Fourth of July. ". . . emence numbers of Deer," Clark observed, "skipping in every direction."

INDEPENDENCE CREEK, so named because Lewis and Clark camped here on Independence Day, 1804. The creek joined the river just right of the dead oak tree. The captains camped to the left of the tree and "closed the day by a Descharge from our bow piece, an extra Gill of Whiskey." The Missouri has changed its channel so that Independence Creek joins it four miles to the east.

There were some hard showers early on the morning of July 14. It cleared a bit by 7 o'clock and the expedition got under way again. At 7:30 the sky was suddenly darkened by a great black cloud. A terrible wind blew, forcing the keelboat sideways toward a sandbar. Throwing out the anchor, the men leaped overboard and shoved the boat against the wind to prevent it being smashed against the bar. The storm lasted only 40 minutes but it blew up waves which splashed two or three barrels of water into the boat. When the disturbance suddenly ceased the river almost instantly became smooth as glass. "A Dredfulle hard Storme," Floyd sagely observed.

The same day Captain Clark's notes blew cverboard. After all the confusion he was hard put to remember the things that had happened during the previous two days.

Often when there was a delay in getting started in the morning one of the captains walked ahead with several of the men. At times they joined the hunters who were constantly on shore with the horses bringing in game. Clark saw wild plums, gooseberries, summer grapes, chokecherries and hazelnuts along the river-bank. The men packed a whiskey barrel with chokecherries. Here the wild turkeys grew fat and the party often feasted on them. On the prairies above the river bottom grew lambs-quarters, a plant good to eat as greens, and cockleburrs, not good to eat and extremely annoying to Scannon. Here the hunters saw their first elk.

On the 21st the party passed the 600-yard sweep that was the mouth of the great Platte River. The two captains with six men in a pirogue explored the waters for a mile. It was swift, they found, shallow and difficult to navigate even in a pirogue.

Early the next morning the expedition set out hoping to find a place where the captains could make observations. Traveling up the Missouri about 10 miles beyond the Platte, they chose a spot on the north side just above a small willow island. The hill across the river, they noticed, was covered with timber: oak, walnut and elm.

The men cleared away the willows, pitched tents and built "boweries &c." Drewyer and Peter Cruzatte were sent to an Otoe Indian village 45 miles away to invite the chiefs to a conference. While they were gone, the remaining men worked hard erecting a flagpole to impress the natives. No sooner was the flag raised than a storm forced them to lower it. This didn't matter, because Drewyer and Cruzatte returned alone. The Indians were away hunting buffalo.

"Nothing worth relating today," said Floyd, but they "continued Hear as the Capts is not Don there Riting."

DEATH AND DESERTION

In a light shower on the morning of July 27 the men loaded the boats to take off again. By 10 o'clock they were fitting the new oars they had made during their five-day rest into place. The hunters "Swam ouer Horses over on the South Side on account of the travilen is beter," Sergeant Floyd said. They made 10 miles that day.

Again the captains hoped to contact the Otoes. A Frenchman named La Liberte was sent ahead to invite the Indians to a conference. While awaiting the Indian guests the party made a camp on the south side of the river. "I think it is the Smothest & prittyset place for a Town I ever Saw," Sergeant Ordway commented.

Several of the men had bad boils. Lancing one, Lewis drained off nearly half a pint of discharge. Most of the party felt much better after their rest. Sergeant Floyd said, "I am verry sick and has ben for sometime," adding hopefully, "but I have Recovered my helth again." One of the two Indian horses they had found along the way swallowed too much water while swimming the river and died the night of the 29th.

August 2, about sunset, the party heard riotous shooting and shouting. Six Indian chiefs and part of their tribes of Otoes and Missouris roared into camp. La Liberte had contacted them, but where was he? "Every man on his Guard & ready for anything," the captains ordered warily as they welcomed the natives.

Next day the chiefs assembled under an awning made from the main sail of the keelboat. As the men of the expedition paraded, Lewis and Clark made long speeches telling the Indians of the wishes of the government, offering advice and instructing them on how to conduct themselves. The captains then passed out medals and presents to their guests. The Indians themselves made "some verry sensable speeches," Ordway said. Lewis concluded the program with a shot from the airgun.

Although everything went well, Clark was worried about La Liberte. He had left the Indian village a day ahead of the chiefs. The captain thought he might be lost on the plains.

The party took to the river again on August 4. Moses Reed, suddenly remembering he had left his knife at the camp, turned back to search for it. When he didn't return that evening, the leaders' worries doubled: two men were missing.

By August 7 the captains grew suspicious and had Reed's luggage searched. His clothes and ammunition were gone. Reed, they decided, had deserted.

Drewyer, Reuben Fields, Bratton and Labich were dispatched to bring him back dead or alive. The main party went on, making 12 miles on the 8th, 17 miles on the 9th, and 23 miles on the 10th when helped along by a good wind.

Next day they visited the grave of Black Bird, great chief of the Mahas who had died of smallpox four years previously. His followers had buried him upright astride his horse. Covering his grave with a 12-foot mound, they had erected an eight-foot pole on top. So great had been his power that Indians still brought gifts to his grave. The captains, respecting tradition, fixed a white flag bound in red and blue on the pole.

Now they hoped to contact the Mahas. After the party made camp on a sandbar August 13, Ordway accompanied by four men went with presents to the Maha village to invite the chiefs over for a talk with the captains. The men returned the

28

SAWYERS. These snags, always a danger to the boats, were called "sawyers" by the men. Usually part of the tree trunk was submerged and caught on the bottom. The pressure of the strong current moved them up and down in the water, giving the appearance of someone sawing. Several times the boats were upset by such snags as these.

"FLOYD DIED with a great deal of composure" on the river bank just below the bluffs on the far side. "We proceeded on to the first hills on N.S. there we dug the grave on a handsome Slightly Round Knob close to the bank," said Ordway. The original "knob" was about where the bushes show at the left but the river cut it away. Floyd's remains were moved back a few rods to a higher bluff.

"WE BURIED HIM on top of the bluff ½ mile below a Small river to which we Gave his name, he was buried with the Honors of War much lamented . . . this Man at all times gave us proofs of his firmness and Determined resolution to doe Service to his countrey." The people of Sioux City erected this shaft at the highest point in a wild, beautiful park.

following day saying they had found the village burned and deserted, with a vast number of graves on the surrounding hilltops. Later an Indian told Clark a smallpox epidemic had taken a terrible toll four years before. The Indians not only burned their village but put to death their wives and children so that all could go together to a better country. Of the original 400 people in the nation only about 100 survived, and they had moved away.

Since the party searching for Moses Reed, the deserter, had not yet returned, the expedition remained in camp on the sandbar. The captains wove willows and bark into bush drag — a kind of seine. Dragging a nearby creek they caught 387 fish one day and 709 the next. Pike, bass, salmon, perch, catfish, shrimps and several unidentified varieties made a change in diet that put the men into high spirits. They danced all evening to the tune of Cruzatte's fiddle while the coyotes on the prairie barked accompaniment in the moonlight.

On the 18th Drewyer and his posse dragged the dejected Reed into camp. They had found Reed and La Liberte in the village of the Otoes, but La Liberte had escaped. The principal Otoe chiefs accompanied the posse.

Meeting the chiefs in the shade near the water, the captains talked briefly with them and gave them presents. They then proceeded to the trial of Reed. Although the deserter confessed and pleaded for mercy he was sentenced to run the gantlet four times while each man of the expedition lashed his back nine times with a ramrod. Dishonorable discharge was to follow. Cruelty was nothing new to the Otoe chiefs but they thought the punishment too severe and pleaded for Reed's pardon. When the unrelenting captains explained the gravity of the crime the chiefs stood by and watched curiously the white man's justice being meted out.

Next day Sergeant Charles Floyd suddenly became seriously ill with "Biliose Chorlick." Nothing in the captains' limited medical knowledge could help him. The alarmed men of the expedition, sober-faced, waited on him unceasingly. He steadily grew worse.

Floyd lay in the boat next morning when, under a gentle breeze, the party moved inexorably onward. He vomited feebly and his pulse steadily diminished. Sensing the end was near the captains pulled the boat to shore. On a Missouri River sandbar Sergeant Charles Floyd, a soldier of the United States, whispered to his leaders, "I am going away."

Crossing the river, his comrades reverently carried Floyd's body to the top of a bluff overlooking the Missouri. Over the grave the men erected a cedar post inscribed, "Sergt. C. Floyd died here 20th of August 1804." After adjusting the post the bareheaded men of the Corps of Discovery stood a moment in tribute. Then silently and slowly they walked down to the boats on the river. They made camp that night at the mouth of a stream, a short distance north, which they named Floyds River.

Aᴜɢᴜsᴛ 21, as the little fleet sailed up the river, a windstorm struck so violently they had to reef the sails. "The Sand blew So thick from the Sandbars that we could not see the channel . . . it filled the air before us about a mile," Ordway said. Scudding before the gale, the boats covered 20 miles of river that day.

Next day Lewis noticed a bluff that he wanted to examine for minerals. The party stopped so he could see the deposits of "Alum, copperas, cobalt, Pyrites." "Copperas and Alum is verry pisen," Clark said, but Lewis sampled both, since he was on the expedition party for scientific reasons. He became violently ill and had "to take some strong medicine to relieve himself." Clark, less delicate, said, "Capt. Lewis took a Dost of Salts."

That night in camp the men held an election. Patrick Gass was chosen to take Sergeant Floyd's place. Bratton and Gibson were runners up.

The hunters had been seeing signs of buffalo for several days. Joe Fields killed a big bull on the 23rd. "The first I ever Saw," Ordway said. "A great curiousity to me." That night the men feasted on succulent buffalo-hump roast.

The Indians had a legend about a high cone-shaped hill on the prairie north of the junction of the Vermilion and Missouri rivers. It was the home of "Deavels" that had "remarkable large heads." These creatures of human form, only 18 inches high, were very wicked and killed with their sharp arrows all who dared to approach their abode.

The captains, with nine men and the lumbering Scannon to back them, decided to investigate. Although they found no devils with sharp arrows, the oppressive heat was almost unbearable, particularly to Lewis who was still weak from the effects of the medicine he had taken the day before. Lewis sent Scannon back to camp, for the dog was suffering from the heat.

After all their labor, they found the hill was remarkable only in that it was the one hill on the plain. But from the top of the mound they saw a beautiful landscape. The plains to the north were dotted with herds of grazing buffalo as far as they could see. The Vermilion River gleamed in the sun nine miles to the south. "If all the timber which is on the Stone Creek was on 100 acres it would not be thickly timbered," Clark said dryly.

When he awoke on August 27 Clark observed the morning star was much larger than usual, but he did not muse long about it for George Shannon, who had been hunting ahead with the two horses, had not returned. Although Shields and Joe Fields were left behind to search for Shannon, the captains became more and more concerned and sent Drewyer ahead. He returned to camp without finding a trace of the 17-year-old boy or the horses. Shannon's father had been lost and had died in the wilderness. Was the boy to follow his father? Any absence worried the captains; besides, Shannon was very young.

"THE MOUND OF THE LITTLE PEOPLE." ". . . in an emence Plain a high Hill is Situated, and appears of a Conic form, and by the different nations of Indians in this quarter is Suppose to be the residence of Deavels," said Lewis. The more practical Clark noticed, "the only remarkable Charactoristic of this hill admiting it to be a natural production is that it is insulated or Seperated a considerable distance from any other, which is verry unusial in the natural order or disposition of the hills."

"EXTENDS WITHOUT INTERUPTION as far as can be seen." This view is from the top of Spirit Mound, as the people of Vermillion, South Dakota call the Mound of the Little People. The prairie, practically treeless in 1804, is dotted with trees that farmers have planted as windbreaks. "A most butiful landscape: Numerous herds of buffalow were seen feeding in various directions."

The next day Shields and Fields rejoined the main party. They had seen signs that Shannon and the horses were ahead, but they could not overtake him. The boy was not an expert hunter, so the captains sent Colter to try to reach him and give him provisions. The main party made camp on the plain to await the coming of the Sioux whom they had sent Pryor and Dorion to summon.

THE SINKING ISLAND

THE SIOUX warily pitched their camp across the river from that of the Corps of Discovery. Peering through the dissolving fogs the morning of August 30, Clark could see the painted buffalo-skin tepees of the Indians. He noticed they were "compact & handsomly arranged . . . an open part in the centre for the fire each lodge has a place for cooking detached." Each lodge, he thought, might hold 10 or 15 persons.

The men of the expedition had erected a flagstaff from which now fluttered the Stars and Stripes. Under a spreading oak tree the captains and the Sioux chiefs met. Lewis delivered his usual speech to the accompaniment of the wild singing of the younger Sioux who circled the camp.

After the speech Lewis and Clark presented medals, a cocked hat with a red feather, a richly laced red coat, a flag and small trinkets to the chiefs. Retiring to a bower of bushes made by their young men during the conference, the red leaders divided their gifts. The captains dined together to discuss further measures. Dorion was miffed because he was not invited to join them.

Later in the day about 30 of the Indians brought an orchestra across the river to celebrate the occasion. The five hideously painted musicians made what Clark called "a confusion of noises" with rawhide rattles and buffalo-skin drums. The whole group then danced about the fire, occasionally pausing while a warrior, waving his scalp-bedecked weapon, chanted of his brave deeds. Ordway was bored with the dances and songs, saying they "always began with a houp & hollow & ended with the same." Late that night when the dancing ended, the Indians "Camped along side of us & behaved honestly & cleaver &c &c."

The following day, with Dorion interpreting, the natives delivered their reply to Lewis's speech. They approved of the theory that they should be at peace with their neighbors and agreed to send someone back with Dorion to see the President. It would be a good idea, they said, if a little Milk of the Great Father were passed around. The captains took the hint and left one bottle of whiskey with Dorion, who was to stay with the Sioux.

Lewis was "agreeably dissapointed" with the Missouri River. Ordway felt the same way, saying "the Missouri river affords us pleanty of fish & country pleanty of all kinds of game." Deer, bear, elk, beaver and now buffalo were everywhere. Herds of an animal not known to science began to appear. They were antelope but the

34

"A VERRY THICK FOG THIS MORNING" but as the mist dissolved Clark could see the tepees of the Yankton Sioux across the river. This view was taken from Yankton, South Dakota, which is on the site of the Sioux encampment.

"ANTILOPE," called by Lewis and Clark goats or ibex, were unknown to science until Clark's description on September 13, 1804. "verry actively made, has only a pair of hoofs to each foot has brains on the back of its head his Norstals large his eyes like a Sheep." Of their habits, Lewis said, "If they happen accedentaly in the woodlands and are allarmed they run immediately to the plains, seeming to plaise a just confidence in their superior fleetness and bottom."

captains called them goats. The men especially enjoyed the catfish which they caught with hook and line. One day's catch of nine fish totaled over 300 pounds.

On September 1 Clark visited a peculiar formation made by the winds which he mistook for an ancient Indian fortification, and used his talent as an artist to sketch it for Thomas Jefferson.

The captains grew increasingly worried about Shannon. The black-haired, blue-eyed boy was popular and the men missed his fine voice in the songs around the campfire. Occasionally they saw his tracks, followed by those of Colter. It was apparent Colter had not as yet caught up with him.

September 7 the party camped at the foot of a round mountain now called *The Tower*. The men amused themselves by trying to flood prairie dogs from their burrows. They labored most of the day, lugging great quantities of water from the river to pour down the holes. By evening they had killed a rattlesnake, caught two frogs and, at last, a prairie dog.

Next day one of the men killed a buffalo and left his hat on it to scare away the wolves. The wolves showed their contempt for the scarewolf by eating the buffalo and added insult to injury by making off with the hat.

The party found a petrified fish 45 feet long, which interested the captains. Sergeant Gass, unimpressed, called it a "ruck of bones."

On the 11th Shannon showed up, weak and half-starved, after having been gone 16 days. He had supposed the party to be ahead of him, and had pushed on attempting to catch them. When he ran out of bullets he had nothing to eat but wild grapes and a rabbit he had killed by substituting a small stick for a musketball. Finally, worn out and hungry, he had turned back, hoping to meet a trader who would give him food.

As autumn approached the days and nights on the river became cooler. The captains issued flannel shirts to the men, and a fresh supply of powder in case of trouble with the Sioux.

On the evening of September 21 the party camped on a sandbar island in the middle of the stream. By midnight the embers of the dying campfires showed only as a faint red glow. A coyote's high-pitched barking from the moonlit hills on the north shore was answered plaintively from the south. It was chilly for the guard walking his post, but at least the cold night brought relief from mosquitoes.

The others lay sleeping in their blankets, lulled by the lap of the current against the sand. Periodically the guard heard a small splash at the upper end of the island. He investigated and found it was caused by little chunks of sand breaking off. He started to turn back, but something seemed wrong. A second look told him the island was smaller than it had been only a few minutes before. It was actually sinking into the river! The alarmed guard wakened Lewis, who was sleeping in the keelboat. With presence of mind even when aroused in the middle of the night, the captain ordered the men off the island. They hastily scrambled aboard the boats and pushed

"BARKING SQUIRIL" the captains called prairie dogs. "those little animals set erect make a Whistleing noise and whin allarmed Step into their hole. we por'd into one of the holes 5 barrels of Water without filling it."

"REATHER DOWN THE RIVER." Frequently the captains on both the outward and return trips climbed to survey the surrounding country from hill tops. A sand bar island like those shown here once collapsed into the river just after the men hastily left it.

off just as the ground under the pirogues dropped into the deep river. By the time the boats reached the opposite shore the entire island had disappeared beneath the surface. Happy that they had not vanished without a trace, the Corps of Discovery spent the rest of the night on the mainland.

OUTFACING THE TETON SIOUX

When the party reached the Big Bend of the Missouri River, Lewis sent a man to pace off the distance of the short cut overland. It was only about a mile and a quarter. The Big Bend was a 30-mile loop. Although they must have had wistful thoughts about the short cut, the heavy boats meant they must make the loop. But the expedition had come a little over 1100 miles and were not daunted by the extra miles.

Along the circle of the Big Bend they saw tracks and old encampments which they judged to be those of the Teton Sioux, a tribe they had yet to encounter.

Three Indian boys swam the river to join them in camp on the evening of September 23. The Teton encampment of 80 lodges, the boys said, was located on the next creek above. The captains gave the youths carrots of tobacco to take to the chiefs and told them to invite their leaders to hear Lewis speak.

Next day the party, moving up the river in high spirits, named an island they passed "Good Humered" Island.

The men anchored the boats offshore at the mouth of the Bad River. The captains allowed only about one-third of them to camp on shore with guards posted. The rest slept on the boats.

The next morning they put up a flagstaff and built a bower for the conference with the Sioux. Since Dorion had stayed with the Yankton Sioux, Lewis was badly handicapped by lack of a good interpreter. However, Chief Black Buffalo, Chief Partizan and Chief Beuffe de Medicine and several lesser chiefs sat down and smoked "agreeable to the useal custom." Lewis delivered his speech and the men paraded, fired the air gun, and showed the Indians the boat "and such curiosities as we thought might amuse them." Although the captains passed around gifts the Indians were difficult. They wanted whiskey and weren't pleased with the fourth of a glass the captains gave each of them when they congregated on the keelboat. They grumbled because there weren't enough presents and finally became so disagreeable that Clark took them, somewhat against their will, ashore in the pirogue. As the boat nudged into shore, three of the young braves grabbed its cable and another hugged the mast. Feigning drunkenness, Chief Partizan lurched against Clark. "His justures were of Such a personal nature . . . I felt My Self warm," said the red-haired captain.

Clark drew his sword and the Indians strung arrows to their bows. As the atmosphere became more tense Lewis, in the keelboat, ordered the men to get their guns and aimed the swivel at the Indians. Chief Buffalo, realizing the white men meant business, ordered his warriors to drop the cable of the pirogue. Its boatmen

"RAISED A FLAG STAFF & MADE A ORNING." Although there was plenty of shade on the shore the captains built a shady spot on a sandbar on the river so they might be safe from the Teton Sioux. This is the site of the council of September 24, 1804, and is just across the river from Pierre, South Dakota.

"PREPARE ALL THINGS FOR ACTION," Lewis said. Here at the mouth of the Teton River the captains cautiously anchored their boats about 70 yards offshore in the Missouri, and left the crews aboard where they remained tensely alert during the council on the sand bar.

immediately put out to the keelboat and returned with 12 well-armed and determined soldiers. Some of the Indian warriors withdrew a short distance but Clark and the chiefs stood glaring at each other. Finally Clark relieved the tension by offering his hand to the two chiefs. Each refused it, but Clark outfaced them. Hesitating a moment, the chiefs asked to be taken aboard. All they had wanted, they said, was to show the boats to their squaws. Clark agreed, and the situation eased.

The boats moved about a mile upriver and anchored off an island. Clark, his mood changed from the cheerful one of the day previous, named it "Bad humered Island."

On the 26th, with the chiefs still aboard, the party moved up to the Sioux village. After a day in council with the Indians, the party spent the evening watching the Sioux perform a macabre dance in which they displayed 65 scalps recently taken from the heads of their enemies, the Mahas, in a raid which also netted them 25 women and children prisoners.

Clark, nervous and uneasy, did not sleep well, and rose early the next morning. After breakfast Lewis and the chiefs went ashore. A Maha prisoner told one of the interpreters that the Sioux intended to prevent the expedition from going farther. Clark issued sharp orders and the men bustled to comply. The sudden activity brought 200 armed, belligerent warriors to the shore. But a chief blandly explained that they thought the Mahas were about to attack the expedition.

Although the captains posted a strong guard aboard the boats, there was no sleep that night. When the party tried to set out the next day the warriors again grabbed the cable, demanding tobacco. Lewis and Clark told the Indians they did not intend to be trifled with but finally gave them two more carrots of tobacco. The truculent Sioux let go of the rope.

When they anchored off a small sandbar up the river that night all but the cooks stayed on the boat. "I am verry unwell for want of sleep," Clark said drowsily, "Deturmined to Sleep tonight if possible."

YORK A CELEBRITY

As the party moved up river they could see great numbers of Sioux watching them from the shore and the hills above. The captains sensed that "they seemed willing to molest us" and ordered extreme vigilance as they traveled during the day and in camp at night.

On October 8 the expedition reached an island three miles long where an Arickara village was located. Captain Lewis, with two interpreters, went into the village while Clark and the others formed the camp. "A pleasant evening," Lewis contemplated, later adding "All things arranged both for Peace or war."

He brought back to camp two Frenchmen, named Gravelines and Tabeau, who were trading with the Indians. Both understood the Indian language well. The captains asked them to arrange the usual conference with the chiefs of the nation.

The Indians came and were amazed by Clark's giant servant, York. He was the first black man they had ever seen. The natives "all flocked around & examind him from top to toe," Clark said. York enjoyed the situation immensely. "He Carried on the joke himself and made himself more turribal than we wished him to doe." He told the Indians he was a wild animal Clark had captured and tamed. A horde of little boys followed him at a safe distance wherever he went. York loved it. He would turn and bare his teeth or growl and the small fry would scatter screaming, only to gather again immediately when he turned his back.

The Arickara men were generous and their wives amorous and pretty. Most of the men withstood the temptation well, but York took full advantage of his popularity. One warrior, considerate of his wife's every desire, invited York to his tepee and stood guard at the entrance. He even refused Clark the privilege of contacting his servant until a reasonable time had elapsed.

Lewis's speech was a success. The Indians promised peace with their neighbors and expressed interest in the fact that they had a great white father. But when the captains offered whiskey the chiefs were surprised that "their father would present them with liquor which would make them fools."

The soldiers had become hardened. Arms inspections now found everything in good order. The men knew what their duties were and how to do them. Discipline was generally good. But John Newman cracked and denounced the captains, the sergeants and the Corps of Discovery, loudly uttering "repeated expressions of a highly criminal and mutinous nature." Sitting in the rain on a sandbar, the court martial found him guilty, sentenced him to 75 lashes and to be discharged from the army, stripped of arms and accoutrements and assigned to the red pirogue as a common laborer.

When the lashes were administered on the evening of October 14 one of the Indian chiefs wept aloud. He felt better when the crime was explained to him but told the captains that in his nation they didn't even whip children.

The party camped near another Arickara village on the 15th. York was still the most popular of the group but Clark said "their women verry fond of carressing our men &c."

"THE COUNTREY IS FINE." This view just south of Mandan, North Dakota, overlooks the site of the abandoned Mandan village. Here the explorers saw several fresh tracks of grizzly bear "which is 3 times as large as a mans track."

"A GOOD DEEL OF WATER." The "Chiss-Che-Tar" (Heart) river at its junction with the Missouri. This photo shows how the clear waters of the contributary streams are absorbed by the muddy waters of the great Missouri. In camp just below here Clark remarked, "a verry Cold night wind hard from the N.E. Some rain in the night which frosed as it fell at Daylight it began to snow."

The leaves were falling fast and a little snow drifted down on the 23rd. Soon, the party for northwest discovery knew, they must make winter camp.

They paddled past the ruins of several old Mandan villages. By October 25 they were approaching the new Mandan camps and frequently noticed Indians "hallooing and signing" them to come to shore. The next day in one of the villages they encountered Hugh McCracken, a British Northwest Company trader who was dickering with the Indians for horses and buffalo robes.

The Indians flocked to see the white men in camp that night on the south side of the river, half a mile below the Mandan village. Lewis walked to the Indian camp to talk to the chiefs but Clark, suffering a bad attack of rheumatism in his neck, decided not to go.

On the 27th they met René Jessaume, a Frenchman who had married an Indian woman and lived with her and their children among the Mandans. He made a handy interpreter for the captains in their talks with the chiefs.

There were a number of good spots for a winter fort, the Indian leaders told them, but the timber was small and scarce. The captains began to get more concerned about where they would spend the cold months.

TRAVELOGUE . . . St. Charles, where the men of the expedition spent their last night in civilization, retains the old world touch. Here many of the buildings were constructed about the time of the Louisiana Purchase, and some of them house the same industries they did decades ago. There is still a printer in the building where, over a hundred years past, Elijah Lovejoy was nearly murdered for the abolitionist views he printed. We wanted a picture of the river, and stopped at a boat set up on blocks which someone was using as a house. A couple of cute dogs greeted us loudly and when we looked up at the boat we were a little embarrassed to see a woman regarding us nonchalantly. "Go ahead," she said, "everyone wants to take pictures from here."

Between St. Charles and Independence we had to duck down crossroads to touch the Lewis and Clark trail. They went by water and we by land and although Highway 24 parallels the river for some distance, most of the time side trips were necessary. We found historic spots all over the place in this part of the country. Here the Santa Fe and Oregon trails began. Here is Marthasville where Daniel Boone was first buried, approximately on the location of La Charette, the little town where the expedition celebrated. Sam Houston once resided at Arrow Rock Park, one of the many state parks along the way. Here is an old tavern that was run by his brother. Lewis and Clark found this country beautiful and fertile, and so we found it today. In spite of hail, lightning and tornado destruction, the over-all picture is of vast corn and wheat fields with lush groves of oak dotting the hills and valleys. It seemed peculiar, as we drove through Kansas City, to realize that the expedition camped just about where the center of the city is now.

When we neared St. Joseph, OUR Joseph (no relation) got the measles. Lewis and Clark had plenty of problems but they didn't ever have to approach a motel operator and ask if they could spend a quarantine period in one of the cabins. Mr. and Mrs. Zoettl, of Faucett, Missouri, didn't hesitate. "Why, when folks are in trouble," Mrs. Zoettl said, "you have to help them out." On the Fourth of July we heard a series of terrific explosions which dumfounded our fretful Joe into complete silence. It was Mr. Zoettl — usually a quiet man — shooting off the biggest firecrackers in the state of Missouri.

This enforced stay was handy for Al's purposes. We were near St. Joseph, which is on the Lewis and Clark trail, and we weren't too far from Atchison, Kansas. Bert and Al had plenty of time to scout around, not only looking for Lewis and Clark sites but also for old Indian campgrounds where they might find artifacts. On July 4, 1949, they stood on a high bluff in Atchison's Jackson Park, knowing that on the same day in 1804 Lewis, too, enjoyed the view of the river from here. The expedition camped that night at the mouth of Independence Creek. When Al and Bert went to Doniphan to look for the creek, old-timers told them the Missouri, which is now several miles distant across the valley, once ran in a big bend close to the town. Sixty years before, they said, steamboats moored just back of where the Doniphan gas station now stands. A large dead oak near the Independence Creek bridge probably was there at the time of the expedition. Independence Creek poured into the Missouri here as recently as 65 years ago. An old man told Bert that when he was a boy he used 54 feet of rope to make a swing from the lowest limbs. Now the branches are only 15 feet from the ground because 12 feet of the trunk is covered with silt from floods. The old channel of the river is now a lush cornfield with groves of oak indicating where the islands once were.

Once the Kansas Indians had a village on a high ridge overlooking this valley. It was abandoned long before Lewis and Clark's visit. A farmer let Al and Bert dig in his field. While curious copperhead snakes rustled in the dry grass, Al dug down about 2 feet and found, among other things, vermilion which some Indian used as war paint 200 years ago. When they came home that day the fellows were as excited about the snakes as they were about their artifacts. Copperheads, it seems, find a hiding place near you and watch, wiggling now and then to keep you on the alert.

At last Joe was spotless and we could move along north. As we approached Sioux City, Iowa, we were thrilled to see the beautiful monument on a high bluff overlooking the Missouri, where Sergeant Charles Floyd is buried. Floyd, the only man who died on the expedition, was first buried on lower ground. The banks of the river fell away leaving his remains exposed. People of Sioux City risked their lives to hang over the bank on ropes and rescue the remains. The shaft to his memory, which was erected in 1904, also commemorates the Louisiana Purchase. It made me think of a long arm pointing straight to heaven.

Near Vermilion, South Dakota, we climbed Spirit Mound, which the captains called the Mound of the Little People. Surely it would be a poor place for Little People to live; the wind nearly knocked Joe over. We remembered Lewis and Clark mentioned the heavy wind, and they also noticed the swallows which still fly about the place. Perhaps that strong howling wind is what gave the Indians the idea the hill was haunted. As we looked out over miles and miles of

44

flat country we saw clumps of trees the farmers had planted as windbreaks to convert what was once a dust bowl into good land. Lewis and Clark saw nary a tree.

There is something fascinating about driving through flat country. A little group of trees, a tiny smidgin of a hill, acquire the grandeur of Niagara. "Seattle?" a farmer exclaimed when we mentioned our beloved home town, "I was there in 1916. Too many hills. I like to be able to stand right here," he pointed south, "and see my brother-in-law's farm." We gathered the farm was miles in the hazy distance, but he could see it and he was glad he could.

As we crossed the bridge into Yankton, South Dakota, Al said, "Look at that city. When Clark peered through the lifting fog of the river he saw the lodges of the Sioux right where we see those buildings." It was easy to capture the picture and to keep it in mind. It seemed ludicrous to be looking for a motel when Clark was across the river worrying about what the Yankton Sioux were going to do.

Toward evening of the next day we came to Niobrara State Park, at the junction of the Niobrara and the Missouri. The expedition camped here and it still looked like a good idea. Little cabins, a fine lawn, a river to fish in. When we stopped to inquire a man told us the whole place was taken over by a church convention. Anyway, Al wanted to stay where the expedition stayed. "This fellow," our man said, "drove 160 miles to be at this meeting." We resisted the almost unbearable temptation to tell how far we had come, and drove off. Paradise lost.

We were beginning to learn, now, that cabins are not always easy to find. It is a good idea to start looking late in the afternoon, get established in a cabin and then scout around all you want, secure in the knowledge that you have a place to pile into bed. It is very hard to remember that. There is always the compulsion to visit just one more place, to add just 50 or 60 miles to the speedometer. How many nights we drove along as the stars and "No Vacancy" signs shone in the darkness, berating ourselves for not learning our lesson.

As Lewis and Clark travelers, we found the Lower Brule the most interesting of the many Indian Reservations in South Dakota. Here is the loop in the river which early explorers called the Grand Detour.

Near Pierre, at the junction of the Bad River with the Missouri, we strolled in the cottonwood grove where the captains held their turbulent council with the Teton Sioux. The large old trees which shielded us from the hot Dakota sun probably also shaded Lewis and Clark's men. It was here, in 1743, that Verendrye claimed the Missouri for France. In 1817 the early fur trading post of Fort Pierre was built.

As we drove through the rolling prairies of wheat and oats toward Mobridge, Al told us there are Indian campsites on nearly every high hill facing the Missouri in this area. A jolly farmer looked amused when we hinted we'd like to dig in his fields a bit. "You sure can go ahead if you want to, but there's not much there. Sometimes when I'm plowing I find broken pieces of pottery and junk like that, but nothing worthwhile." I couldn't look at Al when he said that. Broken pieces of pottery and junk like that were exactly what Al was after. We dug. Not only did we find pieces of pottery, but also a slim, delicate arrowhead. Our benefactor went down the road a way to mend fences, coming back occasionally to see how we were doing. He grinned each time Al put a chunk of pottery carefully into a sack. I'm sure he was just too polite to burst out laughing. But his curiosity was piqued, and I'll bet right now he's digging in that field.

There is a monument to "Sacacawea' near Mobridge, calling her the guide of the expedition. "The name's mispelled, Sacajawea was not here with the expedition and she wasn't the guide," Al commented, "but it's a good looking marker and a good idea." Lil piped up, "I thought Sacajawea WAS a guide." I said, "She just went along to be with her husband but actually she helped a great deal. Imagine a woman taking her baby on such a venture! Imagine the hundreds of miles of hardship. And she just went along being uncomplaining and helping when she could. What a woman." I was looking at Lil but talking to Al — a little trick I had picked up and developed after 17 years of marriage. He tends to discount Sacajawea by 40%. And perhaps I add a cubit to her stature in defense.

45

HOW TO GET THERE NOW . . . See maps 1, 2, 3 and 4.

CAMPSITE OF MAY 16-20, 1804. From St. Charles, the island is toward the south shore. It is above the bridge and can be seen from almost any point in St. Charles. The old part of St. Charles is one or two blocks toward the river from U.S. Highway 40.

ARROW ROCK. From Booneville continue west on U.S. Highway 40 about 8 miles to its junction with Missouri 41. Here turn north 12 miles to little town of Arrow Rock. Go straight through town 4 or 5 blocks to Arrow Rock Park.

GOSLIN (SUGAR) LAKE. From Atchison, Kansas, cross bridge into State of Missouri. On U.S. Highway 50, 4 miles to its junction with Missouri 45. Here turn right (south) .9 miles to gravel road turning right (west). It is one mile to Lewis and Clark Park on the lake.

INDEPENDENCE CREEK CAMPSITE, FOURTH OF JULY, 1804. From Atchison, Kansas, go north on Third Street 2 miles to just south of Deer Creek bridge — the first bridge. Here turn right on gravel road 1.9 miles to Independence Creek bridge, .8 mile south of Doniphan. The second old Kansas village was on the hill overlooking Doniphan to the north and east about .5 mile.

SERGEANT FLOYD'S GRAVE. From Sioux City, Iowa, turn left off the highway at the city limits, about 100 yards. The monument can be seen at a distance as you approach Sioux City from the south on U.S. Highway 75.

THE MOUND OF THE LITTLE PEOPLE (SPIRIT MOUND). From Vermilion, South Dakota, continue west on U.S. Highway 50. .4 mile from the city center turn right on S.D. Highway 19. At 6.2 miles turn left into a farmyard. It is a .3 mile hike to the top of the mound. Ask permission at the farm.

GRAND DETOUR OF THE MISSOURI. From Chamberlin take South Dakota Highway 47, 21 miles north to Fort Thompson. Continue north 2 miles to gravel road, turning straight west to the Missouri River.

CAMPSITE OF SEPTEMBER 24, 1804. From Pierre cross bridge going west on U.S. 14. At end of bridge turn south on U.S. 83 a few blocks to community of Fort Pierre at south end of Bad River Bridge. Turn east .4 mile to picnic grounds. The council with the Teton Sioux was held at the junction of Bad River and the Missouri where the picnic grounds now stand.

COURSE FOR THE DAY. From U.S. Highway 83 on the way to Mobridge, turn left at its junction with U.S. 212. Travel 11 miles to Whitlock's Crossing. Go to bluff on west side of the Missouri for a fine view of the route traveled.

COUNCIL WITH THE ARICKARAS. From Mobridge go east across the Missouri on U.S. Highway 12 to the Sacajawea monument, at junction of U.S. 12 and South Dakota 8. Turn north on gravel road 7 miles to the Grand River where the council was held.

46

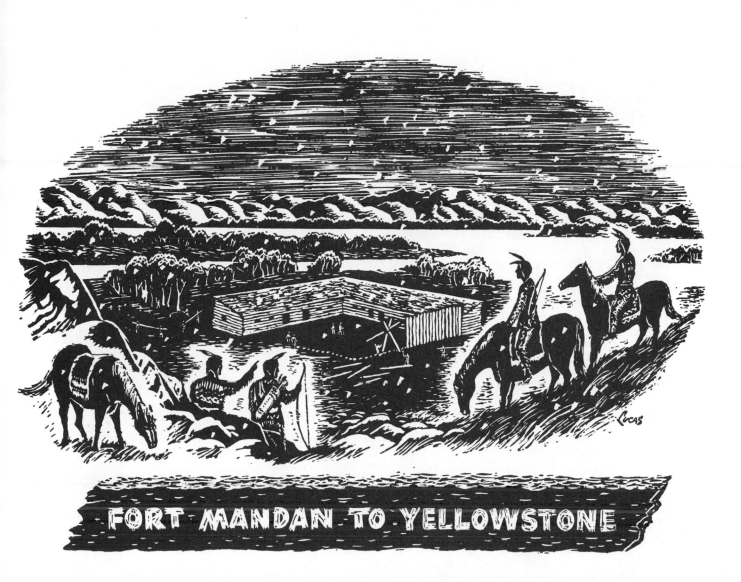

FORT MANDAN TO YELLOWSTONE

ALTHOUGH THE DAYS were bright and clear, the ground was covered with frost each morning, creeks were fringed with ice, and the cottonwood and elm were bright with autumn color. Honking wild geese flew south in great V-shaped formations, a certain sign of oncoming winter. The captains continued their search for a suitable place to build a winter encampment.

On Friday, November 2, Clark found a position on the north bank of the river, sheltered from the north winds by high rimrock. Nearby was plenty of cottonwood and elm, and some ash. The men of the expedition went to work. The ring of their axes attracted the Indians, who gathered in a curious crowd.

Their first day in camp Charbonneau, a Frenchman, came to visit them. He had been hunting up the river with the Gros Ventres and spoke their language well. Lewis and Clark engaged him as an interpreter.

One of Charbonneau's three squaws was Sacajawea, a little Shoshone woman whom the 40-year-old Frenchman had won in a gambling game with the Gros

A REBUILT MANDAN LODGE. Near Mandan, North Dakota. The village that occupied this site was in ruins when Lewis and Clark visited it because smallpox had so decimated the tribe that the survivors had merged with other camps up the river. "fallen earth," Clark said, "some teeth and bones of men & animals mixed in these villages, human skulls are scattered . . ."

INSIDE OF MANDAN LODGE. Clark describes these lodges as being "in a kind of Picket work the houses round and verry large containing several families, as also their horses which is tied on one side of the entrance." The captains found several of these deserted villages before they found one that was occupied.

Ventres. Four or five years previously she had been taken prisoner by a Gros Ventre war party when they attacked the Shoshones near the three forks of the Missouri.

Still just a girl of 17 or 18, she was pregnant when the captains first saw her. Thinking she would be useful as an interpreter when they reached Shoshone country, the captains decided Charbonneau could take her along when they resumed the trip.

It grew colder and colder. The clangorous V's of the southbound geese increased and occasional flurries of snow fell on the frozen ground. An Indian brought in a weasel which had shed its summer coat of brown and was snow-white except for a black tip on its tail.

Snow started falling steadily on November 13, and the river was choked with floating ice cakes. Sometimes the men worked until one in the morning to rush construction of the camp. They built two rows of huts or sheds forming an angle to each other. In each row were four rooms, 14 feet square. The men made floors of puncheon or split plank, covering them with grass and clay. The roofs were built shed fashion so that they would not cave in with the increasing snow. They were 18 feet high on the tall side, which faced out. Seven feet from the puncheon floor was a ceiling which formed a loft under the roof. A high picket stockade fenced off the area not enclosed by the huts.

On the 20th the party moved into the unfinished group of huts which they called Fort Mandan.

The fort was completed none too soon. On November 26 the wind shifted to the north, the mercury in their thermometers dropped and snowflakes again began sifting through the cottonwoods. At first lazily, then whipped with increasing fury by the bitter wind, the snow lashed against the fort walls, powdering through the cracks. "The weather gits colder verry fast," Ordway remarked.

The world outside the huts was blanketed with 13 inches of snow. The party of discoverers settled down, not without anxiety, to wait for spring.

The Indians, who had been almost constant bystanders watching the construction of the fort, started bringing food. They piled this welcome addition to the larder on their squaws and paraded into camp. Clark was surprised when Chief She-he-ke brought about 100 pounds of fine meat loaded on the back of his squaw who was also carrying her baby.

The native women were not only beasts of burden. Sergeant Gass hinted "there were plenty entertaining stories and pleasant anecdotes" which he considered not "prudent to tell." But he "observed generally that chastity is not highly esteemed" and "an old bawd with her punks may also be found in the villages on the Missouri as well as in the large cities of the polished nations."

Sergeant Ordway was loaned a chief's wife for a night. When she returned to Ordway for a second night without her husband's urging, the chief was angry. After stabbing her three times and beating her severely he was inspired to present her to Ordway. It was easier than killing her. Although fond of ladies, Ordway liked the

49

idea of a bow-and-arrow wedding no better than he would have liked a shotgun wedding, and refused the gift. The chief had lost his fervor for killing and left for his camp, pushing and shoving the woman ahead of him.

The natives were moody and unpredictable in their marital affairs. One of Chief Borgne's wives deserted him for a lover she had had before marrying. After a quarrel with her lover, she returned to her father's lodge. Borgne visited the father, ignoring his recalcitrant squaw. He talked in a quiet voice and smoked a pipe or two. His visit over, he walked calmly to his wife, grasped her by the hair, dragged her to the door and tomahawked her. One of his other wives deserted him — he seems to have been an unpleasant fellow. When he next met her and her new lover he inquired politely how they were getting along. They complained of having bad luck and Borgne gave them three horses. Of the Indians, Whitehouse observed, "Some of them & indeed most of them have strange & uncommon ideas."

The Sioux were neither curious nor friendly. They planned to exterminate the Lewis and Clark party at the earliest opportunity. Occasionally they attacked the Mandans and Arickaras. On one of these raids Clark led a party of Indians against them but the wily Sioux escaped. Perhaps it went as Clark planned: the Mandans learned that the white men were their loyal friends, ready to battle their enemies and die for them if necessary.

To greet Christmas morning of 1804 the men fired a round of small arms and a shot or two from the swivel gun. The American flag was raised for the first time in this section. Each man drank a glass of brandy both before and after the ceremony. The captains told the Indians to stay away on Christmas, explaining that this was a great medicine day for the whites. The "merrily disposed" men danced all day long. Even with no women present they enjoyed their square dances, enlivened by a solo jig now and then. The music, made by a violin, a tambourine, a "sounden horn" or bugle and perhaps a mouth organ, may not have been melodious but it was inspiring, for the men danced on the slightest provocation.

New Year's Day the guns again were fired and the men were given drinks of fine whiskey. Sixteen men with "musick" were permitted to go to the Mandan Camp for a New Year's party. York danced for the natives, which Clark said "somewhat

"GREAT NUMBER OF WILD GEES pass to the south," Clark said on November 10, 1804, adding later that "gees continue to pass in gangues as also brant . . . some Ducks also." The men of the expedition frequently feasted on these fowl.

"SAND BARS AND BAD PLACES," complained Clark of this section near Washburn, North Dakota. "Water much divided between them." The boats frequently ran aground on such bars and were deluged. Some times the men had to jump into the icy water to pull them off.

"A PLACE WELL SUPPLIED WITH WOOD," said Clark November 2, 1804. "Cottonwood & elm som ash." This is the site of Fort Mandan, the expeditions winter camp of 1804-05. Flood waters of the Missouri have obliterated the last traces of the fort, which was located on the river bottom in the center of the picture near the sand bar.

astonished them that so large a man should be so active." Six of the men stayed all night with the Mandans and "used them verry friendly," Ordway commented.

Ailments plagued the men throughout the bitterly cold winter, when the temperature sometimes reach 45 degrees below zero. Clark and some of the others had rheumatism. Many, in their depleted state, had boils and abscesses. When Sergeant Pryor dislocated his shoulder, it took four pulls to set it back in place, all this without an anesthetic. One soldier had a violent attack of pleurisy which Lewis, the doctor of the expedition, treated by bleeding and sweating. The man improved and eventually recovered.

Lewis, although apparently skilled in the medical profession as it was practiced in 1804, was eager to add to his store of knowledge and profit by advice from his colleagues. On February 11 Sacajawea labored in childbirth for 12 hours without making any progress. Lewis noted with interest that when an interpreter furnished rattlesnake rattles which were administered with a glass of water, she delivered a fine boy in 10 minutes.

Earlier in the winter when buffalo and other game were fat the captains often hunted, bringing in quantities of meat to add to the store given them by the Indians. There was no cold storage problem — the icy winter took care of that — but they had to build a fence to protect their precious food from the wolves. Later in the winter the blacksmith, over a forge fueled with charcoal, made war axes and hatchets to trade with the Indians for corn.

By early February, when the food supply was nearly gone, a hunting party killed 40 deer, 3 buffalo and 16 elk, but the animals were too lean to eat. One of the hunting parties was surrounded by Sioux. When a Sioux chief interceded for the expedition, the Indians contented themselves with taking the white men's horses and weapons.

Charbonneau, visiting among the British traders during the winter, was tempted to desert the party. He became quite difficult and the captains promptly fired him. He returned in a week or so, asking for his old job and promising to be diligent from that time on. Lewis and Clark took him back and hoped he would keep his promise.

On March 24, when the men heard the welcome clamor of thousands of geese and swans heading north, they started repairing and caulking the boats and building additional canoes.

Soon the ice on the Missouri began to break up, clogging the river with great floating cakes. Occasionally a bewildered buffalo, trapped in the break-up,drifted by on one of the cakes.

On March 31 it rained. This was what the captains had been waiting for: winter was over. Three days later the party loaded a barge with case after case of specimens for President Thomas Jefferson, including skins, skeletons, Arickara tobacco seed, insects, 4 live magpies, a live burrowing squirrel, an ear of Mandan corn and some

"THE AIR KEEN AND COLD." Camped in the river bottom the expedition was sheltered from the bitter north winds by the high rimrock. On cold winter nights the northern lights played over these hills.

"GENERALLY BROKEN" the captains called the Badlands of the Missouri. "a hundred feet high, formed of mixture of yellow sand and clay — many horizontal stratas of carbonated wood."

deer horns. The captains wrote messages for the government and letters to friends. Lewis wrote his mother that he expected to be back the following fall. The barge, carrying gifts and letters, set off down the river with nine men under the command of Corporal Warvington.

Meanwhile the rest of the goods was loaded into the two pirogues and six small canoes. At 5 o'clock the Lewis and Clark expedition left Fort Mandan and headed up the wide Missouri.

INTO THE UNKNOWN

We WERE NOW ABOUT TO PENETRATE a country at least two thousand miles in width on which the foot of civilized man has never trodden," said Lewis. "Our vessels consisted of six small canoes and two large pirogues. This little fleet altho' not quite so rispectable as those of Columbus or Capt Cook were still viewed by us with as much pleasure as thos famed adventurers ever beheld theirs."

Now that the barge had been sent back to civilization the party was smaller. The 31 men included captains Lewis and Clark, sergeants Ordway, Pryor and Gass; the soldiers Bratton, Colter, Reuben Fields, Joseph Fields, Shields, Gibson, Shannon, Potts, Collins, Whitehouse, Windsor, Willard, Hall, Goodrich, Frazier, Cruzatte, Lepage, Labiche, McNeal, Werner, Howard, Wiser and Thompson; the civilian interpreters Drewyer and Charbonneau; and Clark's negro servant, York. Sacajawea carried her baby Baptiste.

There was good sailing wind for awhile. The party made 15 or 20 miles a day. On April 14 they passed a stream Charbonneau previously had followed to its head, which was farther up the Missouri than any other white man ever had gone. They named it Charbonneau River.

As they moved along the captains frequently walked on shore with several of the men. "The country on both sides of the Missouri," Lewis observed, "is one continued level fertile plain as far as the eye can reach in which there is not even a solitary tree or shrub."

One day they sailed past the 120-yard mouth of the Little Missouri, which wound its way down through the picturesque badlands.

When one of the hunters shot a bald eagle, Ordway, the diligent journalist, used its quills as pens to write in his diary. On the 19th several men of the party had the rare treat of fresh eggs from the nest of a wild goose. Later that day one of the men shot a goose. Scannon thrashed out to retrieve it from the swift current. The dog was a great hunter. On April 23rd he spied two antelope swimming in the river. Leaping in at sight of them, he overtook one and killed it in the rushing water. Then, as easily as a smaller dog might kill and retrieve a duck, he swam ashore with his prize.

The men saw carcass after carcass of dead buffalo lining the river bank. The heavy animals had broken through the ice and drowned during the winter. As the

POND BEAVER. Great as was the achievement of the Lewis and Clark expedition, these industrious rodents probably were more responsible for the development of the west than the two captains. Their furs, much in demand by the manufacturers of men's beaver hats, were constantly sought by the trappers and fur traders who steadily pushed back the frontiers.

BEAVER DAM AND HOUSE. Endowed with a natural instinct for engineering, the beaver fells trees, carries in willow brush and packs mud to build a dam like this. His house is the rounded pile of sticks at the extreme right. The beavers' annual damming of creeks and streams has made broad valleys of many places that otherwise would still be narrow channels.

men walked along, or watched from the boats, they noticed many beaver feeding on the bark of trees. Each night the party set traps for them; beaver tails and livers made a special delicacy at the evening meals.

Their arrival on April 26, 1805 at the mouth of the Yellowstone was a time for celebration. The officers gave each man a gill of whiskey, and they all "made merry fiddled and danced &c," Ordway said happily.

Lewis, looking on from the sidelines, said, "they spent the evening with much hilarity, singing & dancing, and seemed as perfectly to forget their past toils as they appeared regardless of those to come."

TRAVELOGUE . . . We arrived at Bismark in a lightning storm that literally illumined the whole countryside. In a flash we saw grain elevators, railways, and farms; then again all was intense blackness. The captains and their men often went through storms like this. How they must have strained to see what the lightning flashes would reveal. This was the home of the Mandan Indians, who had a high culture. It is evident in the replicas of their huts and in the display of their implements at the Fort Abraham Lincoln state park museum. We wanted to spend hours at the park. Here are the remains of General George A. Custer's old home, reconstructed blockhouses from which splendid views are possible, a panorama of the Mandan civilization, one of the Lewis and Clark campsites — several centuries of history confined to a few acres. Al found an old Indian gambling token right on the ground outside one of the huts. By now he had trained us to walk around with our noses practically on the ground looking for artifacts, but he always spotted them first. Even little Joe went around with a pocket full of rocks: one of them turned out to be an Indian sharpening tool.

Bismark has another set of Mandan huts near their water storage plant, which looks almost exactly like the huts. Because of the peculiar terrain we got involved in a maze of little hills and winding roads which led us to the water works, to our disgust. A few signs would certainly help the tourist here.

The ancient Mandan Indian fortifications Lewis found abandoned in 1804 are at the Double Ditch historic site. We saw traces of the ditches dug for defense, the huts and the caches. Someone had been digging here and in their leavings we found several bits of pottery of beautiful, even design and a few arrowheads. We knew we mustn't dig here. Al said, "This is like walking over ground where there's buried treasure and only taking the pennies off the top. If we could just dig . . ." As he steps on soil where Indians once lived, Al's mind pictures what is under that soil. One foot down, artifacts a century old; two feet down, two centuries old. We had to get our minds out of the dirt and move along to Williston.

57

We found that with a good highway map we could see a lot of the Lewis and Clark route between Washburn and Williston. A side road took us to where the expedition camped the winter of 1804-5, about 20 miles from Washburn. It was here, at the encampment they named Fort Mandan, that the captains hired Charbonneau and agreed to take along his mate, Sacajawea, and her baby, Baptiste. Occasionally someone asks if Clark was the father of Baptiste. We don't know anything about Clark's love life, but we do know Baptiste was born a few weeks after the captain met Sacajawea — and 1805 was not the atomic age.

The bridge on Highway 85 crossing the Missouri is named for Lewis and Clark. It is probably about where the captains rejoined, after separating at Traveler's Rest Camp on the return journey. We were determined to go to Fort Union, which would have been a good idea on a dry day. Lewis had recommended this spot at the junction of the Yellowstone and Missouri as well suited for a fort, and soon after, a fort had been built. It was one of the most popular fur-trading posts in the west. As we slithered along we were again reminded of what rain can do to clay roads. We made it. Here was a big cornfield at the site of the fort. All that plowing, we thought, should unearth something. We tiptoed among the young corn shoots, picking up a few artifacts of both Indian and white culture. If that farmer across the road saw me digging I hope he didn't think I was treasure-hunting in his corn patch. We wouldn't be so crass as to dig on someone's land — at least within sight of his house. I was merely burying one of Joe's diapers.

HOW TO GET THERE NOW . . . See maps 4 and 5.

OLD MANDAN VILLAGE. From Mandan, North Dakota, take North Dakota Highway 6, 4.5 miles south to Fort Abraham Lincoln. The old Mandan village is just back of the museum at the entrance of Fort Abraham Lincoln.

DOUBLE DITCH INDIAN VILLAGE. From Bismark, take river road at east end of bridge on U.S. Highway 10. Go north on road running along east bank of the Missouri 9.2 miles. Double Ditch State Park is on the east side of the road.

SITE OF FORT MANDAN. From Washburn, North Dakota, instead of turning north on U.S. Highway 83, continue straight ahead (east) on gravel road 14 miles to monument marking site of Fort Mandan. A few farm lanes cut off, but keep to the river side on the road The site of the fort is below the monument in the river bottom.

JUNCTION OF YELLOWSTONE WITH MISSOURI. From Williston, North Dakota, on U S. Highway 2, continue 2 miles west of junction with U.S. Highway 83. Take gravel road to left 15 miles to site of Fort Union.

YELLOWSTONE TO GREAT FALLS

As the little fleet of the Corps of Discovery sailed and rowed up the river the men saw great flocks of geese, brant, swans and ducks of every description. Frequently they saw beaver swimming in the water or peering cautiously at the boats from their holes in the river bank. Deer, antelope, moose, elk, buffalo and bighorn sheep were everywhere. Lewis said he honestly believed two hunters could supply a regiment; the hunters restrained themselves and killed only enough for food.

All along the shore they saw wolves, coyotes and the great silver-tip grizzlies of the Missouri, feeding on the carcasses of the winter-killed buffalo. The big savage grizzlies were almost impervious to the stone-pointed spears and arrows of the Indians. Even the poor guns which traders furnished some of the Indians were useless against this mammoth prey. "The natives frequently miss their aim & fall a sacrefice to the bear," Lewis said, adding that the animals were more likely to attack than flee when approached by man.

By April 29 Lewis had become casual about the danger of the grizzlies, saying "in the hands of a skilled rifleman they are by no means as formidable or dangerous as they have been represented." That same day he wounded a small bear and had to take to his heels with the injured animal hot after him. He was fast on his feet and sprinted 70 or 80 yards, reloaded his gun and killed the beast before he himself nearly "fell a sacrefice."

Farther up the river Clark and Drewyer shot a bear five times in the body. It still had strength to thrash through the water to a sandbar where it died 20 minutes later. Lewis estimated the weight of the "tremendious looking anamal" at 600 pounds. The captain's opinion of bears improved when he found it was 8 feet 7½ inches tall and 5 feet 10½ inches around the chest.

Bratton, on May 11, had a sore hand and, since he couldn't ply the oars, walked along the shore. About five in the evening Lewis saw him dashing back toward the canoes "hollowing as if in distress." When he got his breath he told them that he, too, had tried to kill a grizzly. The men were beginning to learn not to attack single-handed the "white" bears, as they called the silver-tip grizzlies, even though they were prized for their oil.

Several days later they saw a huge bear on the open prairie about 300 yards from the river. Six of the best hunters went out to get him. Creeping up behind a small knoll they were able to get within 40 paces before he saw them. This time they had a plan. Four fired simultaneously while two held their guns in readiness. Their aim was good but the animal, with four musket balls in him, reared toward them open-mouthed. The other two hunters fired and hit but still the brute kept coming. Two of the party fled to the canoe with the bear chasing them while the other four quickly hid in the willows and reloaded their guns. When they fired several more shots into the beast the only effect was to reveal where they were hidden. The bear seemed invincible!

Two of the hiding hunters threw away their guns and streaked for the river, diving 20 feet into the muddy water. The bear plunged in after them. Just as he was about to overtake the swimmers one of the hunters on shore reloaded, took desperate but careful aim and sent a ball into the old fighter's brain.

"I must confess I do not like the gentlemen," Lewis finally admitted, "and had reather fight two Indians than one bear."

MISADVENTURES OF THE WHITE PIROGUE

As the boats worked their way up the channel usually one of the two captains walked on shore. Although they seldom both left at the same time, on the evening of May 14 Lewis and Clark were ashore together. Drewyer, who had been the helmsman on the white pirogue, relinquished his seat to Charbonneau, "perhaps the most timid waterman in the world." Charbonneau could not swim. He was not noted for his quick reactions except in anger. He, as helmsman, almost had upset a canoe just below the Yellowstone. Nevertheless steering boats had a fatal

60

GRIZZLY BEAR AND CUB. Although these huge bears were greatly feared by Indians, the explorers at first didn't take them very seriously. After a few narrow escapes, the explorers learned not to approach them unless there were several riflemen together. Often it took eight or ten bullets in vital spots to stop the charge of a grizzly. Modern photographers, even when backed with a high-power rifle, are wary of getting close to them.

BLACK BEAR AND TWIN CUBS.

charm for him and here he was at it again. Not only were his wife and baby in this pirogue, but also the medicine, books and other indispensable items of the expedition.

All went smoothly until a sudden squall struck the sail, turning the pirogue sideways. "Instead of puting her the wind" the panicky Charbonneau "lufted her into it." As the wind snatched the brace of the square sail from the hands of the man who was holding it, the pirogue turned on her side. The captains, watching from shore, were frantic. Lewis even thought of plunging into the river and swimming to the rescue but realized he could do nothing. The pirogue, now full of water, righted herself. "God have mercy on our souls," screamed the terror-stricken Charbonneau while the rudder swung loose.

Cruzatte, though his powder was wet, forced the craven helmsman to regain control by threatening to shoot him. Sacajawea, the little squaw, sitting in water to her waist and holding her baby, calmly reached out and gathered the packages that were floating away from the boat. With Charbonneau and the pirogue under control, Cruzatte and three others started bailing out water and put the boat to shore.

Only a few things were lost. Lewis, who usually ignored Sacajawea, said, "The Indian woman to whom I ascribe equal fortitude and resolution to any person on board . . . preserved most of the light articles which washed overboard." Soon after he named a creek for her.

Clark was almost bit by a rattlesnake on May 17. That night a large tree burst into flame, ignited by campfire. The sergeant of the guard wakened the men, who scurried away from the giant torch. The captains moved their tent just a few minutes before the tree came crashing down where they had been sleeping. A hard wind blew sparks in every direction, endangering the whole camp, but at last the crackling died away.

Next morning the wind was from the west and the sails were of no use. The party labored along shore, pulling the canoes with elkskin tow cords. They were always a little leary of towing the boats from shore — if the cords stretched and snapped apart it was no easy job getting the boats in line again.

The huge Scannon enjoyed loping along the shore. He, the antelope killer, was afraid of nothing. But he met his match when he tried to kill a wounded beaver. The rodent bit him on the hind leg and cut an artery. Lewis, trying to check the flow of blood, thought his big dog might die. The bleeding finally stopped and Scannon pulled through.

Still tugging the tow ropes two days later and 2270 miles up the Missouri the party reached the junction of the Musselshell River where they made a camp on the south bank. Great swarms of blowflies buzzed here. "We are oblige to brush them off what we eat," Clark moaned, and was inspired to name a nearby stream Blowing Fly Creek.

They noticed the countryside was broken although there were some plains up the Musselshell. As they proceeded up the river cottonwood grew thick in the bottoms. On the hills to the south were scrubby pine and dwarf cedar. They were surprised to see that the rich soil on the plains produced mainly prickly pear.

On May 25 Drewyer and Clark killed three bighorn sheep — the first to be taken by the expedition. During the day they saw the first polecat they had seen for some time. Perhaps the memory of the little skunk lingered on when Clark later remarked in the camp they made a few miles up river, "The air of this quarter is pure and helthy."

Next day Lewis, climbing the hills on the shore of the Missouri, saw a great distance to the west the snowy crests of the Rocky Mountains shining in the sun. He called them the Shining Mountains but as he gazed at them he thought of what a terrible obstacle they would be. Might the great adventure end in those gleaming crags?

As the men lay sleeping around four smoldering campfires late in the night of May 28 a lone buffalo bull swimming from the opposite shore blundered into the white pirogue. Frightened by the unfamiliar object he stampeded blindly into camp, his heavy hoofs missed the men's heads by inches. The sentinel screamed a warning, Scannon barked and the bull charged first one way then another. When he headed directly for the two captains' tent, Scannon yipped and growled him into greater confusion. Finally the frantic buffalo charged away into the black night leaving the camp in complete uproar. Wandering around with guns in hand, the dazed men asked one another what had happened.

Next morning they found the damage was slight although the bull had smashed two guns.

"It appears the white pirogue which contains our most valuable stores is attended by some evil genii," Lewis mused.

WHICH WAY?

"THE HILLS AND RIVER CLIFTS which we passed today exhibit a most romantic appearance," Lewis observed the evening of May 31.

Wind and water had eroded the 300-foot sandstone cliffs along the river into a thousand weird and grotesque shapes. In Lewis's active imagination they were like

63

a mighty city with great tall buildings. He could see "their parapets well stocked with statuary" and liked to think of the erosions as "columns of various sculpture . . . supporting long galleries in front of these buildings."

While Lewis dreamed of beautiful ancient cities the men strained on the tow cords, hauling the heavy canoes. Ordway said they were "compelled from the rapidity of the current in many places to walk in the water & on Slippery hillsides on the Sides of rocks &c on gravel & thru Stiff mud bear footed and we cannot keep on moccasons from the Stiffness of the mud & decline of the Steepp hills."

Lewis was not too preoccupied to notice "their labour is incredibly painful and great, yet those faithful fellows bear it without a murmur." Ordway, however, did grumble, "We to be sure do have a hard time of it oblidged to walk on shore and haul rope 9/10 of the time barefooted."

At noon the captains refreshed the men with a dram of whiskey. They covered 18 miles that day and 23 the following.

The Corps of Discovery made camp on the south side of the river June 2. Opposite them was the mouth of a river coming in from the north. The captains were puzzled. Here was a branch that discharged almost as much water as the main stream. The Indians had mentioned no such river. Which was which? What was the best route to the Pacific? A mistake now might be fatal to the expedition.

The party moved camp the next morning to the point of land between the rivers. While most of the men rested and nursed their bruised feet, Gass with two others went 15 miles up the south river and Pryor and two men explored the north river. When each party returned to report its findings, the captains still didn't know which was the Missouri. They knew they must choose the right river or spend weeks of useless toil on the wrong route and perhaps end their expedition in some far-off wilderness. The following day Lewis took six men to investigate the north river more thoroughly. Clark with five others went up the south river. Both parties were gone several days and explored about 40 miles.

Arriving back at camp, the captains discussed their findings and became convinced the south fork was the Missouri. The other river, they agreed, came from too far north to be an easy access to the Columbia. Lewis named it Marias River after Maria Wood, his cousin with whom he thought he might be in love.

The men were equally convinced the north river was the Missouri. But by now they were so well-disciplined a unit that they were willing to follow their officers anywhere.

THE GREAT FALLS OF THE MISSOURI

As THE CURRENT had grown swifter in the river channel the party found it increasingly difficult to navigate the large red pirogue. The captains decided to cache her, with all of the heavier baggage they could spare and with some provisions to be picked up on the return trip, at the junction of the two rivers.

64

"WHITE CLIFTS" between Arrow Creek and the Marias Junction with the Missouri. ". . . the Hills and river Clifts of this day," Lewis said May 31, 1805, "exhibit a most romantick appearance on each side of the river is a white soft sandstone bluff which rises to about half the hight of the hills."

". . . THE WATER IN THE COURSE OF TIME in decending from these hills and plains on either side of the River trickled down the soft sand clifts and woarn it into a thousand grotesque figures. which with the help of a little immagination are made to represent eligant ranges of lofty freestone buildings."

"IN THE FORM OF VAST PYRAMIDS of conic structure bearing a serees of other pyramids on their tops becoming less as they ascend and finally terminating in a sharp point. nitches and alcoves of various forms and sizes are seen at different hights as we pass."

". . . HAVING THEIR PARAPETS WELL STOCKED with statuary: collumns of various sculpture both grooved and plain, are also seen."

"IN OTHER PLACES on a much nearer approach and with the help of much less imagination we see the ruins of eligant buildings: some collumns standing and almost entire: others retaining their pedestals but deprived by time of their capitals."

"AS WE PASSED ON it seemed as if those seens of visionary inchantment would never have and end . . . so perfect indeed are those walls that I should have thought nature had attempted here to rival the human art of masonry had I not recollected that she had first began her work."

Both Lewis and Clark still thought the south river was the Missouri, but they wanted to be sure. Lewis decided to take Drewyer, Joe Fields, Gibson and Goodrich scouting ahead to search for the great falls the Indians had described, while Clark and the main party prepared the cache.

Although sick with dysentery Lewis started out with his men about 8 a.m. on June 11. They hadn't gone far when the captain became worse. Although Lewis had failed to bring medical supplies, his mother had been a famous herb doctor and he remembered her cures.

The men gathered chokecherry twigs which he cut up and boiled in water until he had brewed a "strong black decoction." He drank two pints every hour for several hours.

While the captain was treating himself Goodrich, who never missed a chance to fish, caught several dozen pike, perch and Missouri herring. Next day Lewis, feeling better but still too weak to travel, was tempted to join in the sport.

At last able to move on, the party arrived at the first of the great falls of the Missouri at noon June 13. The beauty and grandeur of the falls took Lewis's breath away. Viewing them from the top of a rock he tried to draw them; later he attempted to describe the wonderful sight in his journal. He longed for the pencil of Salvator Rosa or the pen of Thompson that he "might be able to give to the enlightened world some just idea of this truly magnificent and sublimely grand object which has from the commencement of time been concealed from the view of civilized man."

Goodrich, surveying the falls with a practical and calculating eye, soon found an excellent fishing hole where he caught half a dozen trout 17 to 23 inches long. The other men killed three fat buffalo cows.

"My fare is really sumptuous this evening," Lewis said, "buffaloe's humps, tongues and marrowbones, fine trout parched meal pepper and salt, and a good appetite." Mindful of his recent illness he added thoughtfully, "the last is not considered the least of the luxuries."

Next day he explored further and with each successive falls was more impressed. The series of five cascades brought the Missouri River down 400 feet. He had trouble comparing the two largest, finally deciding one was "pleasingly beautiful" and the other "sublimely grand." About this time he stepped on a prickly pear which brought him out of his reverie.

Continuing to the head of the falls he shot a buffalo. Again in a dreamy mood he leaned on his empty gun and pitied the dying animal. A grizzly bear moved in on his daydreams and the captain, trying to maintain his dignity, retired at a brisk walk. The bear charged full speed, his huge mouth open and fangs flashing. Lewis, with the grizzly bear hot on his heels, sprinted 80 yards to the river and waded out to his armpits. He turned and, with his spear, faced the bear. The brute changed his mind and ran away.

"SMOTH UNRUFFLED SURFACE," agreed the captains, "its bottom is composed of round and flat stones." The Gros Ventres called this stream the Amahte Arzzha — the river that scolds all others. Having trouble with this pronounciation, white men simplified the name to Missouri. This view is just above the Marias-Missouri rivers junction in central Montana.

"STROLED OUT TO THE TOP OF HIGHTS in the fork of these rivers." This is what the captains saw as they viewed the junction of the Marias with the Missouri. Lewis named the former after his cousin Maria Wood, although its muddy waters "but illy comport with the pure celestial virtues and amiable qualifications of that lovely fair one."

Later the same day Lewis saw an animal "of the tiger kind," presumably a panther, ready to spring on him. He shot the beast, and it crawled into its hole. Still later, three buffalo bulls charged him. When within a hundred yards of the captain they stopped, stared stupidly, turned tail and ran.

Lewis began to think all wild things were in conspiracy against him. He was convinced when he found a large rattlesnake coiled on the slanted trunk of a tree under which he had slept for an hour during the heat of the day.

By now Lewis's party had made enough observations to feel sure they were on the right river. He sent Joe Fields back to meet Clark and tell him this was indeed the Missouri.

SACAJAWEA–ILL

CLARK, MEANWHILE, back in the main camp at Marias River, appointed Pierre Cruzatte to build the cache while he treated Sacajawea who had become seriously ill. He gave her temporary relief by bleeding her. She soon relapsed and Clark's concern for her grew.

Cruzatte, who had had experience making caches, searched for the right spot on a high plain above the river bottom, for dry ground which was imperative for a cache. He found a spot about 40 yards from a high bluff. He cut a circular piece of sod about 20 inches in diameter, being careful, when he removed it, to disturb it as little as possible. The men dug a hole straight down about a foot. As they dug in deeper they carefully widened the hole until it was about seven feet deep and as many feet wide. The resulting shape was like a huge buried kettle.

The men carried each scoop of earth and threw it into the stream. They wanted no tell-tale fresh dirt near their secret cache. When finally satisfied with the size of the hole they made a floor four or five inches thick of dry sticks and covered it with dry grass and hide. On this they placed the articles to be hidden. They then put more sticks around the walls to protect the supplies from dampness. After piling more hides over the cache they meticulously replaced the original piece of sod and hoped that neither Indian nor white man would see that the earth had been disturbed.

The party drew the red pirogue onto an island in the mouth of the Marias River. They pushed the heavy boat into a hiding place among the willows and tied it securely to a tree to prevent high water from sweeping it away.

After the day's work Cruzatte got out his fiddle and the men sang their favorite songs while they danced around the campfire. All "were extremely cheerful" except little Sacajawea who steadily was growing worse.

When the party moved upriver on June 12 Sacajawea was so ill Clark laid her in the covered part of the white pirogue where it was cooler. She had great pain in the lower abdomen which led the captain to guess her trouble was stoppage of the menses. Clark tried everything he could think of to help her. The "doste of salts"

"THE GRANDEST SIGHT I EVER BEHELD," Lewis said of the Great Falls of the Missouri. ". . . a perfect white foam which assumes a thousand forms in a moment sometimes flying up in jets of sparkling foam to the hight of fifteen or twenty feet and are scarcely formed befor large roling bodies of the same beaten and foaming water is thrown over and conceals them."

"THIS SUBLIMELY GRAND SPECTACLE . . ." . . . "Such a cascade would probably be extolled for its beauty and magnificence" Lewis thought, if he had not just seen the Great Falls, Crooked Falls and Rainbow Falls. These are Colter Falls, and Lewis passed them by, paying little attention.

"RATTLESNAKES LIKE THOSE OF THE UNITED STATES." Said Captain Lewis, "this snake is smaller than those common to the middle Atlantic states . . . about 2 feet 6 inches long . . . it is of yellowish brown color and sides variagated with one row of oval spots of a dark brown colour."

"ON THE LIST OF PRODEGIES of this neighborhood" thought Lewis. "I think this fountain the largest I ever beheld." The center of Giant Springs boils out directly under the pier overhanging the pool, and then cascades down to dissolve its clear waters in the muddy Missouri. A park has been built around it for the people of Great Falls, Montana.

he gave her did no good. He gave her opium and applied poultice of bark but still she grew weaker and could hardly hold her baby.

The men worked in the water from morning until night hauling the heavy boats against the current. Rattlesnakes buzzed from the least expected places. One of the men slipped and clutched at a bush to steady himself. He was horrified when he felt his hand close over the head of a rattler that lay along the limb. Quick as a snake is in striking, the man was quicker in letting go. When there was a chance for a pause the exhausted travelers dropped in their tracks and were asleep instantly.

Sacajawea was now out of her senses and would take no medicine. Clark finally got the indifferent Charbonneau to help him. "If she dies it will be the fault of her husband as I am now convinced," the captain commented disgustedly.

When Lewis rejoined the party on June 16 he found Sacajawea extremely ill and very weak. "This gave me some concern as well as for the poor object herself, then with a young child in her arms, as from the consideration of her being our only dependence for a friendly negociation with the Snake Indians," he worried.

Arriving at the foot of the first falls the captains decided the portage was too long for the men to carry the heavy boats past the five falls on their shoulders. Clark took six men to find timber large enough to make wheels so the boats could be hauled overland on carts.

Lewis continued his partner's treatment of Sacajawea, adding water from the mineral springs at the falls. The woman's pulse became stronger and from that time she began to improve. The next day Lewis said, "I think . . . there is every rational hope of her recovery."

NATURAL PHENOMENON AND THE PORTAGE OF GREAT FALLS

THE PARTY CAMPED below the Great Falls on the north bank the first night. Next day they crossed over and hauled the canoes as far as they could up Portage Creek where they established Portage Creek Camp.

The six men sent to build wagons found only cottonwood available. They cut circular sections from logs for wheels. The soft wood was not ideal for axles, tongues and other parts that carried stress, but they used it for want of something better.

Sacajawea was much better. Most of June 18 she sat up. The next day she overate and her fever returned. "I rebuked Sharbono severly for suffering her to indulge herself," the exasperated Lewis said, "he being privy to it having been previously told what she must only eat." The captain continued giving her laudanum and applying bark poultices. He insisted she drink only sulphur water from the mineral springs. In addition he gave her 30 drops of vitriol and after her fever returned added doses of diluted nitre to the treatment.

Clark wanted to see the falls, too. While the work party was building the wagons, he took five men to explore them. The individual falls were not high

73

compared to Niagara and other famous waterfalls; Clark measured the highest at 87 feet. But the great volume of water flooding over five successive cliffs was spectacular. Clark continued exploring and found Great Spring, a natural fan-shaped fountain over 300 feet wide. Watching it bubble and roar up from its deep pool he noticed it formed a small river of its own as the crystal clear waters ran into the muddy Missouri.

Clark selected a campsite for the upper end of the portage on the south bank opposite the smallest of three islands. That night in camp the men were attacked by bears. Colter escaped by diving into the river. They named the spot White Bear Island because there were so many "White Bears," as the captains called the silver-tip grizzlies.

On their way back to lower camp Clark and the men staked off the best route to pull the wagons over the hills.

The work party finished the crude wagons June 21 and loaded the canoes aboard to start the long portage.

It was hard, grueling work. The soft cottonwood axles broke. The men replaced them, but the wagon tongues broke. As they labored up the hills and through rocky ravines studded with prickly pear their moccasins wore out in one day. In camp that night they resoled them with double thicknesses of leather only to have to throw them away the next evening, completely worn out.

The earth, churned rough by thousands of buffalo hoofs while muddy, then baked hard by the sun, was worse than frozen ground to the men's feet. "Added to those obstructions," Clark said, "the men has to haul with all their strength wate & art." Pulling, slipping and stumbling they grabbed at bunches of grass or rocks to anchor themselves with one hand while they strained at the tow cords with the other. "Maney limping from the soreness of their feet," Clark sympathized, "some become fant for a fiew moments, but no man complains all go chearfully on."

The men were delighted when a wind storm blew on top of one of the hills. They put up sails and enjoyed the help the wind gave them. "This is saleing on dry land in every sense of the word," Ordway commented.

Clark frequently traveled back and forth the 17¾ miles between White Bear Island Camp and Portage Camp, cheering the men on, although he himself was having troubles. "I feel myself a little unwell with looseness &c &c," he commented on June 25. "I had a little coffee for brackfast which was to me a necessity as I had not tasted any since last winter."

Three days later, Clark took several men to build a cache before they abandoned Portage Camp entirely. They pulled out of the water the white pirogue which had been brought up the creek and hid it in the willow thickets on an island. Then they moved on to establish Willow Run Camp slightly past the half way mark on the portage where there was plenty of wood and water.

74

"IT IS A PRETTY LITTLE GROVE in which our camp is situated." White Bear Camp, a short distance up the Missouri from Great Falls, Montana, was the upper end of the expedition's portage past the Great Falls. The camp was about where the white house shows across the river to the south.

"WE SHOT AT A LARGE WHITE BEAR," said the explorers late in June, 1805. ". . . past a small island in the middle and one close on the Larboard shore . . . those 3 islands are all opposite." The island on the far (north) side of the river has filled in and now is part of the mainland. The small island in the middle of the river has been washed away, but the one "close on the Larboard shore" is shown here. The willows, which are still here, made a wonderful home for the grizzlies which infested White Bear Island.

Just at dusk that day a "most Dredfull wind" came up and it rained heavily during the night. In the morning, the captains gave the wet and shivering men a dram of whiskey to warm them. Clark realized it was too wet and muddy to continue portaging. Instead he sent the men to Portage Camp to bring the remaining baggage while he, Charbonneau, York and Sacajawea, carrying her baby Baptiste on her back, went again to the falls. The captain wanted to do more exploring and replace the lost notes he had made on his previous investigation.

A great black cloud blew over the sun as they reached the falls, and a violent wind told them they were in for one of the upper Missouri's terrible storms. The little party of four and the baby took shelter under some shelving rocks in a ravine a quarter of a mile above the falls. The storm grew steadily worse until "A torrent of rain and hail fell more violent than ever I saw before . . . the rain fell like one voley of water falling from the heavens." Clark knew the ravine was a dangerous place during such a cloudburst. Peering around the edge of the rocks he was horrified to see a flooding torrent roaring toward them.

Charbonneau, as usual thinking first and only of himself, scrambled out in a hurry. Clark grabbed his rifle and pouch in one hand; Sacajawea grabbed her baby. With his free hand the captain pushed Sacajawea ahead of him through the torrent which was already up to their waists. The two struggled through the sweeping waters toward the top of the ravine. Charbonneau, perhaps because of the cursing of the red-haired captain, finally turned and took his wife's hand. "Much scared and nearly without motion," he probably was more a handicap than help.

With grim effort they pushed through the terrifying flood. When they clambered to the top of the boulders they saw a raging river 15 feet deep plunge through the gulch.

York, who had somehow escaped, was running along the hillside. Certain that all had been drowned, he was hoping to catch sight of his master's body.

All the baby's clothes were lost. Sacajawea, still weak from her illness, was wet and chilled. Clark ordered York and Charbonneau to rush to camp for dry clothes while he gave the shivering woman some whiskey from York's canteen.

After the four, with little Baptiste, finally straggled back to camp, the men who had been working at bringing the baggage over the portage came tumbling in with great confusion. They had been working hatless and naked when hail stones seven inches in circumference and weighing three ounces began to pelt them. Lewis said the stones came down with such velocity that some of them bounced 10 or 12 feet in the air. One man had been knocked down three times by the falling balls of ice; several men were bleeding and all were bruised.

Clark "gave the party a dram to console them in some measure for their general defeat."

Four days later the bruised and battered men got the canoes and baggage to White Bear Camp. They had spent 10 days going 17¾ miles.

76

BIG HORN SHEEP. These were a great curiosity to the explorers. They sent skins and skulls to President Jefferson for him to inspect. Lewis told of seeing a large herd on an "emmencely high and nearly perpendicular Clift," near the river. "They walked about and bounded from rock to rock with apparent unconcern where it appeared to me no quadruped could have stood and from which had they made one false step they must have been precipitated at least 500 feet."

"THE PRICKLY PEAR IS NOW IN FULL BLUME" said Lewis, "and forms one of the beauties as well as the greatest pests of the plains." They were particularly torturesome after the men's shoes wore out and they had to resort to moccasins.

AT WHITE BEAR ISLAND camp Captain Lewis finally put into effect "The Experiment" he had nursed three quarters of the way across the continent. He and some men assembled the 36-foot iron boat frame he had had made at Harper's Ferry. Many times the practical Clark must have looked at the 100 pounds of metal with a prejudiced eye, but by now "The Experiment" had become almost an obsession with Lewis.

The iron frame was covered with skins brought in by specially assigned hunters. Since there was no tar for calking, Lewis collected pitch from pine trees to seal the seams of the skins. He was worried, because the sewn hides tended to pull apart as they dried.

While the men worked on the boat, the grizzlies became more and more of a nuisance. They stole meat and otherwise harried White Bear Island camp until 12 men, led by both captains, went on a punitive expedition against them. The party invaded the island stronghold of the animals where the willows were thick. Perhaps the men didn't hunt too carefully for only one bear was killed.

On July 4 Clark spent the morning "drawing a copy of the river to be left at this place for fear of some accident." He may have made another kind of copy also, as all during the expedition he shamelessly peeked at Lewis's journal, Ordway's diary and perhaps Gass' and Whitehouse's as well, often repeating their entries word for word. Writing did not come easy for him.

The men celebrated their second Independence day of the trip that evening, growing gay when the captains portioned out the last of their whiskey stock. It made "several verry lively," Clark said. Cruzatte got out his fiddle and the men danced until 9 o'clock when "a heavy shower," according to Lewis, "put an end to that part of the amusement tho they continued their mirth with songs and festive jokes and were extremely merry untill late at night."

Five days later "The Experiment" was launched. Lewis, happy as a mother duck watching her ducklings take to water, stood on shore. It floated! His joy was short lived. As the water soaked into the hides the pitch that sealed them worked loose. Water poured through the holes made by the great sewing needles. Although Lewis still believed his idea would work if —, the next day he had "The Experiment" dismantled and buried in a cache.

Clark, without a word, took some men with axes and went about eight miles up the river to build dugout canoes of cottonwood.

Lewis and the main party, having cached some baggage, abandoned White Bear camp on July 13 and joined Clark.

Two days later the men completed and loaded the canoes and the Expedition for Northwest Discovery started traveling again. Of the men Clark said, "All appear perfectly to have made up their minds to succeed in the expedition or perish in the attempt."

78

TRAVELOGUE . . . We were edging along the river most of the way between Williston and Fort Peck, Montana. We knew that any resemblance between the Missouri now and the Missouri of the captains' time would soon end in the tremendous Fort Peck Dam. Here, not a century and a half after the expedition, the PWA and the Army Engineers had restrained the tempestuous Missouri with a dam over three and a half miles across. Near here, in 1867, Fort Peck had been established as a trading post and Indian agency by Comdr. E. H. Durfee and Col. Campbell K. Peck. Our guide book told us 100-pound sacks of flour were issued to the Indians as one of the attempts to mollify their attitude toward the gold-seekers who were pouring into Montana. As ingenious as the housewife who makes an apron from her flour sack, the Indians cut holes for their arms and heads and romped around with "Durfee and Peck" stamped in bright red letters on their war dress. Was it possible that here, in 1805, that tiny band struggled up this very river? Here, just after the Civil War, only a little trading post broke the lonely expanses? And here, now, is this dam, one of the biggest constructions of its kind in the world. It is almost too much for the imagination to encompass.

The road breaks away from the Missouri on the way to Big Sandy, but a number of state highways intersect the main route, where one may cut south and ferry across the river.

Near Big Sandy, with the help of the captains' old maps and an enthusiastic farmer's wife — she generously offered Al pictures if he failed to get some — we found the white "clifts" that so fired Lewis's imagination. Here the river is edged with the peculiar sandstone formations that made the captain think of ancient cities, and inspired one of the greatest flights of fancy in his journal. We were all thrilled with the sight and Al let out a regular war whoop of joy. "You just relax and enjoy this; I'm going to be taking pictures a long time," he said as he walked away.

It was so strange and beautiful here we didn't care how long he took until he called back, "Remember the rattlesnakes." Relax? Just a few minutes later Bert pointed out a mass of something and said, "There's one." We don't have rattlesnakes in western Washington and I find it quite impossible to believe in them even when I see them. Bert heaved a stone at it. The rattlesnake uncoiled in a flash and slid away, its tail full of rattles stiffly erect. We saw several snakes and learned they don't always rattle at your approach. No, this is not a place to relax but surely a place to dream and let the imagination play. It has an out-of-this-world quality with its weird statuary, its lovely blossoming cacti and the milk-chocolate river.

Al suddenly rounded us up and said, "Let's get out of here quick. Looks like it might rain." We could see where one road had washed out in the ravine that cuts through to the shore. If another was going to, we certainly didn't want to wash out with it.

On our way to the expedition's campsite near Loma we saw a tombstone in a huge oatfield. Backed by a clump of trees and surrounded by the tall grain, the grave looked lonely. No tombstone remains ignored with Al around. Plunging through the green field, he came back to tell us it was the common grave of 10 men killed by Blackfeet Indians in the Friend's Massacre.

In this area on the way to Fort Benton we noticed strip farming is practiced; long parallel rows of wheat with fallow land between the rows. Looking at the curious striped pattern we wondered how in the world they ever kept those rows straight. Next year the pattern will be the same but moved over a notch. Wheat will sprout from the now-fallow land, and the now-planted land will rest.

The town of Fort Benton is right on the river. In 1846 — just 42 years after the expedition passed through a wilderness here — Fort Lewis was established. Four years later Major Alexander Culbertson of the American Fur Company rebuilt and renamed it for Senator Thomas Benton of Missouri. The ruins are preserved in a pleasant little park.

At Great Falls, the hub of so many Lewis and Clark landmarks, we hardly knew where to go first. There are the Great Falls themselves, changed somewhat by a dam but still surely as beautiful and spectacular as in the captains' day. We strolled in the fine park just below the falls and looked up at the bluff where Lewis viewed them and went into raptures over their splendor. The falls meant a long portage to the expedition, and a tough one. It was in the Great Falls area that Sacajawea and Clark nearly drowned in a cloudburst.

There is a park, too, at the Giant Springs. These springs bubble up through submerged bushes, giving the effect of a little underwater jungle. Looking into the depths we could imagine Lewis's delight with what he called its blue-tinged waters.

In spite of Clark's map we had a tough time finding White Bear Camp. The road actually crosses the first White Bear Island. I asked, "Isn't this the island where Lewis chased out the grizzlies?" "Yes," Al answered, "but where is *this* little island." He pointed to Clark's sketch of an island in the middle of the river. It had disappeared entirely. The larger island on the west side is now a peninsula jutting out into the river. The Missouri calmly swallows islands and changes landmarks, to the confusion of people trying to locate spots where there is no sign nor marker to help them.

Old Town, at the Great Falls auditorium, is a fascinating place to spend an hour or so. Here are houses rebuilt with original timber from frontier times. A little village has been set up with a barber shop, saloon, fire department, general store and even a shadowy "lady" peering from a second story. Lil put her nickels in what must have been the granddaddy of all jukeboxes, and with a great whirr it tinkled out old-time music.

We left this region with reluctance, to continue our expedition.

HOW TO GET THERE NOW . . . See maps 5 *and* 6.

WHITE CLIFFS. From Big Sandy, Montana, go south through Big Sandy; turn right just past the second church. Keep to right on good road 10.9 miles to Roy Pegar's ranch on the right side of the road. Inquire here about road conditions down to the river. The road, merely a track through the sagebrush, goes 5.1 miles to the Missouri.

MARIAS RIVER JUNCTION. From Loma, Montana, cross Marias River bridge just south of the town on Montana Highway 29. At end of bridge take gravel road to left, 1.9 miles to junction of Marias River with the Missouri. The campsite of (date) was on the point of land between the two rivers.

GREAT FALLS OF THE MISSOURI. From Great Falls, Montana, go east on Montana Highway 29, 10.5 miles to gravel road marked "Ryan" that cuts off to the south. Follow this road 1.9 miles to the Great Falls.

GIANT SPRINGS. From Great Falls, Montana, turn right at the bridge on U.S. Highway 87 and go 3.4 miles to the springs park on the south side of the river. Six miles farther east on the same road is Belt Mountain Creek, the "Portage Creek" of Lewis and Clark.

WHITE BEAR ISLAND. From Great Falls, take the river road on the south side of the river at the approach to the U.S. 89 bridge. Go east 4.4 miles to slough that is Sand Coulee Creek. Lewis's camp was in the little meadow back of the house that stands just to the north and east of the slough. The highway crosses one of the White Bear islands just before getting to the slough.

THREE FORKS TO THE GREAT DIVIDE

T HE MISSOURI grew swifter and more perilous, its waters swirling around and over huge boulders. In the rocky river channel the powerful current smashed violently first on one side and then the other. "Every object here wears a dark and gloomy aspect," Lewis said. "The towering and projecting rocks in many places seem ready to tumble on us." Although they could see snow banks on the distant mountain peaks the heat shimmering in the confined and narrow canyon was almost suffocating.

Sometimes the party had to keep traveling after dark to find a few feet of ground level enough to make camp on. They had entered the Gates of the Rocky Mountains.

The sweating men, naked from the waist up, took turns toiling up the boulder-strewn banks as they towed the canoes with ropes. Where the river was less swift they poled the canoes. Lewis, who had learned to "push a tolerable good pole," encouraged the men with his help.

The captains were concerned about the approaching autumn. Soon the mountain passes would be choked with snow.

"I CALL IT THE GATES OF THE ROCKY MOUNTAINS," said Lewis. "We entered much the most remarkable clifts we have yet seen these clifts rise from the waters edge on each side perpendicularly to the hight of 1200 feet." The dam at the lower end of the canyon has raised the level of the water, but many of the formations described by Lewis are immediately recognizable.

"THIS HOWLING WILDERNESS" Gass called what is now Meriwether Camp. Lewis said there was not ". . . a spot except one of a few yards in extent on which a man could rest the soul of his foot." The party made camp here after dark. It is now a picnic grounds for the people of Helena, Montana.

It was certain that water travel could not continue much longer. How was the heavily-laden party to push on? With increased anxiety they scanned the country upriver after each bend, searching for Sacajawea's people, the Shoshones. "If we do not find the Shoshones or some other nation with horses," Lewis worried, "I fear the success of our voyage will be doubtful." Besides horses to carry supplies, they needed guides to help them through the Rocky Mountains to the headwaters of the Columbia. The Shoshones were timid, and perhaps the gunshots of the main party hunting for game had frightened them into fading away to their homes in the mountain fastnesses. The captains, in grave council decided that Clark, with Joseph Fields, Potts and York should set out cross-country to try to contact the Indians.

On their shortcut overland, where wood was scarce, the men prepared meals over campfires of long-burning, aromatic, dried buffalo dung. They were tortured by mosquitoes and gnats, while sharp flint rock and prickly pear penetrated their moccasins. Clark spent one whole evening picking seventeen prickly-pear thorns from his bleeding feet. Of the mosquitoes and gnats he said, "These animals attack us as soon as the labours and fatigues of the day require a rest and annoy us until several hours after dusk."

Clark and his companions found old Indian encampments, tracks of Indian ponies and even a wild Indian horse. Although at times they felt as if they were being watched by native eyes, they never saw an Indian. One afternoon in the distance they saw clouds of smoke billowing away from the river. They knew then that Indian scouts had indeed seen them and were setting the dry grass afire to warn the main encampment somewhere upriver. Discouraged, the weary men rejoined the main party. The captains were short of food, short of knowledge about this strange new country, short of almost everything but courage.

Clark treated his bleeding feet, put on a new pair of moccasins and again started out ahead, this time with four men, Charbonneau, Frazier and Joe and Reuben Fields. On July 25, 1805, despite blistered and wounded feet, the five reached a place where the Missouri divided into three forks, each contributing about an equal amount of water.

Because the Columbia was somewhere to the west, Clark concluded the most likely course was to follow the branch of the Missouri coming from the southwest. Leaving a note for the main party, they went up this branch to check Clark's guess.

They pressed on through the scorching heat. Charbonneau and one of the other men gave out and rested while Clark, with two men, climbed a mountain to scout for Indians. During the descent they came to a cold mountain spring. Clark, overheated, took the precaution of bathing his hands, face and feet before drinking the icy water. He still drank too soon and became violently ill. But sickness could not conquer his curiosity and he decided to go back and explore the middle fork. While wading the river, Charbonneau, who could not swim, stumbled and almost drowned. The weakened Clark rescued him.

"WE ARE NOW SEVERAL HUNDRED MILES within the bosom of this wild and mountainous country," said Lewis. "The hills or reather the Mountains again recede from the river and the valley again widens." This view is taken looking down the Missouri just below Three Forks. Lewis particularly described the canyon in the lower center. "The river was again hemmed in by high clifts . . . solid Limestone rock which appeared tumbled or sunk."

"I COMMANDED A MOST PERFECT VIEW." This is what Lewis saw from the limestone cliff pictured above. "The country opens suddenly to extensive and beautiful plains and meadows . . . ," he said of the Madison Valley.

"I WALKED UP THE S.E. FORK about ½ mile and ascended the point of a high limestone clift." It was from this rock that Lewis first viewed the valleys of the Gallatin, Madison and Jefferson rivers on July 25, 1805.

"A DISTANT RANGE OF LOFTY MOUNTAINS." In the foreground is the Gallatin Valley. Sacajawea Peak is the snow-capped mountain in the center. Clark went this way on his return trip and crossed over to the Yellowstone through Bozeman Pass, in the distance to the extreme right.

The main party under Lewis came upon the three forks Saturday, July 27. Going up the first fork about half a mile Lewis surveyed the situation from the top of a limestone cliff. Here the country opened into a beautiful wide valley with green meadows and grassy plains. On every side rose the snow-covered mountains. Descending the cliff Lewis rejoined the party and they went upstream a mile to the next fork where they found Clark's note. They camped on a point of land half a mile up the third fork. "This is a verry handsome pleasant place," Whitehouse commented, "fine bottoms of timber &c."

Sacajawea recognized the campsite as the very place where, four or five years before, the Gros Ventres attacked the huts of her people. She told how the Shoshones, outnumbered, fled three miles up the river, made a stand, but were overwhelmed with the first rush. Four men and four women were killed and many were wounded. The remaining Shoshone warriors mounted their horses and fled into the hills leaving their women and children at the mercy of the Gros Ventres. Sacajawea was overtaken and made prisoner as she tried to wade the river at a shoal.

She was neither pained by these recollections nor enthusiastic at her return to her own country. "For she seems to possess," said Lewis, who never liked her, "the folly or philosophy of not suffering her feelings to extend beyond the anxiety of having plenty to eat and a few trinkets to wear."

Weary and ill, Clark rejoined the main group that night. Lewis gave him a dose of Rush's Pills, a cure-all which the party carried. Whether these pills were named for their effect or for Dr. Benjamin Rush, a leading physician of the time, is not certain. But the formula was 10 grains jalap and 10 grains calomel and they were a violent physic. Anyway the morning of the 29th found Clark improved but still very weak.

Since the "three noble streams" were the same size, the captains could not decide which was the Missouri. Perhaps with the boss and payroll man in mind, they named the first fork the Gallatin for Albert Gallatin, secretary of the treasury; the second fork the Madison, after Secretary of State James Madison; and the third fork the Jefferson, for the President of the United States.

By the next day Clark was "much restored." The canoes were loaded and the party, with many misgivings, began the ascent of the Jefferson. The elusive Shoshones with their horses and their all-important knowledge of the mountains were still somewhere to the west. But the question of the moment was: Is this or is one of the other two rivers the way to the headwaters of the Columbia?

THE WRONG RIVER

THE URGENT NEED for horses drove the party on relentlessly. Usually they broke camp as the first streaks of dawn showed on the eastern horizon. Leaving without breakfast they paddled, poled or towed their canoes as the river permitted. Because game was getting more and more scarce, the hunters now nearly always

THE THREEFORKS OF THE MISSOURI. The Jefferson is the stream taking off to the lower left. The Madison joins it at the lower center. The Gallatin comes in from the right. The expedition camped for three days just to the left of where the railroad bridge shows on the Jefferson. The "handsome site for a fortification" that Lewis described is between the Madison and the Gallatin right of center: the high limestone cliff he climbed is just beyond and across the Gallatin. The men had lunch on the point of land below this rock, between the road and the Missouri, on July 27, 1805.

"A VERREY HIGH MOUNTAIN which jutted its tremendous clifts on either side." Clark shot a bighorn sheep in these rocks and it tumbled into the river. "The water swift and very sholey," he said, of this stretch of the Jefferson between Three Forks and Whitehall, Montana. The canoes could ascend the river only when pulled with towropes by the men on shore.

"GANGUE OF BUFFALOW." A few small, privately-owned herds still roam Montana and there are large herds near Polson and in Yellowstone Park, but they are a pitiful remnant of such herds as Meriwether Lewis described on July 11, 1806. It was mating season and the "bulls keep a tremendious roaring we could hear them many miles and there are such numbers of them that there is a continuous roar . . . I sincerely beleif that there are not less than 10 thousand buffaloe within a circle of 2 miles." Notice how the big bull stands guard by himself at the left of the herd.

A PISHKUN OR BUFFALO JUMP. The fleetest of the young men in an Indian tribe, disguised with buffalo skins, horns and all, would place themselves between the herd and a precipice like this one. The other Indians surrounded the grazing herds on the high plateau and, waving blankets and screaming, stampeded the herd. The buffalo-disguised young men then would run toward the cliff and the stupid animals would follow their false leaders, those behind forcing those in front over the cliff. The Indian runners usually swerved behind a rock just in time. Sometimes, however, their bodies were found among the mangled carcasses at the foot of the jump. Lewis and Clark described one of these jumps near Judith River, saying there were a "vast many carcases of Buffalow . . . they created a most horrid stench . . ." and that there were "great many wolves in the neighborhood of these mangled carcases" which were fat and "extreemly gentle." At this jump near Logan Montana the soil in the middle draw is almost pure bone and blood meal for a depth of at least four feet.

preceded the party. When they made a kill of elk, bighorn sheep, bear, deer or antelope they hung it in the shade of a tree. Not until the exhausted and hungry members of the main party reached this spot could they breakfast. On August 1 Clark shot a mountain sheep on which they feasted and, because it was his 35th birthday, gave each of the men a little flour. As a rule they traveled 10 or 11 miles on a rough stretch of the river, or 18 to 20 miles if the current was less swift.

The upper Jefferson in the high mountain valleys meanders a good deal. On some days after a strenuous 20 mile voyage they found themselves only two or three miles as the crow flies from their campsite of the previous night.

Lewis by himself undertook the job of scouting ahead, because Clark was confined to his canoe by a "rageing fury of a tumer" on his ankle. One day Lewis, while exploring, got involved in a series of beaver dams along the river. Wading around them waist-deep he fought underbrush until exhausted. That night he camped by a fragrant driftwood fire alone in the great wilderness. As he lay in his bed of willow twigs after a dinner of roast duck the moody Lewis probably actually enjoyed the plaintive barking wail of the coyotes.

On August 3 Clark saw the pigeon-toed moccasin tracks of an Indian near camp. They were fresh. He followed them and found they led to a hill overlooking the previous night's camp. The native had spent the night watching these strange people as they moved to and fro around the campfire. Then he had noiselessly drifted away in the darkness to warn his brothers to move still farther back among the mountain crags. But it was encouraging to the party: at least the Shoshones had been near them.

Lewis formerly had attempted to return to camp each night. Now, heartened by the Indian tracks, he decided on a longer excursion and with packsacks he, Sergeant Gass, Charbonneau and Drewyer started ahead. Clark writhed in pain each time a twig or rock touched the carbuncle on his ankle. He was in no condition to travel, so stayed with the canoes.

On Sunday, August 4, Lewis and his three men came to a fork in the river. He examined the two streams, and decided which was the most logical course for the main party. Sergeant Gass cut a green willow wand, attached to it a note for Clark and jammed it into the marshy ground. Then Lewis and the three set off exploring again.

When the main party under Clark reached the fork the note was gone; probably a hungry beaver had made a meal of the stake. "We was not certain whether Capt. Lewis was up the left fork or the right," Ordway said, and they went up "The right hand fork which is amazeing rapid." It was not only rapid: it was the wrong fork. Willow and cottonwood brush grew out into the channels. At some places where the beavers had been busy gnawing, the brush choked the stream. The men hauled the canoes by pulling on the branches of the overhanging brush. At times they were forced out into the water where "we could scarsely kick our feet for the rapidity of the current."

They had gone only a mile from the junction when they camped that night. Wet and shivering, they built willow beds to keep them off the clammy, recently-inundated ground. To go further seemed impossible, but Clark and his men had done the impossible before. They started out the next morning to do it again.

They had gone nine miles when Drewyer, who had been sent up this stream by Lewis to guard against Clark's taking the wrong fork, came upon them. The mistake was easier made than corrected. Clark had sent young Shannon ahead to hunt. The men blew the horn and fired several shots but Shannon couldn't be located. They had "difficulty in gitting the canoes down over the sholes and rapids," Ordway commented. Joe Whitehouse was thrown from a canoe as it lurched in the swift stream. As he lay on the rocks under the surface the current swept the heavy dugout over him. The boat missed crushing him by a scant two inches; however, he was lamed by the fall.

When they finally reached the forks they spent a day unloading their canoes and drying the contents. Several things were damaged and "one kig of powder spoiled." Clark sent Drewyer upriver again, this time to find Shannon. Failing, he returned and Reuben Fields went out. When Fields came back without him, it appeared that Shannon was really lost for a second time.

FRUSTRATION

On August 9 Sacajawea pointed to what she said the Indians called the Beaverhead Rocks. The discouraged men took heart when she told them this marked the high mountain valley that was the summer home of her people. At this time of year they almost certainly would be on this river or on the one over the ridge. The party felt further relieved when young Shannon, whom they had about given up for good, found his way to camp. He was in fine shape, having killed and fed on four deer.

Lewis and his three companions had rejoined the party because the lazy Charbonneau claimed to be unable to go farther. Now with renewed enthusiasm Lewis took his knapsack and again swung out ahead, this time with Shields, Drewyer and McNeal.

The very next day this advance party came upon a well-beaten Indian trail. They followed it all day. Coming to another fork in the river Lewis correctly took the branch to the west, but incorrectly assumed it was the Jefferson River. It was Horse Prairie Creek.

To advise Clark of the decision he again left a note on a willow stake for the main party. This time he was careful to use a dry, not a tempting green stake.

Next day the advance group saw a man coming down off higher ground onto the plain about two miles away. Looking through his spyglass Lewis saw an Indian

90

". . . A FIEW ISLANDS and maney gravelly sholes." Among the willows this looks like the junction of the Beaverhead and Bighole. It is actually an island but it demonstrates the puzzling problems of which river to take that confronted the captains at this point.

JUNCTION OF THE BIGHOLE AND BEAVERHEAD RIVERS. At this point the Jefferson becomes the Bighole (left) and Beaverhead (right). Lewis and Clark tried the Bighole and rejected it and went up the Beaverhead. Either river would have taken them to the Continental Divide.

THE BIGHOLE RIVER. Because beaver destroyed Lewis's message, Clark and the main party came up this river by mistake. The current was so swift that the men had to tow the canoes. There was more water in the river than is shown here and because the shores are so brushy the men had to wade in the water. "This increased the pain and labour extremely," Lewis said.

BEAVERHEAD ROCK. Sacajawea pointed this rock out to the captains saying that beyond it was the summer home of her people, the Shoshones, and that it was called Beaverhead because of a "conceved resemlence of its figure to the head of that anamal." As the expedition passed this spot they ran into a violent electrical storm with rain and hail. The men took refuge in the bushes but got "Perfectly wet." Clark said, "This clift the Indians call the Beavershead, opposite at 300 yards is a low clift 50 feet high which is a spur from the mountain."

"SHORT BENDS constituteing large and general bends," Lewis said of this section of the Beaverhead River near Twin Bridges, Montana. "We travel briskly and a considerable distance yet it takes us only a few miles on our general course," he complained.

"OF THE TIGER KIND." Cougars were and still are common anywhere deer abound. The hunters killed one and several times saw others. Once two of the men wounded one. Clark said, "Two of our men fired at a panther a little below our camp. this animale they say was large, had caught a Deer & eate it half & buried the ballance."

"STEEP UP FROM THE RIVER." Rattlesnake Cliffs, south of Dillon, Montana, were so named by Lewis because of the great number of rattlesnakes he saw. Drewyer, hunting with Lewis, killed a deer here. Clark, coming along later, agreed about the snakes. "They were fierce," he said.

whose dress was different from any he had ever seen. He was armed with a bow and a quiver of arrows. The Shoshone was mounted on an "elagant" horse! The native apparently did not see the group for he rode unconcernedly toward them until only about a mile distant. Catching sight of them he stopped. Lewis stopped also and tried to signal his warm friendship for the Shoshone nation. Sign language, difficult to understand at best, probably was impossible to grasp at the distance of a mile. Lewis said dryly the "signal did not have the desired effect."

The Indian was suspicious but since a whole mile separated him from the party and since he was mounted and the party was on foot he apparently felt he could keep the situation under control.

Lewis moved toward him, frantically waving a looking glass, a string of beads and other trinkets calculated to delight the childish heart of the native. Drewyer and Shields, who were off to the left and right of Lewis, were moving up also and they weren't waving anything interesting. Desperately Lewis motioned them to stop. Drewyer got the idea but Shields kept moving up. The Indian's suspicion of Shield's motives grew faster than his curiosity about the trinkets. Lewis, who usually studied each Indian language, hadn't spent much time on Shoshone because he relied on Sacajawea to interpret for him. Shouting the only Shoshone word he knew, "Tabba-bone," meaning white man, while feverishly trying to signal Shields to stop, waving the trinkets and pulling up his sleeve to show his white skin, Lewis undoubtedly won for himself the distinction of being the first white contortionist in the Rocky Mountains. It must have been a good performance because the Shoshone let him get within 100 paces. But Shields by this time had continued until he was slightly in back of the Indian. No Indian who loved life and liberty and was in his right mind would permit strangers to be both in front and back of him at the same time, no matter how entertaining the one in front. The Shoshone suddenly wheeled his horse applied the whip, leaped the creek and disappeared in the willows.

There was no humor in this for Lewis. It was bitter tragedy. He felt the chances of success for himself and his expedition were riding the "elagant" horse off through the thickets.

Supposedly what Lewis told his men was unprintable. What he wrote in his diary that night was, "I now felt as much mortification and disappointment as I had pleasure and expectation at the first sight of the Indian . . . I felt soarly chargrined at the conduct of the men." It must be remembered that Lewis and Clark were preparing their journals to be read by the President of the United States.

SHOSHONES AND HORSES

THE FATE of the ". . . expedition [which] I have ever held in equal estimation to my own existence" seemed to hang in the balance for Lewis. He built a campfire on a hilltop and surrounded it with beads, trinkets and mirrors hung on stakes, futilely trying to decoy the Indian into coming back, but the medicine show was rained out. McNeal marched ahead waving a small American flag; if the Shoshone saw him he was not interested. They were unable to trail the lone Indian rider because the sudden rainstorm had washed away the tracks.

Gloomily the group followed along an Indian road, their clothing soaked by rain and their spirits dampened by the thought of failure.

Horse Prairie Creek divided. The Indian trail followed Trail Creek, which dwindled to a mere rivulet. McNeal, in what Lewis called a "fit of enthusiasm" but more likely was a fit of hysteria, straddled the stream shouting his thanks to God that he had lived to "bestride the mighty and heretofore deemed endless Missouri."

Passing over Lemhi they realized they had crossed the Continental Divide. On descending a steep slope they came to a "handsome bold creek" of clear cold water. Lewis, in better spirits now, stopped to taste for the first time the waters of the Columbia. As twilight's long shadows crept up the ravines of Lemhi Pass, they made camp without comfort and with very little food, but on the Pacific slope!

On the morning of Tuesday, August 13, Lewis, Shields, Drewyer and McNeal started out again with their backs to the rising sun. Still following the old Indian road they traveled about nine miles. On a hill a mile away they saw an Indian man and two women surrounded, as usual, by dogs.

The Indians saw them but apparently distance lent enchantment, for they sat down and watched Lewis as he approached. Cautious, this time, he ordered his men to stop. Then, because his antics had interested the Indians two days before, he unfurled his little American flag and waved it as he advanced. But the women were nervous and disappeared. They were soon followed by the man, leaving Lewis hopelessly pleading "Tabbabone, tabbabone" to his echo among the hills.

Desperately Lewis tried to capture one of the dogs. He hoped to tie some trinkets around its neck to be carried to its master. The dogs were as wild as the Shoshones, and Lewis's "tabbabone" didn't interest them either.

Lewis and his companions trudged disconsolately down the dusty Indian road in the hot sun. They were following a little stream into which frequently converged deep ravines. Coming suddenly onto one of these, they surprised three Indians. A young woman fled like a deer. An old woman and a little girl, seeing no chance to escape, bowed their heads, seeming "reconciled to the death which they supposed awaited them." The persistent Lewis again repeated his unmagic word "Tabbabone" but the woman was reassured only when he put down his rifle and raised her up. She became interested when he gave her a few trinkets and downright friendly when he painted her cheeks with vermilion. This was one of the few times in his life when Lewis displayed a little understanding of the feminine sex.

The young woman who had run away apparently hadn't gone far. On seeing the treatment accorded the old woman she came back all out of breath.

Cooperation of the Shoshone women was now assured so Lewis, through the interpreter Drewyer, asked to be led to the Indian camp. Following down the same

96

"ONE OF THE HANDSOMEST COVES I EVER SAW." Here, just west of Armstead, Montana, is where Lewis saw the lone Indian rider. "At the apparent extremity of the bottom above us two perpendicular clifts of considerable hight stand on either side of the river and uppers [appears] at this distant like a gate."

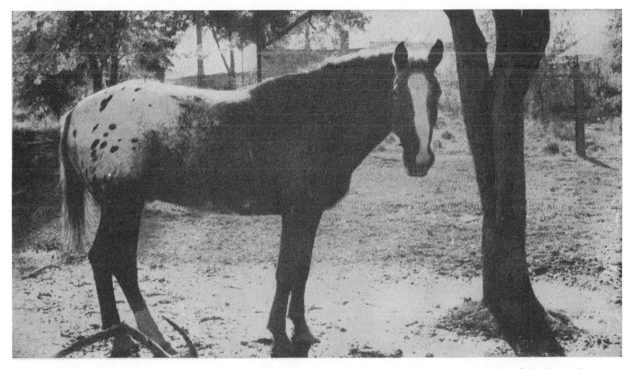

AN "ELIGANT" HORSE. This is a typical "Appaloosie," so called because these horses were bred by the Palouse Indians as well as the Nez Perce. This horse is a descendant of the horses brought across the Atlantic by the Spanish in their galleons to Mexico. Partly of Arabian stock, the horses were much coveted by the Indians. They traded or stole them and brought them north where they flourished on the grassy hills of the Nez Perce country. It was horses like this that the two captains saw among the Nez Perce and Yakimas.

"HERETOFORE DEEMED ENDLESS MISSOURI." This is the head of Trail Creek just below Lemhi Pass. Here McNeal stood astride what he thought was the headwaters of the Missouri and thanked God that he had lived to do so.

"THE MOST DISTANT FOUNTAIN of the waters of the mighty Missouri." From Lemhi Pass looking east over the route that the expedition came by. The ancient road of the Shoshones followed down here to the headwaters of the Jefferson and from there to buffalo country.

"EMENCE RANGES OF MOUNTAINS still to the west of us." From Lemhi Pass on the Continental Divide looking into the Salmon River country. Lewis rested here a few minutes, then descended into the ravine, "to a handsome bold runing creek of cold clear water. Here I first tasted the water of the great Columbia river."

road about two miles, they were met by a wildly-riding band of sixty warriors, fully armed and ready to fight the abductors of their women. Possibly Lewis was alarmed at their warlike approach but more likely his thoughts were on the "excellent" horses they were riding. At last the Shoshones! And at last the horses!

The women soon explained that the "tabbabones" were friends. The chief and two other men leaped from their horses shouting "Ah hi e! Ah hi e," the Shoshone version of "I am glad to meet you." The three Indians embraced and rubbed cheeks with Lewis and his men. Then the whole party of 60 warriors came forward to greet the whites. Lewis ruefully remarked that the motive was much more agreeable than the manner, adding "we wer all carresed and besmeared with their grease paint until I was heartily tired of the national hug."

After these enthusiastic ceremonies the Indians seated themselves around Lewis and his men, looking expectantly at them as if to say, "Now you do something interesting." Lewis lighted his pipe and started to pass it around. The unpredictable Indians all solemnly removed their moccasins. This must have been disconcerting to Lewis but he made the next move and it was the right one. He passed around gifts and to the chief he gave the little American flag. The Indians then led the way to their camp on the bank of a river. In the camp were an old buffalo-hide lodge and about 25 "huts of conical figure made with willow brush." They must have seemed beautiful to Lewis and his men.

The Shoshones danced and yelled all night long in celebration of having guests. But the guest of honor slept soundly in the leather lodge on the western side of the Continental Divide.

SHOSHONE INDIANS

THE OLDER SHOSHONES could remember when the tribe had been proud inhabitants of the plains. But they fared badly in their wars with the Blackfeet and had to flee the rich buffalo and game country for the mountains. At the headwaters of the Columbia and Snake Rivers, where they spent most of the year, fish and roots were their diet; only occasionally their stone-pointed arrows sank into a deer, mountain sheep or goat. Each September they joined forces with the Flatheads and, finding strength in numbers, invaded the buffalo country for meat and skins. After their annual forays they retired again to their meager life on the mountains.

Although poor nourishment kept them physically undeveloped they were honest, hospitable and courageous in spirit. Lewis and Clark found they behaved with "the greatest decorum."

Fine horses were the greatest wealth of the Shoshones. Largely of Arabian stock, these animals originally had been traded for or stolen from the Spaniards in the south. Some bore Spanish brands and a few of the Indians sported Spanish saddles and bits. The Shoshones, mindful that their horses were their point of superiority over other tribes, carefully and expertly bred them.

100

TRAIL ALONG LEMHI PASS. This is a part of the Indian road that Lewis, with Drewyer and McNeal, walked down and over. The main party passed a few days later with their Indian companions, on their way down the Columbia side of the Continental Divide.

The tribal government was a pure democracy with each warrior his own master. The chiefs were simply men whose acts of valor or great wisdom had elevated them to a position of respect. They were looked to for advice rather than orders.

As in most Indian tribes, the women performed most of the camp chores. Some Shoshones had several wives to share the work and share the warrior. Girls often were betrothed by their parents when they reached puberty. Before being captured Sacajawea had been so betrothed.

Shoshone children scampered around the lodges doing as they pleased, for their elders thought discipline would break their spirit.

Lewis awakened in his hide hut the next morning to face a day of negotiation for horses and information. Although he got meager information and no horses he had a bit of success. Some of the tribesmen agreed to accompany him on an expedition back to meet Clark and the main party who were still toiling up the river.

The Shoshones were short of food, as usual, and Lewis said, "this morning I arrose very early and as hungary as a wolf." When they started out with Lewis to meet Clark the Indians were suspicious of a trap. "They looked as surly as so many imps of Satturn," said Lewis. Growing more alarmed as they went along some of them sneaked off to the home camp. Curiosity and hunger for the food provided by the hunters, Drewyer and Shields, kept 28 Shoshone men and 3 women with the party.

Two days later, Lewis, already worried by the Indians' flightiness, was dismayed when the whole band suddenly lashed their horses and started racing away through the sagebrush. He was especially concerned because he was riding double with one of them.

Fearing wholesale desertion he was relieved when he learned the wild excitement was caused by a deer one of his hunters had killed. His fear allayed, he suddenly realized that riding double on an Indian horse going full tilt over rough ground was somewhat less than comfortable. Pulling up the horse he ordered the native to stop whipping the animal. The Indian was really in a hurry. He jumped off the horse and ran nearly a mile to the place of the kill. He proved he was a distance runner of no mean ability by arriving before Lewis.

When Lewis came riding up to the scene the Indians were scrambling about and tumbling over each other like a pack of hungry dogs, tearing away with their bare hands at the warm, still quivering flesh. Lewis noticed one native feeding a 9-foot length of entrail into his blood-smeared face with one hand while squeezing the entrail's contents onto the ground with the other. "I really did not until now think that human nature ever presented itself in a shape so nearly allied to the brute creation. I viewed these poor divils with pity and compassion," said Lewis.

Another deer was killed; another feast, then still another. Finally Lewis was able to get his group, in better humor now, started again on their way to help Clark and the main party.

102

"THE RIVER VERRY CROOKED." Looking toward the junction of Prairie and Red Rock creeks which form the Beaverhead river Captain Clark saw this view August 16, 1805, and said, "I assended a mountain from the top of which I could see the river forked near me the left hand appeared the largest & bore S.E. the right passed from the west thro an extencive valley, I could see but three small trees." Clark and his men camped that night to the left of the island shown in the center of the picture.

"RUND ON THE LARBOARD SIDE," Ordway called Clark's canyon. Tugging their canoes against the strong current with tow cords, the men were forced into the water by the thick underbrush and became "fortigued." Clark climbed the hill where this picture was taken and viewed the forks of the Beaverhead.

All went well until they reached the forks of Horse Prairie Creek and the Beaverhead River. Here Lewis expected to meet Clark. He had told the Indians that Clark would be there and they grew wary of the whole affair when they found no Clark and no main party.

The Indians had not yet spied the note Lewis had left for Clark on the willow stake. Darting to get the note, Lewis read it aloud claiming it was a message from Clark saying he would be up tomorrow. The ruse temporarily satisfied the suspicious natives. Nevertheless when the captain hastily dispatched Drewyer to locate Clark and tell him to hurry, most of the Indians went along just in case.

SACAJAWEA'S BROTHER

THE RIVER became shallower and swifter as the main part of the expedition approached the Great Divide. The men were almost constantly in the water, sliding and falling over the slippery rocks as they hauled the large canoes. "The water is verry cold," grumbled Sergeant Ordway, "we have to waid in it which makes our feet and legs ake with cold. We expect it is made of springs." The men were almost exhausted but Captain Clark "engouraged them and passifyed them."

Nor was the water the only hazard; rattlesnakes lurked on the shoreline. Sacajawea was almost bitten once, and twice Clark narrowly escaped. Once when fishing he discovered a large rattler between his feet, ready to strike. The snakes were a very real danger. Certainly Rush's Pills wouldn't help a snakebite.

On August 15 they passed two high pillars of rocks on each side of the river, literally crawling with snakes. Lewis, who had passed by a few days before, named them "Rattlesnake Clifts." The party caught what Ordway called a "nomber of fine trout" and picked up deerskins left by Lewis.

In the valley beyond, Sacajawea gathered service-berries for their dinner. The food-conscious men called it Service-berry Valley. When they passed a "verry bad rockey rapids" they were "obliged to hale the canoes over large rocks etc." The mountains huddled close to the river. Clark, climbing the hill on the right, viewed the splendid scenery and saw, shining in the distance, another fork in the river.

They started toiling up the river again about 7 o'clock on August 17, 1805. Clark, Sacajawea and Charbonneau walked through the dew-covered grass along the banks of the stream. Clark, his ankle still lame, fell behind about 100 yards. He saw Sacajawea jump suddenly and begin a dance of joy, sucking her fingers and pointing at several Indians riding toward her. "This is my tribe," she was saying in sign language, "the people among whom I was suckled."

As the Indians approached they broke into a wild song. Drewyer was with them, for these were the Indians who went with him to find the main party. They rejoined Lewis and then all journeyed to the Indian camp where they were soon seated in council. Having removed their moccasins the Indians were now in a position to discuss anything intelligently. Sacajawea, allowed in council only because she

"A HIGH KNOB OR HILL at the forks of the Jefferson." . . . ". . . in the level plain between the two forks," Lewis described on August 10, "and about ½ mile distant stands a high rocky mountain . . . it has a singular appearance." The council was held here between Lewis and Clark and Chief Cameahwait. The canoes were filled with rocks and sunk in the pond.

THE PINTO OF THE PLAINS INDIANS. These horses, either red and white or black and white, were one of the types obtained by Lewis and Clark from the Shoshones. It is probable the Shoshones also got some Appaloosies, because they traded with the Nez Perce and because they too had contact with the Spaniards.

could speak Shoshone, came into her own. She translated her native tongue into Gros Ventre. Charbonneau translated Gros Ventre into French. Labiche translated the French to English. It is surprising that a war caused by misunderstanding did not start on the Continental Divide that day. Each side tried to be tactful, but tact is lost when three languages removed. The lank face of the Indians' Chief Cameahwait showed suspicion.

Suddenly Sacajawea leaped to her feet. Streaking for the dour Cameahwait she embraced him, threw her blanket over him, alternately weeping and chattering Shoshone. In the great wilderness she had found her brother, one of her only three relatives who had survived the Gros Ventre attack at Three Forks. Her interpreting from then on was interrupted by frequent bursts of tears. Cameahwait himself was moved.

The expedition had found a common ground, if not a common language with the Indians.

CLARK ON THE LEMHI RIVER

Lᴇᴡɪꜱ ᴀɴᴅ Cʟᴀʀᴋ earnestly set about the business of getting horses and information. The Indians loved entertainment and they loved gifts. Lewis and Clark provided both. First they gave the more important tribesmen honorary gifts of medals, a uniform coat and tobacco. Lesser presents of awls, beads, moccasins and mirrors were scattered around among the other natives. Now and then Lewis or Clark carefully, casually interjected a question about the country ahead or a request for horses. But they must not hurry, they must not be too businesslike. Hastily, when an answer was given, they changed the subject by giving an exhibition of some sort. What impatient urgency the captains must have felt as the questions piled up inside of them. But they must wait while the airgun was shot, or one of the men went into a jig or someone struck up a tune on the violin to keep the Indians in a negotiating mood. When they ran out of diversions, a display of York's black skin and wiry curls made a good show. "We have learnt by experience," Lewis explained, "that to keep the savages in good humor their attention should not be wearied by too much business . . . matters should be enlivened with what is new and entertaining."

Cameahwait and the other chiefs succumbed to this thoroughly sound sales procedure. They not only agreed to furnish information, but for a consideration, the horses.

While the two captains were in council with the chiefs, the men of the expedition were discovering that the Indian husbands would, as Lewis said, "for a trifle barter the companion of his bead for a night or longer." The captains cautioned the men to be careful not to give the Indians cause for jealousy, but could not "prevent this mutual exchange of good officies," said Lewis sensibly, "particularly on the part of our young men whom some months abstanence have made very polite to those

106

MONUMENT TO OLD TOBY. This monument located on the Salmon River side of Lemhi Pass is in commemoration of Lewis and Clark's Shoshone Indian guide, who, with his sons, showed the two captains the way to and over Lolo.

tawney damsels." He added, "No evil has as yet resulted and I hope will not from these connections."

The white men were not the only ones who had ideas. The Indian man to whom Sacajawea had been betrothed before her capture stepped up and claimed her. But he changed his mind when he found that she had had a baby by Charbonneau.

Clark had recovered from the carbuncle on his ankle. The captains decided he should take 11 men across Lemhi Pass, about 40 miles distant, and then go down the Columbia to see how navigable it was. Actually the river was the Lemhi, a tributary of the Columbia. If river travel seemed feasible, the 12 men planned to make canoes and send a messenger back to Lewis telling him to come with the rest of the men and the baggage.

With a uniform coat, two pair of leggings, a few handkerchiefs, four knives and an old checkered shirt they bartered four horses from the Indians and were on their way. The narrow gap where they camped August 18 they named Shoshone Cove. Next day an Indian with two mules and a Spanish saddle came into their camp. An old waistcoat convinced him that he should carry Clark, who had no horse, over the pass on one of his mules.

They reached the Indian encampment on the west side of Lemhi Pass August 20. Here the Indians graphically described the country on ahead by drawing maps on the ground with sticks, indicating mountains with handfuls of sand.

The Lemhi River, they said, was unnavigable. So was another river far to the southwest, which Clark concluded was the Colorado. But there was a route following the high ridges used by the Nez Perce even though it was "very rough, much timber, no game." Clark decided if the Nez Perce could do it, so could he and his men.

They pressed on, passing through a valley rich and wide. The hills, Sergeant Gass worried, soon "assumed a formidable aspect." Closing in, the "amazeingly high" and rugged mountains towered over the swift river with its frequent "dreadful narrows."

There were no trees fit for canoes. Had the Indian guide taken them past the route of the Nez Perce? Clark decided to return to the Shoshone encampment near Lemhi Pass to find out.

LEWIS AND PARTY TO LEMHI

August 18, 1805, was Lewis's 31st birthday. After the day's work was done the captain, protected from the driving rain only by the temporary shelter the men had built, reflected "I had in all human probability existed about half the period which I am to remain in this Sublunary world . . . I had as yet done but little, very little, indeed, to further the hapiness of the human race, or to advance the information of the succeeding generation. I viewed with regret the many hours I have spent in indolence, and now soarly feel the want of that information which those hours would have given me had they been judiciously expended . . . resolved

108

"A VERRY LONESOME PLACE." . . . "so Steep that the horses could Scurcely keep from Slipping down, Several Sliped & Injured themselves verry much," said Clark of this spot. The timber is dense in the canyon so the party had to keep to the side hills where rock slides like the one shown at the right were prevalent. Snow and sleet also made this part of the trip extremely difficult. The "fur" trees Clark mentioned still are abundant near Salmon, Idaho.

in future, to redouble my exertions . . . to live *for mankind,* as I have heretofore lived *for myself.*"

There was pressing work to be done before Lewis and the main party could leave the forks to join Clark at Lemhi Pass.

First they must cache the surplus baggage some place where the Indians would not find it. Scouting around, they found a suitable spot three-fourths of a mile below camp, where three men dug a pit while a fourth did sentinel duty in case any inquisitive Indians came around. After dark they warily moved the baggage into the pit. It was cold work. "The ground is covered with white frost," Ordway wrote, "the ink freezes in my pen now."

Hiding the canoes was a matter of outwitting the atmosphere rather than the Indians. Lewis decided to fill the canoes with stones and sink them in a pool in the river to prevent their drying out and cracking in the high altitude. The Indians promised not to disturb them. Even the skeptical Lewis accepted their promise, feeling sure that the work involved in raising the canoes would be just too much bother for the natives.

After buying nine horses and hiring two more and a mule, they moved on toward Lemhi on Saturday, August 24. At Shoshone Cove, Wiser was taken suddenly and violently ill with "colic." Lewis dosed him with essence of peppermint and laudanum. He got better with this medication and they might have moved on but the Indians had already unpacked and turned loose the horses. Although the sun was still high, they made camp at the cove.

Next day, starting early, they made 17 miles and camped about two miles from Lemhi Pass. Here Lewis was disturbed to learn that Cameahwait and his chiefs were planning to forsake the party and go off hunting in the buffalo country. Lewis changed their minds and won them back with some additional presents.

Next day when they arrived at the Shoshone camp they found John Colter waiting for them with the message that Clark and his part of the expedition were returning.

OLD TOBY LOSES THE TRAIL

When Clark and his 10 men rejoined the party at the Shoshone camp on Lemhi Pass, he reported that on the western side of the divide the streams were small and swift, tumbling from one cataract to another. They were "beat into a perfect foam," he added, "as far as the eye could see." It would be impossible to descend them in canoes. Horses were what they needed for the trip across the mountains — horses from the Shoshones.

Trading the Indians out of their horses took a bit of doing. The tribe was poor because of the wars with the Blackfeet and had only a few extra horses. But they had acquired a great respect for the white men, partly because of a "bush drag" which netted Lewis and Clark's men 528 fish in one morning from a stream near the

110

camp. The Indians, who fished only with their bone spears, thought this was a miracle.

Even with miracle men the natives drove sharp bargains. For one horse they demanded a pistol and ammunition; for another a musket. The Indians shrewdly reasoned that with weapons they could replenish their horse herds from those of their enemies. Perhaps they thought they could even Indian-give their horses to Lewis and Clark.

When the two captains finally had 29 horses they knew they could start searching for the pass through the mountains to the Columbia River. They set off on Friday, August 30, under the guidance of a Shoshone dubbed Old Toby, and his four sons.

It was rough going. The first Indian trail they followed swung off in the wrong direction and the men had to cut their way through the heavy timber. "The creek is become small and the hills come close in upon the banks of it," Sergeant Gass noted, "covered thick with standing timber and fallen trees." But there was a little compensation in finding "wild or choke cherries . . . which eat verry well."

Sometimes to by-pass a particularly dense thicket they went up a side of the mountains which Whitehouse said were "nearly as steep as a roof of a house." It was hard on the horses. Several of the heavily laden animals were pulled over by the weight of their packs and sent rolling down the precipices. The last of the party's thermometers was broken in one of these accidents. Although only one horse was seriously crippled, the men themselves had to carry several of the beasts' loads up the sheer mountainsides.

On Tuesday Old Toby led them up a small creek on a journey which Sergeant Gass called "fatiguing beyond description." It was the wrong creek and certainly the wrong weather. Rain began falling on the tired men and weary horses. At dusk it changed to snow which "continued until the ground was covered with two inches of it." During that sleety night of September 3, they did not need a thermometer to tell them their camp in the heart of the Rockies was cold.

"This," remarked Ordway, "is a verry lonesome place."

TRAVELOGUE . . . Following the Missouri most of the way to Helena we found the road good, and the campsites well-marked by the Montana Highway Department, bless its heart. Helena is one of my favorite cities; I knew that as we drove toward it on the long straight highway across Prickly Pear Valley. Here sits Helena at the end of the road, and she seems to say, "Well, it's about time you came to see me." Little byways out of town lead into the hills where, in a few minutes, we saw dozens of old mines. The town is backed by them, and its main street was once the fabulous Last Chance Gulch. Spring rains still upheave nuggets into the street.

The Gates of the Mountains boat ride on Hauser Lake, near Helena, is a lovely and often spectacular two-hour trip. At two o'clock each day, and oftener on weekends, the little excursion boat chugs through the channel in the mountains. The expedition went through here. From some angles it looks as though there were no opening through the great rugged rocks, which must have been disheartening to the party.

Leaving Helena, we weren't far along when antelope seemed to spring up from everywhere. Although there were only eight or ten of them altogether, they appeared so rapidly and from so many directions that we felt surrounded. They dispersed quickly enough when they saw Al with his camera. Animals seem to take a fiendish delight in escaping photographers. These creatures posed beautifully until just before the shutter snapped, then off they would go. We sat in the car and wished we could help as Al ran over fields and little hills after the prancing animals.

Al was collecting animal pictures for the book. He likes to get his own, but in some cases planned to use pictures from the game department or from photographer friends. Lewis and Clark spent hundreds of pages in their journals describing the animal life they saw, in the minutest detail. Thinking of the two captains mixing their powdered ink and painstakingly writing their descriptions, I'd often commented it was too bad they didn't have a candid camera to take quick snaps of the animals. When Al came sweating and panting back to the car, I decided the captains didn't have it so bad after all.

A little side road led us to an old buffalo jump. Here hundreds of buffalo had tumbled to their death after being stampeded over by the Indians. Bits of the animals' bones are thick through the ground. Standing on a hill Al pointed to several circles of rocks. "Tepee rings," he said. "That's where their camp was." I for once pointed to the right place to dig and Al came up with a delicate white arrowhead and several crude tools.

We were nearing the headwaters of the Missouri. As we drove along we found the Madison, the Gallatin and the Jefferson rivers gleaming before us. How strange to think that melted snows and tiny springs trickle down distant mountains, each rivulet joining the descent until a river is rushing toward the plains. And here were three, uniting to make the Missouri, so that the people of St. Louis see the melted snows of Montana pouring into the Mississippi.

All along the road to Dillon we could see the meandering Beaverhead River, up which the expedition toiled with their heavy canoes. When we reached Beaverhead Rocks, where the road crosses the river, Al pointed to the landmark which Sacajawea had recognized and which had helped her locate her people for Lewis and Clark. "I think Sacajawea was indispensable," I said somewhat truculently, "because who knows how the expedition might have turned out without her guidance." "You're partly right," Al replied, "but I still say she just went along for the ride and happened to be helpful. If she was so vitally necessary why didn't the captains mention her oftener in their journals?"

This road is historic for other reasons. Vigilantes camped here, and this was a landmark on the old stage-coach road. At Dillon Al reminded me that President Rush Jordan of Western Montana State Teacher's College had helped him locate many historic spots not too easy to find on a map. Quite often local residents are a wonderful help in searching out obscure places, and it pays the traveler to inquire at the town's high school or college when he is stumped.

On the way to Armstead we passed Fortunate Camp where Clark met the Indians and cached their canoes. Armstead is a real old-fashioned western town. No drugstore cowboys here, but actual cattlemen who whoop it up in traditional western style.

112

"MOUNTAINS CLOSE ON EACH SIDE OF THE RIVER." The explorers camped on this little creek in Rosses Hole September 4 and 5, 1805, about where the willows are in the center of the picture. They left through the high saddle on the mountain ridge to the right.

"A CLOUDY & RAINIE DAY . . . & DRISLEY." The captains got a poor impression of the Bitter Root Valley, saying incorrectly that there were no fish in the river and the soil was poor.

The road over Lemhi pass is at times terrible. There is no other word for it, and the only consolation is that we traveled it a lot faster than Lewis and Clark. In the fall a traveler must drive with caution as he may meet great herds of prime white-faced steers being driven to the shipping point at Armstead. A herd of buffalo roams the hills in this area, too, and last year Al had the thrill of photographing it. As he walked toward them they kept drifting away. He snapped some pictures, disgustedly wishing the animals wouldn't be so shy, when suddenly they got the same idea. In one concerted action they swung around and started moving toward him. He claims he never ran so fast in his life.

HOW TO GET THERE NOW . . . See maps 6 and 7.

GATES OF THE MOUNTAINS. From Helena, Montana, take U.S. 91, 16.4 miles north to where gravel road turns off at right. On gravel road go 3 miles to Gates of Mountain boat club. Trips by boats down the gorge leave every day at 2 o'clock, oftener on weekends. At Meriwether Camp, about half way down the gorge, Lewis and Clark camped July 19, 1805.

THREE FORKS OF MISSOURI. From Three Forks, Montana, take U.S. 10, 2.2 miles east. Take gravel road on left to where the Gallatin unites with the Madison and Jefferson rivers to form the Missouri.

JUNCTION OF THE BIG HOLE AND BEAVERHEAD RIVERS. From Twin Bridges, Montana, take Montana 41 across the Beaverhead to just past the orphanage. Here take road to right and cross the Big Hole River bridge. Turn sharp right at end of the bridge and go 3 miles over rough road to where road skirts the river. Here walk across field to right, about 115 paces, to the junction of the two streams.

BEAVERHEAD ROCKS. From Twin Bridges, Montana, take Montana 41 west 14.5 miles to Beaverhead Rock, a narrow gorge where the road crosses the Beaverhead River. The Vigilante Trail (Montana 41) follows the route of Lewis and Clark all the way from Whitehall to Dillon.

RATTLESNAKE CLIFFS. From Dillon, Montana, continue south 7 miles on U.S. 91 to a monument to Beaverhead Gateway. Rattlesnake Cliff is the high rock just beyond the monument and on the left side of the river.

Clark's Canyon, 9.7 miles farther, can be seen to the left of the road as it crosses over a bridge. The canyon is steep and the river swift at this point.

LEMHI PASS. From Armstead, Montana, turn off U.S. 91 on gravel road running straight west 21.8 miles to Trail Creek road. Here turn right 11.7 miles to summit of Lemhi Pass. The road is narrow and unimproved but goes through the pass about 35 miles to Salmon, Idaho.

LOST TRAIL PASS. From Salmon, Idaho, go 47 miles north on U.S. 93 to Lost Trail Pass. From the pass go 9 miles down into Rosses Hole to reach the Lewis and Clark campsite. It is ½ mile from the ranger station, down the little creek that goes through the station.

TRAVELERS REST CAMP. From Missoula go 6 miles up U.S. 93 to the town of Lolo. Continue south through town and cross Lolo Creek bridge at the edge of town. Walk west ¼ mile through a farmer's field to the railroad tracks. The campsite was below the railroad bridge on the north side of the stream.

LOLO PASS. From Missoula go 6 miles on U.S. 93 to Lolo. Here go west on Montana 9, a gravel road, 30 miles to Lolo Hot Springs where Lewis and Clark stopped on both the westward and return journeys. Several campsites are well marked along the road. From Lolo Hot Springs go 7 miles to Lolo Pass. Here turn left on road leading along ridge to Packer's Meadow — the Glade Creek of Lewis and Clark.

Road straight ahead goes to the Powell Ranger Station on site of Colt Killed Camp. About ½ mile back toward Missoula from the Powell Ranger Station, the Lolo Trail Highway turns sharply up mountain and follows very close to the Lewis and Clark trail to the west side of the Bitter Root Mountains.

The road is not passable except for a short period in late summer.

114

THE BITTERROOTS TO THE PACIFIC

The men shook snow out of their blankets the morning of September 4. "Our moccasins froze," Ordway said. "We have nothing but a little pearched corn to eat. The air on the mountains verry chilley and cold. Our fingers aked."

After the sun thawed their frozen baggage covers, they set out on the slippery trail. Crossing a divide and descending into a valley they came to a large encampment of Ootlashoots, as the captains called the Flatheads. These Indians were as friendly as the Shoshones had predicted. Eyeing a fine herd of nearly 500 horses, Lewis and Clark speedily arranged a council with the chiefs. The Indians threw white robes of dressed skins over the soldiers, and the peace pipe was passed.

The parley began, with the Flatheads speaking what Ordway called "the most curious language of any we have seen before. They talk as tho they lisped, or have a bur on their tongue. I suppose they are the Welch Indians if there are any Such." Lewis said it resembled "the clucking of a fowl or the noise of a parrot."

The captains had learned to overcome language difficulties. It was not too remarkable that they were able to buy 11 more horses. But to trade their weaker horses, probably those injured the previous day, for seven "tollerable good" horses proved that practice had made them skilled horse traders.

During the two nights they spent with the Flatheads the men were plagued by the swarm of hungry dogs. "They eat several pair of the mens Moccasons," Ordway remarked ruefully.

The morning of the sixth the party went over a mountain and camped in the Bitter Root Valley on a river which they named after Clark. The Flatheads, on their way to buffalo country, traveled down the valley with them. It was easy going although they had to cross and recross the river several times. They made 18 miles the first day and 20 the second. Finding lots of game, they stopped at a "fine bold clear creek." Here, at what they called Travelers Rest Creek, they stayed two days hunting and repairing clothing. They knew the trip ahead, over Lolo Pass to the country of the Nez Perce, was a hard one.

JOHN COLTER always was a bold one. Hunting a few miles from Travelers Rest Camp he saw three Flathead Indians with drawn bows about to make him an archery target. Instead of using his rifle for defense he laid it on the ground and calmly walked toward them. Although the Indians were in a bad mood because someone — probably their friends the Shoshones — had stolen 23 of their horses, they did not shoot. A man with so much nerve was to be admired. They stopped looking at him down the shafts of their arrows and became friendly. As a reward Colter asked them to dinner.

The Shoshone Indians had told Lewis and Clark that game was scarce on Lolo Pass. The captains were worried. Their grub sacks were about empty. Moving up through the pines the first day on the Lolo Trail they noticed an ominous sign. The Indians had peeled many of the trees so they might eat the tender inner bark.

Friday the 13th started out as it usually does. When the horse herd was rounded up in the morning, Lewis's horse was missing. They set out anyway and soon came to Lolo Hot Springs. The Indians had built a dam across the warm stream formed by the nearly boiling springs so that they could bathe. Many trails coming from all directions indicated the place was popular with both Indians and animals. Leaving the springs, the Indian guide selected the wrong trail. It cost them three extra miles of rugged travel to get back on the main trail.

On the 14th Lewis was happy when the man who had stayed behind to look for his horse caught up with them. He had found the horse.

Their only game that day was three or four pheasants, "on which," Sergeant Gass said, "without a miracle it was impossible to feed 30 hungry men."

116

"SEVERAL ROADS led from those springs in different derections." Deer, elk and Indian trails converge on Lolo Hot Springs, confusing even the expedition's guide who took them three miles out of their way on an "intolerable route."

TRAVELERS REST CREEK. Today this creek is called Lolo, which some think originated with the Indians' clumsy attempt to call it Lewis or, in Indian jargon, Lou Lou. The expedition camped just across the creek near its junction with the Bitter Root River, and camped here again on the return journey from June 30 to July 3, 1806.

The trail was along steep rocky mountainsides, over and under fallen timber, through dense forests where, the captains were not too weary to note, grew eight different species of pine.

Snow began falling heavily; as much as 10 inches in one night. With their moccasins worn thin, the men constantly feared frozen feet. Evenings, huddled around campfires, they mended their moccasins with fingers made awkward by the numbing cold. "This," said Gass, "is a horrible mountain desert." Clark went on ahead, looking for game and for the Nez Perce.

One night the men killed a colt for food "which appeared to me to be good eating," Gass wistfully remarked, although he ate none.

On September 19 Ordway said, "We eat our verry last morcil of our provision except a little portable Soup." Later, "We killed a wolf and eat it." Clark found no game ahead except a stray Indian horse which he shot and hung up for the party. By this time Gass's stomach was not so squeamish. He ate both wolf and horse meat.

The main party, on a high ridge, sighted a prairie in the distance which Ordway said "put us in good spirits again." The spirits were better but the flesh was getting weaker. The prairie, which they supposed was at the headwaters of the Columbia was a long, long way off.

The next day Lewis's horse was lost again, this time with all Lewis's personal possessions. Two men with one horse between them were left to search for it. The party moved on.

Two days later the nearly starved and thoroughly exhausted men came out of the mountains at last onto Weippe Prairie.

WEIPPE PRAIRIE

Weippe Prairie, Ordway said, "is Smooth and mostly handsome plains." Here and there groves of pine extend into it from the surrounding heavily-wooded hills and ridges. For many generations the flat prairie, ideal for horse racing, was a favorite meeting ground of the Nez Perce. Here camas grew thick among the grass. The Indians cured and ground the bulbs to make into bread. "Sweet," Ordway commented, "and good to taste."

When the depleted men of the expedition stumbled out of the timber they found the prairie dotted with Indian lodges, well stocked with camas root and dried salmon.

Perhaps they foundered themselves eating, or perhaps the wolf, crows and roasted horse's head on which they had subsisted while traveling the Lolo Trail proved too rugged a diet. At any rate most of them, especially Lewis, became quite ill.

Clark, now interested in practicing medicine, naively "gave the sick a dose of Rush's pills to see what effect they would have." Gass did not elaborate on their effect, but it is not hard to guess.

118

"A PRETTY LITTLE PLAIN of about 50 acres plentifully stocked with quamash," the captains said of what is now called Packers Meadow. The expedition camped here on their westward trek September 13, 1805, and named it Quamash Meadows because of the many camas flowers. It is located almost exactly on the Montana-Idaho state line.

"HAVING TRYUMPHED OVER THE ROCKY MOUNTAINS" Lewis found his pleasure almost impossible to express. Clark, exploring ahead, first came onto Weippe Prairie from the timber at the left.

The two men who had been searching for Lewis's horse staggered into camp not only without the captain's horse but also minus their own. They had found first the saddlebags, then the horse but that night both Lewis's horse and their own broke away and they were too weak to try to follow the animals. The men did have the captain's saddlebags.

Although the Nez Perce were distrustful at first, the old formula of passing out medals and presents worked again. Soon they were trading food and information for trinkets.

On Tuesday the 24th the party moved on down the Clearwater looking for good timber to build canoes. The men were still weak and sick. Lewis was so ill he could hardly keep seated on a horse.

Clark, who had gone ahead, rejoined them to report he had found "pitch pine," which he thought would be suitable canoe material, four or five miles farther on near a fork of the river.

Having just descended from the wintry weather of the mountains, the sick men found the heat at the lower altitude an additional affliction. But they camped at the forks of the Clearwater on September 27 and immediately started making five canoes.

CANOE BUILDING CAMP

Called by the Indians Kooskooske, The Clearwater River well deserves its name. It is crystal clear and about 200 yards wide at the forks and from two to five feet deep. When Lewis and Clark saw it the deeper pools and eddies were alive with salmon.

Game continued to be very scarce. Only occasionally were the hunters able to bring in a deer. The fish and camas roots furnished by the Indians seemed to make the men sick. Since horses were no longer of immediate importance the captains butchered one of their best animals. "We eat the meat," Whitehouse said, "with good stomacks as iver we did fat beef in the states." They also ate a fat dog. The disgusted natives promptly dubbed them "dog eaters."

Because many of the men were still sick and weak the captains gave up the idea of hewing out the canoes in favor of the cruder but easier Indian method of burning them out. "Indians collect about us . . ." said Lewis, "to gaze at the strange appearance of everything about us."

The Nez Perce men were "well looking" and the women generally handsome. Of the same stock as the Flatheads, they had quite similar language. Their dress also was similar except that many of their clothes were decorated with white beads which they said came from white men a long way to the west. "The dress of the female is modest . . . the other sex is careless of the indelicacy of exposure," Lewis said primly. These Indians were the only ones along the whole route who "do not exhibit the loose feelings of carnal desire," said Gass perhaps regretfully.

120

"HILLS HIGH AND RUGED." The ailing men of the expedition in Canoe Camp on the Clearwater needed fresh meat. Clark said, "I walked out with my gun on the hills which is verry steep & high could kill nothing." One of the hunters killed a small coyote, but horsemeat was the main bill of fare. "woods too dry to hunt deer," Clark explained.

CANOE CAMP. Searching for pine trees to build canoes, Clark found a grove of yellow pine at this spot. Here, opposite the forks of the Clearwater, the captains distributed the axes and the men worked September 26-October 7 building the dugouts.

NEZ PERCE COUNTRY. The Clearwater in 1805 probably carried a much greater volume of water than it does now. Rapids like these, one following another, were troublesome to the expedition.

SITE OF THE CACHE. A canister of powder, a bag of musket balls and the packsaddles were cached here. This also was where the tree stood from which Shields cut his canoe. Old timers on the Clearwater remember when the stump was still visible. The weather during the canoe building was, according to Clark, "verry worm."

On Sunday, October 6, the party cached their packsaddles, a canister of powder and a bag of bullets about half a mile below camp at a place marked by a broken tree. Branding their horses with an iron stirrup, they arranged with the Indians to care for the animals until their return.

Next day one small and four large canoes were loaded with supplies and the horsemen became rivermen again as they shoved off down the Clearwater.

DOWN THE CLEARWATER

CANOEING DOWN the swift, sparkling Clearwater River, the party made good time until one of the boats struck a rock and began leaking. The whole party stopped while the canoe was unloaded and repaired.

Next day the party swirled successfully through 15 rapids but the 16th was their undoing. Again one of the heavily-laden canoes struck a boulder which punched a large hole in its side. It filled and sank, throwing the men into the rushing water. Peculiarly, although Lewis and Clark so carefully selected their men for their special abilities on just such a trip, many of them could not swim. However, they clung to the dugout and were rescued without casualties. Again the party had to stop, dry out baggage and repair a canoe.

Old Toby, the Shoshone guide, and the only one of his sons still with the party had no liking for this mode of travel. After the second mishap they disappeared. "I suspect," Gass guessed, "he was afraid of being cast away passing the rapids." Perhaps he was homesick, too. Leaving without pay, he and his son were seen running full speed toward the east and their fellow Shoshones. Lewis, wishing to pay Old Toby, thought of sending a Nez Perce horseman to overtake him. A Nez Perce chief blandly quashed this generous plan when he pointed out that his people would take everything Old Toby had when he passed the first Nez Perce camp.

On the night of October 9 the party camped a short distance above the junction of the Clearwater and the Snake rivers.

DOWN THE SNAKE RIVER

WHEN THEY ARRIVED at the Snake River the captains exulted for the third time over having reached the Columbia.

They guessed wrong on the river, but there was another cause for exultation. There was enough food. The river swarmed with salmon and the air was thick with ducks and geese; the men no longer had to sicken themselves on crows and roasted horse head. They did get a few dogs from the Indians because four-footed game was practically nonexistent. Wood for campfires was the biggest problem. The high barren hills along the river yielded very little. Most of the Indian camps were built of split timber. "We have made it a point at all times not to take anything that belonged to the Indians, even their wood," Clark said, "but at this time we were Compelled to violate that rule." And they took the wood.

124

"KOOS KOOS KE." Here the men of the expedition first floated their newly-made canoes. Clark said, "All the canoes in the water, we Load and set out after fixing all our Poles &c &c. The afternoon cloudy proced on passing maney bad rapids . . . which wer dangerous."

"THE HILLS OR ASSENTS from the water is faced with dark ruged stone." The men of the expedition found this part of the Snake very hazardous, with rapid after rapid, but they made good time in the swift current. At this point they camped on the north shore while they examined the Texas rapids—the worst on the river—which were just ahead of them.

"THE RIVER RAN LIKE A MILL RACE." The Snake river with its many rapids was one of the most dangerous stretches of river navigated by the explorers. High waves splashed water into the cargo; several times the canoes ran into rocks and split, damaging the supplies; valuable trade goods were lost when a canoe overturned.

The Snake River at its junction with the Clearwater is 860 yards wide, and "Goslin green" in color, according to Gass. But as they went on down the Snake they found it narrowed to only about 15 yards in some places, where the green water ran like a millrace. The swift river thrust them along until sometimes they made forty miles a day. At one place they had to portage the baggage while the men who could swim ran the rapids in the canoes.

On October 14 one of the canoes was swept crosswise against a big rock. Although the men got it off, a wave dashed against it and the boat started to sink. Scrambling up on the rock the men were able to hold the boat for a while. Soon some of the baggage floated off and the dugout, lightened by its loss, broke away leaving her crew standing on the rock in the middle of the river. One of the other crews put into shore, unloaded the boat and hastened to the rescue. Although most of the baggage was recovered the mishap caused delay because they were again forced to open the bundles and spread them out to dry.

When crossing the last rapid before reaching the Columbia on October 16 another canoe ran on a rock, resulting in the usual soaked contents. This time when they stopped to repair the damage they did so on a point of land at the junction between the Snake and the Columbia — the real Columbia at last.

CAMP ON THE COLUMBIA RIVER

ALTHOUGH THERE already was a large encampment of Yakimas at the junction where the party camped, scarcely had the evening fires been lighted before nearly 200 Indians from up the Columbia marched in to join the throng. "Singing in their way," as Ordway wryly remarked, and beating drums, they danced around camp while the white men cooked their evening meal.

After dinner the captains sat in council with them, smoking and passing out gifts. When the council was over, they traded for food until late in the evening. The party netted 20 pounds of dried fat horse flesh and seven dogs, the captains' walking food supply.

The next day Clark and two men explored up the Columbia in a light canoe. Passing Indian villages on the shore, they soon acquired an escort of 18 Indian canoeists. Paddling first in front then in back and then on both sides of Clark's canoe, the natives gaped at the bearded white men. At times they dropped back to watch Clark go by, then sprinted ahead furiously to get a second look.

In the crystal clear river where Clark and his men could see to a depth of 15 feet, they noticed a multitude of salmon. The shores, too, were covered with "an immense number" of dead fish. The Indians had merely to pick up their dinner from the ground and cook it over a fire of older fish carcasses. The fires probably were not as aromatic as the driftwood fires the party was used to, nor as long-burning as the buffalo chips they had used on the great plains, but the oil in the sun-baked fish burned fiercely.

UP THE COLUMBIA. "In every direction from the junction of those rivers," Clark said, "the country is one continued plain low and rises from the water gradually, except a range of high Country which runs from S.W. & N.E. and is on the opposite side about 2 miles distant from the Columbia."

"ON DOWN THE GREAT COLUMBIA RIVER." The party camped here at the junction of the Snake and Columbia rivers surrounded by Indians who were "singing and beeting on their drums Stick and keeping time to the musik," according to Clark. The campsite, now Sacajawea Park near Pasco, Washington, had been a campground for Indian fishermen and a council place for neighboring tribes for hundreds of years.

Clark continued up the Columbia about 10 miles to a point where he could see the mouth of the Yakima River in the distance. This was desert country. There was not a tree in sight and scarcely a shrub except for great masses of prickly pear.

When Clark returned to camp the party feasted on "prairie cocks" the hunters had shot that day. The birds were plentiful, nearly as large as small turkeys, and very tasty.

The following morning, Lewis made celestial observations and took notes on the language and customs of the Yakimas. Clark spent the forenoon measuring the 475-yard width of the Snake River and the 860-yard width of the Columbia just above the junction. At noon the men loaded the canoes and the expedition moved down the wide Columbia.

DOWN THE COLUMBIA

THE NEXT TWO DAYS the dugouts swept past scenes of wild beauty where the wide river cut its way through a gorge of brilliantly hued rocks. The party could enjoy the sunny afternoons while the current did the work for them. They got a hint of the ocean when they saw rocks formed into grotesque shapes by the winds of the ages blowing up the Columbia from the Pacific.

The spirits of the men rose with each swiftly passing mile. The two captains, who often must have hit the depths of discouragement, now realized their mission would soon be accomplished. Eagerly they watched for signs of tidewater — the Pacific was not far away. When they had to portage several rapids their enthusiasm made the canoes seem lighter.

The party often stopped among small groups of Indians. At one place Clark didn't know how to handle them. The natives were frightened, "crying, ringing there hands, . . . hanging their heads . . ." The captain offered his pipe and small gifts. Although "Somewhat passified," the Indians still thought these white men strange and dangerous. But when they caught sight of Sacajawea ". . . all came out and appeared to assume new life, the sight of this Indian woman . . . confirmed those people of our friendly intentions, as no woman ever accompanies a war party of Indians in this quarter."

"THE COUNTRY RISES HERE about 200 feet above the river and is bordered with black rugid rocks," Clark said of the Columbia near its junction with the Walla Walla River. As the expedition passed they saw several lodges of Indians on these islands.

SALMON JUMPING WIND RIVER FALLS. Lewis and Clark called Wind River pouring into the Columbia from the Washington side the Cruzatte River. They didn't pause to explore it but noted "the bottoms above the mouth of this little river is much covered grass & firn . . ." Salmon was an important item in the diet of the explorers, as it had been for generations among the Indians.

The Corps of Discovery passed the mouth of the Umatilla River coming in from the south. Farther down the Columbia the party saw things familiar to white men: a scarlet coat, "salers clothes," a string of beads. The Indians pointed west and said they got the articles from white men.

On the morning of October 20, 1805, from their camp six miles below the John Day River, the captains inspected an Indian burial ground on an island in the Columbia. Here was a building 60 feet long and 12 feet wide, made of six-foot poles planted in the ground. The curious captains and their party noticed exactly how the building was constructed. Across the forks at the top of the poles a ridge pole was laid the whole length of the building. Boards or broken canoes were leaned against it to form a shed. Each end was open. Entering the eastern end, the party saw bodies carefully wrapped in leather robes lying side by side in rows and covered with a mat. Going farther into the shed they found older bones scattered about, then a great heap of them toward the eastern end. They found 21 skulls arranged in a circle, symbolic of only the Indians knew what.

From the roof hung baskets of trinkets, fish nets, wooden bowls and other personal possessions that might be needed by Indians in the great beyond. Outside they noticed skeletons of horses offered as sacrifices, perhaps so the vanished warrior could ride on his long journey.

Moving down the river the party portaged Celilo Falls. At the bottom of the cataract they took time out to "Strip naked . . . that they might have an opportunity of brushing the flees off" which they had picked up among the fishskins and straw of the Indians.

Some of the natives at the falls told them that Indians nearer the ocean planned to exterminate the expedition. The captains saw to it that their men had plenty of ammunition, inspected arms and felt they were alert enough for any trouble.

They moved on down river, coming to the Short Narrows, which Gass said were "terrifying with vast rocks . . . and the river foaming thru channells." The Indians were shocked that they planned to shoot these rapids. The river was only 45 yards wide for a quarter of a mile, and Clark observed the water "boiling and whorling in every direction." Here was all the water of the mighty Columbia pounding through this narrow gap. But portage by land was almost impossible and the captains trusted the direction of Cruzatte, the expert boatman. While the natives watched apprehensively from the rocks above, the five canoes shot swiftly and safely through the rapids.

On October 25 the captains, alert to danger of unfriendly Indians, made camp in a strong position on top of a high point they called Fort Rocks.

Some of the time it rained as they moved closer to the ocean. Frequently in the morning heavy fogs drifted up the Columbia. The drumming roar of the water

"CROUDED WITH HUGE ROCKS scattered in every derection" . . . "the passage verry difficult," Clark described this section of the Columbia near Wishram, Washington. This was a favorite fishing spot of the Indians. The captains saw them in their canoes pulling salmon with gigs. Clark counted "20 parcels" of drying fish on the upper point of this island.

CELILO FALLS from the Oregon side. The river tribes to this day congregate at the falls during the salmon run, netting and spearing the big Columbia River salmon.

increased, seeming to threaten them from behind the grey fog banks and to form a barrier to the Pacific.

Many of the islands of the Columbia were Indian burial places. The captains named a large rock in the middle of the river "Sepulchar Island." The Indians called this and others like it Memaloose, or place of the dead.

On the night of October 30, 1805, the party camped on an island just above the Upper Cascades. Clark investigated and decided the hazard of navigating the cascades with loaded canoes was too great. Ordway, gazing on them said they "look shocking."

Next morning the captains ordered the canoes to be unloaded on the shore. Each man shouldered all he could of the burden. With Sacajawea carrying little Baptiste, the party started off single file through dense timber, following the Indian portage trail to the foot of the falls.

With tremendous effort they managed to float the empty canoes down the cascades. Gass called it the most "fatiguing business we have been engaged in for a long time."

Three days later the last of the rapids was behind them. They passed Beacon Rock. Again the canoes floated smoothly on the silvery bosom of the great river — the river that was widened now by the tidewaters of the Pacific Ocean.

THE STORMY PACIFIC OCEAN

The Great Plains, the Rocky Mountains and the Columbia River Gorge behind them, the little party glided swiftly down the now mile-wide Columbia, delayed occasionally by fog in the morning. There was a profusion of deer, fish, geese and ducks. Sometimes game was almost too plentiful. One night the men were kept awake by the cacophony of vast flocks of geese and brant roosting nearby.

They saw more and more evidence that other white men had been there before them, at the mouth of the river. There was a British musket, a copper kettle, beads, and finally Indians who spoke a little English with a liberal sprinkling of curses. The natives told of three ships down the river and a sea captain named Haley. The party was exuberant; certainly some of the men were thinking, at least secretly, of a ride home aboard ship.

But situations changed rapidly with the expedition. On Sauvies Island the Indians were especially unfriendly. "Those fellows we foun assumeing and disagreeable," complained Clark. They hung around the evening camps offering very little food, poor advice and women with flattened heads.

The captains' usual strategy of gaining friends by giving gifts didn't work. The natives saw no point in trading for trinkets when they could steal them. They stole everything: beads, a soldier's great coat, a hatchet and two of the sleeping men's rifles. To top it off, when Clark in council passed the peace pipe, it also was stolen.

"REMARKABLE HIGH DETATCHED ROCK." On the westward journey the captains referred to this as "Beaten" Rock, but on the return corrected it to Beacon Rock. They viewed it from about this very spot near North Bonneville, Washington and said it "Stands in a bottom on the Starboard Side . . . about 800 feet high and 400 paces around." At this point the captains first noticed the effect of tidewater on the Columbia.

INDIAN PICTOGRAPHS. There are many such rocks along the Columbia, some with the pictures painted on them and others with the art cut into them as in this case.

SNOW GEESE. At the camp of November 4, 1805, the geese were so thick on a sandy island just offshore in the Columbia that Clark said next morning, "I could not sleep for the noise kept by Swans, Geese, White & Black brants &c . . . they were emencly numerous and their noise horrid." The "white brant" were snow geese.

"SOMEWHAT IN THE FORM OF A SUGAR LOFE." Clark thought Mt. St. Helens was "perhaps the highest pinical in America." When the explorers first saw this mountain they had it confused with "Mt. Rainy" as they called Mt. Rainier further north in Washington.

MALLARD DUCKS TAKING OFF. Lewis and Clark called these birds "Duckinmallard." Generally they were the most plentiful of the wild ducks. Occasionally, when members of the party shot these ducks, the captains enjoyed a feast.

Lewis and Clark finally told the Indians they would shoot the next one who stole anything. The pilfering stopped immediately and some of the stolen articles were returned. A bit miffed, the natives piled into their canoes and left for the other side of the river "thru the highest sees I ever saw a small vestle ride," Clark said with grudging admiration; "certain it is they are the best canoe navigators I ever saw."

Rain began to fall on the 6th of November, wet rain, lots of it and continuous. The men, soaked clear to the skin, were chilled by the high winds. The baggage was wet; everything was wet and it never got dry.

As they came closer to the ocean good campsites were few and far between. Five nights later, they were pinned against the cliffs by the tide with scarcely room between the rocks and the water to lie down. During that completely miserable night they moved the canoes often to keep them from being smashed against the rocks or carried away.

Although the Indians got about nicely in their canoes which Gass said were "admirably calculated to ride waves," the heavy Rocky Mountain dugouts were dangerous in the storm which continued all the next day.

The party huddled cold and wet on their narrow stretch of beach. In the driving rain they warmed their fronts at the campfire while their backs got soaked, and then reversed the process. This went on hour after hour as the rain kept pouring down on the following two days. The water-soaked clothing began to rot on their backs.

On the next day the weather modified a little. They pushed on, and found a good campsite three miles farther down.

When the 16th of November dawned bright and clear, the relieved men crawled from under their sodden robes. Directly to the west they saw, roaring, churning and crashing against the rocky shore, the Pacific Ocean.

"Oh the joy," breathed Clark.

TRAVELOGUE . . . Going down the Bitter Root Valley is an experience that even a confirmed seacoast dweller appreciates. It smells like heaven. The valley folks looked a bit surprised when I kept raving about the warm pine fragrance. Like a woman who always wears perfume, they'd become used to smelling good.

Lewis and Clark indicated they didn't think much of the Bitter Root Valley soil. Thanks to a promise of irrigation there was a great fruit-growing boom here in 1910. Logged-off land, where there were once stands of yellow pine and fir, produced wonderful McIntosh Red apples and bing and lambert cherries. Although there still is some fruit-growing here, most of the land has been converted to heavy sugar beet production. At times we passed orchards whose trees were dried, twisted and stunted. "Some rancher's dream in 1910," Al said. "Some man planted those trees and thought his future was secure. But transportation was the problem. He got apples all right, but it cost too much to ship them." It's sad to see a man's hopes dried, twisted and stunted. We decided to quit thinking about it.

The cities of Montana seem to have greater variety than those of other states. Butte is staggered down a hillside, Helena nestles at the far edge of a great flat valley and Missoula looks like she was poured right out of Hellgate Canyon. The Blackfeet Indians used to trap their enemies in this canyon, and other Indians called the section Issoul, meaning horrible, from which the musical name Missoula came. Until I saw one of Montana's many fine highway signs explaining it I thought Missoula was the name of a beautiful Indian maiden.

There are a number of historic spots around Missoula. Near here is Hellgate, one of the first towns in this area. It looks like it won't last much longer; the little old store is caving in and the one-time saloon is now a barn. Off in another direction is St. Mary's Mission and Fort Owen.

On our way to Lolo Pass Al stopped to visit Travelers Rest Camp. From the road we could see the cottonwood-shaded glade where the expedition camped. Al piled out and across an alfalfa field. We felt a little envious as we sat in the hot car where Joe was sleeping, until he came back. "Did you get your pictures?" "Yes," he said disgustedly pointing to his muddy boots, "but the darn alfalfa field was irrigated." "Don't lose your grip," I replied, "I remember the time you waded in mud to your knees in a business suit to get a picture of three deer, and when it was developed it looked like three small snags. And when I handed your suit to the cleaner he gave me one of those looks cleaners always give when you explain how a suit got in that shape. It's a knowing sort of look that says 'I don't believe ya'."

The Hot Springs in Lolo Valley, where the expedition luxuriated in a warm bath, are still a favored swimming place. We sat with our feet in a tepid little spring while Al took pictures, not knowing that a few hours later our feet would be plunging into the snows of Lolo Pass.

In the Lolo region the Nez Perce leader, Chief Joseph, played a neat trick on the United States Army. A barricade had been erected in the valley to keep Joseph and his people bottled up and prevent their flight toward Canada. The Indians merely walked up the hills and around the obstacle, and it became known as Fort Fizzle.

The Lolo Pass Highway follows the same high ridges that Lewis and Clark traveled on both the westward and eastward journeys. This is some of the ruggedest country in North America. There is wild game here, but there wasn't in the expedition's time. In those days buffalo were not mountain animals, deer lived in valleys and the elk fed on grass. Pressed back into the mountains by civilization the animals became browsing beasts, eating willows and alders. Now this region, where the expedition had to eat their own horses, is rich in game of all kinds.

Packer's Meadow is quite easy to reach and certainly worth the effort. High and flat, it stretches for several acres, giving us the feeling we were on top of the world. We almost hated to walk over it; every step meant crushing some cluster of wild flowers: camas or dogtooth violets. We stayed as long as the mosquitoes would let us; even they had a hard time driving us from the lovely rich meadow.

The people at the Powell Ranger Station, which is located on the site of Lewis and Clark's Colt Killed Camp, were exceptionally helpful in giving us directions and information about the area. The Lolo Trail is no broad highway. It is narrow, rutty and hangs on the edge of the mountain. Great pines, fir and cedar are thick at the lower levels. Masses of trilliums and dogtooth violets carpet the ground. There are a few campsites for travelers in the area. As we went higher we saw snowbanks glistening in the sun. We slid down snowbanks right where the expedition fed grass to their starving horses. Cities usually hold more fascination for me than the country-side. But standing on top of a peak and looking out over the range after range of Bitter Root Mountains, something happens inside of you. Maybe your soul expands.

138

As we drove westward we were almost constantly, to the children's disgust, talking over the various problems of our book. For example, what geographical terms should we use? The Indian names which cause so much confusion with the many varieties of spelling were actually descriptions. The captains, picking them up by sound only, sometimes inadvertently changed them a bit. Then, years later, someone else might have given the spots entirely different names. What were WE going to call the Clearwater River, for example. The natives called it Koos-Koots-Kie to Lewis and Clark, but did not intend it as a name. They were merely trying to tell them the river was a small branch of the great river ahead of them. The captains took it as a name, and twisted it a bit to Kooskooskie. Now it is the Clearwater, "and that," said Al, "is what we're going to call it. It's the way it appears on the map. Besides, it's too tiresome and confusing to read three different names for a place unless there's a particular reason for giving them all."

We recalled that Wheeler in his *Trail of Lewis and Clark* was somewhat resentful that more places weren't named after the captains. But we had already seen several places named in their honor, and were now passing through Lewiston, Idaho, right across the river from Clarkston, Washington. It seemed they weren't exactly neglected when it came to honors. But we knew how Wheeler felt. Reading the captains' journals, a person is so impressed with their thoroughness, their modesty and their great delight in all things, that he is almost convinced the U.S.A. should be renamed the United States of Meriwether.

Out of Washtucna, Washington, we dipped down a dusty road to Riparia. The town was once named Texas Ferry and is just above the Texas Rapids of the Snake River — rapids which were no small problem to the expedition. The railroad changed the name to Riparia, meaning pile of rocks, apparently in recognition of the great wall of stone which forms the opposite shore of the Snake. The postmistress, who is also the librarian of Riparia, is deeply interested in the history of the territory. She told us a lot about the county and we agreed as we drove away that she was one of the pleasantest persons we'd met on the trip.

It was a beautiful golden evening when we drove into Sacajawea Park, near Pasco; the picnic dinner was locked securely in the trunk of the car. Al pointed to the Columbia. "Clark paddled right past here," he said, "and went on up ten miles, just about to where the Hanford Atomic Project now stands." This spot was an Indian gathering place for many years because it is at the junction of the Snake and Columbia, where the natives might easily observe what their friends and enemies were up to. The museum has hundreds of arrowheads, pestles, knives and other artifacts, many of which were picked up in the area when the park was being laid out. At dinnertime we found the car trunk locked only too securely. It wouldn't open. Al can live on arrowheads. While he sat on the grass wishing he could plow up the park to see what more lay under the ground, we ate hot dogs and tried not to think of what the heat was doing to the food in the car. Al was becoming almost morbid thinking about the park covering up such rich artifact territory. "Look, Al," I said, "if a community commemorates an historic spot with a park you say it removes the old natural feel of the place and covers up the artifacts. If the community doesn't lay out a park or memorial of some sort you say the people are ignorant of their history, or too casual about it. Which do you believe?"

"I believe them both," he said.

Traveling down the Columbia we were so enthusiastic about the spectacular scenery Al had to keep reminding us that the expedition had tough going here. We drove along a good road; they portaged around falls and battled bad weather. We stopped to chat with friendly river-dwellers; they stopped to dicker with suspicious or terrified Indians in this area.

On a river it is always baffling which side to travel. We chose the Washington side just because we had to make some choice, and we were already on that side. Al has made many trips along the Columbia in Oregon, and when I asked which he preferred — the Oregon or Washington route — he said there was no choice; they are both magnificent.

The Maryhill Museum was on our side. Built by Sam Hill, it was said to have been a castle for a queen. But the queen never came to it. High on the bluff, it surveys miles of the river and a great sweep of the northern Oregon hills.

The Bonneville Dam, named for Captain B. L. E. Bonneville, early nineteenth-century explorer of the northwest, spans the Columbia like arms stretched out to join the two states. When we look at any tremendous project such as this, first conceived, then planned, then executed, we come to only one conclusion. People can do anything.

Near Camas Al took a side road toward an Indian village he saw on Clark's map. Just at the brink of the village site there was a sign saying, "Keep out. M. Sams." We also saw M. Sams. He let us poke around, was pleasant and eventually showed us boxes of fish-net weights, pestles and many other things he and his brother had recovered. It wasn't long before we learned why this kindly man had such an abrupt sign on his property. The sign said "Keep out" and people kept pouring in. One man wanted to fish, another to hunt grouse, several others had different requests. I still wonder how Mr. Sams gets any work done and what would happen if he didn't have any sign up.

We drove past Fort Vancouver; probably the first time Al has ever done such a thing. He can photograph a fort from every direction and still find something to intrigue him the next time he visits the place. But we, like the expedition, were beginning to be anxious to see the ocean. The difference was, we knew right where to expect the Pacific.

HOW TO GET THERE NOW . . . See maps 6, 7 and 8.

CANOE CAMP. From Orofino continue west on Idaho 9 on the south side of the river about six miles. The Idaho highway has the Canoe Camp marked with a big sign on the river side of the highway.

The community of Ahsahka is almost directly across the river. The site of the cache is marked by a stone cairn on the river's edge .3 mile beyond the sign.

KAMIAH CAMPSITE. From Kamiah, Idaho, cross the Clearwater River bridge and turn sharply left on rough gravel road about ½ mile to sawmill which occupies point of land where Lewis and Clark made their camp.

JUNCTION OF COLUMBIA AND SNAKE RIVERS. From Pasco, Washington, go 2.3 miles east on U.S. 410. Here turn right at road sign marking Sacajawea Park, and go 2.2 miles to the park where the expedition camped October 16 to October 18, 1805.

TWIN SISTERS ROCKS. From Pasco, Washington, go east on U.S. 410 to Wallula. Here turn right on U.S. 730. The rocks are to the left, towering above the road just as the road and river enter the gorge.

The islands where Lewis and Clark noted the Indian fishing villages can be seen in the river to the right at this point.

CELILO FALLS. At Celilo Falls, Oregon, on U.S. 30. Or they can be seen from Wishram, Washington, across the river on U.S. 830.

BEACON ROCK. From North Bonneville, Washington, continue west on U.S. 830, 3.8 miles to Beacon Rock.

From rock continue west 1.6 miles to small sawmill on left. Here turn left on wooded road across tracks, .3 mile to end of road. The site of an old Indian village described by Clark is on the private property of Will Sams of North Bonneville. Permission can be obtained to inspect four lodge pits still clearly visible and Indian pictographs on a rock on the riverbank.

140

WINTER ON THE PACIFIC OCEAN

İт нᴀᴅ ʙᴇᴇɴ more than 18 months since the 32 gaunt, bearded men of the Lewis and Clark expedition had seen civilization. They had come 4,100 miles from St. Louis; 4,100 miles of prairie, river, creek, Indian trail and mountain pass. Miles up the Columbia they noticed the Indians displayed white men's articles. Drawing closer to the Pacific they had further proof that the natives had contacted white men before when they met an Indian who said "son of a pitch" and "damned rascal." Maybe they could ride home on shipboard.

But the wet, shivering men in their rotting leather clothing found no white traders. Camped along the driftwood at the edge of the surf they saw nothing to the west but the grey, surging waters of the great ocean. First Lewis and then Clark, with a few tired volunteers, explored the shore north of the Columbia for the ships the Indians had described. Lewis found where the traders had camped but, as Sergeant Gass said sadly, "they have all sailed away."

It rained unceasingly. At times, for variety, the rain was accompanied by wind so violent it tore great trees from the forest and flung them thundering to the ground.

NORTHWEST INDIAN CANOE. Craft of this type were used by most of the coastal Indians. This old one is on display at Coupeville, Washington.

"AT THIS DISMAL POINT" at Megler, Washington, the men of the expedition, pinned down by wind and storm formed a camp on what dry land they could find "in the crevices of the rocks & hill sides. . . . With most tremendious waves brakeing with great violence against the Shores, rain falling in torrents." The men got as "wet as water could make them." One can picture Sacajawea trying to shelter her baby here.

The Pacific, the party agreed, was poorly named. "Oh how disagreeable our Situation dureing this dreadful winter," groaned Clark.

They began to wonder whether to spend the winter on the north or south of the river mouth. There were more deer, the Indians told them, on the north side but more elk on the south. Elk, Lewis thought, were more nutritious than deer and certainly they were bigger, with better hides for clothing. The elk made a strong argument. Too, the captains thought trading ships would more likely visit the south side. But the crowning advantage was that it was warmer.

The captains allowed the men to settle the matter with a vote. Even Sacajawea, or "Janey" as Clark now called her, had a voice in the issue. She, with the majority, cast her vote for the south because she wanted to go where there were plenty of wappatos, a root resembling potatoes, which she liked.

High waves crashed around the canoes when they first tried to cross the mouth of the Columbia. After one boat nearly swamped, the captains decided to go back to where the river was narrower. They went 15 miles upstream before they found a suitable place to cross. Reaching the southern shore, they made camp on a little neck of land. Wind and rain roared about them. The water-soaked wood burned poorly. They spent most of that cheerless night sitting in a huddle because whenever they lay down rain filled the hollows their bodies made in the soft ground.

On November 29 Lewis and five men in their Indian canoe went searching for a good winter campsite. Not until six days later did they return to the anxious main party to report that they had found "a tolerable good place for our winter quarters."

On December 8 the entire party moved to the new location which was on the first high point of land on the west side of the Lewis and Clark River, about three miles from its junction with the Columbia. Clearing out the dense growth of spruce and fir, they built the foundation for the winter camp. There was plenty of good cedar and fir that split easily into long planks for the buildings. Perhaps conditioned by taking wood from the Indians on the Snake River, the formerly meticulously honest captains also used boards they found in a nearby Indian encampment.

Several of the men had "enfluenzey." Some were sick from drinking salt water. Sgt. Pryor dislocated his shoulder, and Werner strained his knee lifting and hauling the heavy planks. The constant rain was both a drawback to their efforts and a spur to finish the buildings.

Meanwhile Clark and five of the men, who had left the campsite immediately on arrival to search for urgently needed salt, were working their way over a ridge toward the seacoast. Pushing through dense timber for about five miles they came out on swamps which quaked for a whole acre at the vibration caused by one footstep.

The first day they killed an elk. That night, camped on a small knoll in the dismal swamp, they were partially sheltered from the driving rain by the goaty-

A BULL ELK WITH HORNS in the velvet. On the plains, in the mountains and on the seashore elk nearly always were plentiful. Their flesh, although "pore" in the winter at both Fort Mandan and Fort Clatsop, formed a large part of the expedition's diet. The Indians found them hard to kill with their arrows, too fleet to be overtaken on horseback and too wily to be driven over cliffs as the buffalo were. When they managed to get an elk they prized it highly, using its teeth as money, its horns for tools, its hide for clothing, its hoofs for rattles and its meat for food.

smelling raw hide of the freshly killed animal. The next morning they arose "perfectly wet with rain," as Clark said. Making their way through swamps and thickets of underbrush they at last reached the seashore and found an encampment of Indians.

Clark was amused that evening by the natives' bone gambling game. Shifting a bone from one hand to the other, the Indian distracted his watchers with loud and raucous singing. Finally the gamblers bet which hand held the bone. Tiring of the game Clark lay down to sleep. He immediately wished he hadn't, for there was no gambling as to the whereabouts of the Indians' fleas.

After a busy night, Clark spent the morning examining the seashore, and amazed the Indians by shooting the head completely off a duck with his rifle. After finding a good location for making salt, the small party returned 15 miles to the main camp.

A terrible storm occurred six days later. "Winds violent Trees falling in every derection, whorl winds, with gusts of Hail & Thunder," worried Clark; "Certainly one of the worst days that ever was!"

The huts were roofed on December 24 and the men moved into their winter home on Christmas Day. The Fort consisted of two parallel buildings each 50 feet long. They were connected on both ends by a high wall made of pickets driven into the ground which completed a 50 foot square with a gate at the south end. The men's barracks on the west side had three rooms, each about 16 feet square, and each with a fireplace in the center. On the east side directly across the 48-foot-long, 20-foot-wide parade ground was officers' row. Each of the two captains had a small room for himself with the meat house and storehouse filling out the balance of the building. The men hoped the split planks chinked with moss and mud would keep out the cold rain and the fog that rolled off the Pacific.

The captains awakened in their new headquarters to "a salvo of gunns" fired by the men, "followed by a song as a compliment to us on the return of Christmas." The party tried to celebrate without liquor and nearly without food. "We have no ardent spirits," Ordway complained. Clark too, lamented, "We would have spent this day the nativity of Christ in feasting had we anything to raise our spirits or even gratify our appetites."

They divided the last of the tobacco among the men who used it and presented silk handkerchiefs to the seven who did not smoke. Sacajawea gave Clark two dozen weasel tails. Lewis got nothing from the "squar," perhaps because she sensed he didn't like her. Their Christmas dinner of "pore elk meat," spoiled by moisture, and of rotten pounded fish they got from the Indians was washed down with nothing but pure cold water. What a difference a sailing ship with its meager comforts would have made on that dreary Christmas!

But the expedition, camped three miles up a tributary, saw no eagerly-desired trading ships. During the time of the party's worst suffering a sailing ship, the Lydia, under Captain Hill, arrived in the Columbia. The Indians, displaying the medals they had been given, told the skipper that Lewis and Clark had been there and had left.

Between Christmas and New Year's the men put the finishing touches on their winter home. They found their cabins "smoaky," because only the captains' quarters had chimneys, and wet, because the rain probed through the roof. They worked to correct these defects. By December 30 the captains could post a guard and organize the camp on the basis of military procedure which would help keep up the men's morale during the dreary winter months.

A salute of rifle fire to the officers in front of their quarters greeted New Year's Day, 1806. "A little sunshine" which Ordway said was "verry uncommon to this place" started the year off right. Though New Year's dinner was a little better than their Christmas meal, Lewis wryly remarked that their pleasure "consisted principally in the anticipation of the 1st day of January 1807." Reuben Fields, Potts and Collins, who had been hunting since December 28 and were still away from the post, "killed a very large raven which they eat on New Years Day."

Indians had been congregating since the party arrived, and, although they were expelled from the fort at a regular hour, continued to camp nearby. The Chinooks, the Clatsops, the Wahkiakums, the Tillamooks and other tribes were putting their heads together to figure out these white men. These Indians were real flatheads, their heads having been strapped between boards during the first years of their life and permanently flattened. They were the most unprepossessing of all the Indians the expedition had seen, with their shoulders and arms overdeveloped by constant paddling of their canoes, and their legs short and some observers thought deformed by infrequent use.

The most prized possession of these Indians were their beautiful canoes ranging in length from 15 to 50 feet. The smallest ones held only two people, but the largest ones accommodated 30 or more. Chiseled out of solid cedar or fir, the canoes were truly works of art. The captains often marveled at the skill with which both the Indian men and women drove their tricky craft through the high waves and violent storms of the Pacific.

One Indian, sitting in the stern, steered the canoe with a paddle. The others, kneeling side by side, rowed in perfect synchronization, their bodies showing no movement but that required to thrust and pull the paddles. If a large wave threw the canoe over on her side so precariously that a watcher would be sure it was lost, the men on the windward side steadied the craft by throwing their bodies in unison toward the upper side, thrusting their paddles deep into the wave and righting the boat with a sharp pull. To the Chinook the canoe was what the horse was to the Shoshone. It was his means of travel, his way of getting food, his best and often his only possession.

146

CAMPSITE, WINTER OF 1805-1806. The broken trees are ancient cherries planted by a settler early in the 1850s. The ruins of Fort Clatsop were still in the clearing but the settler burned them to make way for his buildings, which have in turn moldered away leaving scarcely a trace.

"THE MOST ELIGABLE SITUATION for our purposes." The site of Fort Clatsop near Astoria, Oregon. The stream is what the Indians and the early explorers called the Netul. It has been renamed the Lewis and Clark River.

Five men of the expedition went to the seashore with a large kettle to make salt. On January 5 two of them returned with a jar of salt to report they had found the right place about 15 miles to the southwest on the ocean beach, near a village of scattered Indian houses.

They also brought pieces of blubber from a whale that had washed ashore near the saltworks. The men of the expedition tasted the blubber and liked it. The next day Clark organized a party of 12 men to go to the seashore to see if he could get more. The captain permitted Sacajawea to join the party because she begged to go saying "She had traveled a long way with us to See the great waters, and now that the monstrous fish was also to be Seen, she thought it verry hard that she could not be permitted to See either."

Only the skeleton of the "whail" remained when the party arrived at the ocean; the bones had been picked clean by the ravenous Indians. Even so it was an experience for the men to see the 105-foot-long remains of the huge mammal.

At the salt cairn the men had made several bushels of coarse but good salt. Although the captains did not describe the process it is thought the salt was made by filling an Indian dugout canoe with sea water which they allowed to settle. Pouring the fresher water off the top, they boiled the remainder until all moisture was evaporated. The salt, encrusted on the sides and bottom of the kettle, was scraped out and sealed in kegs for the return journey.

The Indians were troublesome at both the saltworks and the fort. Since neither sex hesitated to take anything they wanted, they had to be watched every minute they were near anything of value.

Striking up an acquaintance with McNeal, a native plotted to murder him for his scanty valuables. The simple McNeal, going arm in arm with his treacherous Indian friend, was about to walk straight into the trap when a squaw he knew stopped him and tried to tell him something. Many of the Indians were infected with "Venery" disease. Perhaps the woman had given McNeal something more than her friendship. Anyway McNeal brushed her aside and started to enter the hut of the plotter. Standing by the door the woman screamed and was soon joined by some friends who also screamed. The murderer may have been hardened but he did not appreciate the applause. As several white men plunged across the creek to see what the excitement was about, he left by the back way still carrying a long knife. Coming out of the dark hut the bewildered McNeal stood blinking in the daylight, still unaware of what had been averted.

The Indian women wore skirts of white cedar bark tied around their waists, "the whole being of Sufficient thickness, when the female Stands erect to conceal those parts usially covered from familiar view, but when she stoops or places herself in any other attitude this battery of Venus is not altogether impervious to the inquisitive and penetrating eye of the amorite," said Lewis. Sergeant Gass also

148

"THIS EMENCE MOUNTAIN the top of which was obscured with clouds" Clark's Indian guide told him was Pe Shack, or bad. This is Tillamook Head, near Seaside, Oregon. Clark, with Sacajawea and party, climbed it on their way to see the whale.

THE SALT CAIRN. Clark had been without salt for so long he didn't care if he had it or not. Lewis, although he observed, "I have learned to think that if the chord be sufficiently strong which binds the soul and the boddy together it dose not so much matter about the materials that Compose it," craved salt, and so did the rest of the party. This is the oven or stove built of stones where Joe Fields, Gibson and Bratton boiled the salt from the sea water.

peeped and observed that the skirts were "some use as covering while ladies are standing erect and weather calm, but when in any other position or when the wind blows their charms have but a precarious defense."

However their charms did have a very lively and active defense. Wherever the women went they left a trail of fleas. Lewis said the little animals were almost a calamity to the Indians. They were more than that to the white men for "they attained mastery of our house and it is impossible to expell them."

On the plains, mountains and upper Columbia the Indian women had given freely of their favors because their husbands wished it, or because, as Lewis said, "Their kindness exceeded the ordinary courtesies of hospitality," or just for fun. Now on the coast the men for the first time met Indian women engaged in prostitution, sometimes aided by husbands who eagerly drummed up trade for them. A chief came to the fort hoping to trade a mat and bundle of roots for a file and some beads. When the captains refused the barter the chief offered his two wives, one to each captain. Lewis and Clark weren't interested in women. The chief, longing for the file, became irate and his disappointed wives joined him in his anger. Assuming as much dignity as possible, the Indian leader, his wives and his tribe stalked away from the fort.

"The person is in fact the only property of the young female," Clark commented, "therefore is a medium of trade." Lewis thought them poor indeed and sourly said, "a Chinook or Clatsop beauty in full attire is one of the most disgusting objects of nature." Whatever their looks, their wares appealed to the men of the expedition. The captains had to issue little pieces of ribbon to be used as means of exchange to prevent the women from bankrupting the party.

An elderly madame whom the men called "the Old Bawd" first met the men on the north side of the Columbia, offering six of her daughters and nieces. Trade was brisk so she and her girls, supplemented by three of her nieces, followed the white men to the fort on the south side. Several of the men had by this time contracted venereal disease so Lewis "therefore gave the men a particular charge with respect to them [the girls] which they promised to observe."

A light-skinned Indian with red hair and freckles and another with 'J. Bowman' tattooed on her arm indicated that the Lewis and Clark expedition were not the first white men on whom the women had practiced their arts.

The sun upon rare occasion would break through the clouds during the dreary winter and then "as if it were impossible to have 24 hours of pleasant weather" the rain would resume. At the saltworks in the wind and rain "the sand flew and waves rolled" and "the sand cut our faces," Ordway said.

There were many elk but they were hard to get. Only Drewyer, raised in the wilderness and an infallible marksman, was consistently successful. In the meat house, one of the first buildings constructed at the fort, the smoking and salting were no

"THIS EMENCE OCIAN." Driving rain and stinging sand made the explorers feel the western sea was anything but "passific." But Clark said, "The men appear much Satisfied with their trip beholding with astonishment the high waves dashing against the rocks."

". . . A MOST ROMANTIC APPEARANCE," Clark said of these "nitches and points of highland." He and his party viewed this section of the Pacific coast just north of Cannon Beach, Oregon.

match for the humidity. The meat spoiled so quickly that 150 elk and 20 deer were no more than adequate food for the party that winter.

Between spells of heavy colds, influenza, boils and indigestion from spoiled meat, the men at the fort whiled away their time making clothes for the return journey. Out of the fine elk skins they made 338 pair of good "Mockasons."

The captains planned to leave their winter fort about April 1, believing snow would block the mountain passes until early June. They hoped, too, that some of the sailing ships would return so they could replenish their supply of trade goods which they needed for dickering with the Indians on their return journey. Partly because of the shrewdness of "the Old Bawd" and her girls, the party's bartering articles had dwindled so they could almost be tied up in two handkerchiefs.

As winter wore on, elk were more and more difficult to get, and in poorer condition when they were killed. Therefore, the captains decided they had better start homeward about the middle of March.

They repaired their canoes and augmented their supply by stealing an Indian craft. No longer were they so scrupulously honest with the natives. They merely reminded themselves that the Indians had stolen some elk meat.

On March 22 hunters were sent on ahead. Next day the canoes were loaded for departure. They were ready to leave the place where, Clark said philosophically, ". . . we have lived . . . as we have any right to expect . . . 3 meals of some kind a day either pore elk meat or roots."

The dreary winter was over. "Huckleberrys leafing out remind us of spring," said Clark. The answers to Thomas Jefferson's questions about the amusements, morals, customs and languages of the coastal Indians filled Lewis's and Clark's bulging notebooks. The report on the climate if monotonous with its description of rain, rain, rain certainly was accurate. They had explored both north and south of the Columbia, obtained maps from the Indians and drawn some of their own. A record of their exploration was left with the Indians to give to the first ship that came to the Columbia. Although Lewis and Clark probably did not know it, the foundation for The United States' claim to the Oregon country was established.

At noon on March 23, with the sun giving a brief benediction, they put their loaded canoes into the river. Two men were sick; Bratton so violently ill he had to be carried. Hardship and new dangers lay ahead of them, but they were on their way home.

TRAVELOGUE . . . It was a lovely sunny day. High time, we decided, to head for Cape Disappointment. Even though the cape is in Washington we crossed over to Portland because the Oregon road heads more directly toward the ocean from here on out. Al was sidetracked once or twice by graveyards. Whenever we stop to look at an old cemetery he is immediately captured by some ancient family plot, and conjures up pictures of the lives of these people who died so long ago. I invariably notice first a tiny headstone with, perhaps, a lamb chiseled on it. Instead of sternly refusing to look at it, knowing what it does to me, I doggedly read the inscription. "Our darling. Age 3 years 4 months 5 days," one will say. Once there were three headstones all with the same family name, one for an infant, one for a two-year-old and one for a big sister of five. Fire? Plague? What had carried away those three, decades ago? So many little ones went, in those days.

When we ferried across the river from Astoria to Megler the annual salmon derby was on. Here were hundreds of fishermen struggling to capture the fish that might win one of the many prizes. "Imagine," I said, "deep down in that water the big Kings are pushing home to their spawning grounds. And here on top men and women are trying to snag them. It makes quite a picture when you think of the depth of the water, the thousands of fish and the boats skimming along the top." Al said, "More fish win than lose. They'll swim up falls, they'll half-kill themselves to get back where they were born. People have been taking these fish for centuries and still they pour back." The children were wild to go fishing but we were too near journey's end for such delays.

Clark indicated Indian villages on his maps with little groups of teepees, much like the "principal products" maps youngsters use today. In the lower Washington coastal area there are a number of these drawings on his map. Of course we saw no villages, but it was easy to visualize the party going from one group of natives to another to try to figure out whether they would winter here, or go south of the Columbia. Because they went south, we headed south again after investigating Cape Disappointment.

At Seaside is the salt cairn used by the party; it is probably the one man-made relic left on the Lewis and Clark trail, with the exception of Clark's name which he carved in Pompey's Pillar. The cairn is nestled among the modern houses of the little resort town, and is just a few steps from the ocean beach. Still it is far enough from the shore so it must have been quite an effort for the men to lug gallons of water to the fire. Al has tried many times to get a good picture of the cairn. With trees shadowing it and an iron fence protecting it, the pile of rocks is not photogenic. But without that fence some happy toddlers would have toted those rocks away long ago.

Not far down the highway we found Ecola State Park where there are magnificent views of the ocean when the fog is not rolling in. It is truly a rockbound coast. I reminded Al that a photographer had drowned trying to get unusual pictures here, but Al's early-day forest service training was not lost. He strolled around the steep rocks unconcernedly while the rest of us looked the other way.

Toward evening we pulled into Fort Clatsop. Although we'd visited this winter camp several times, it was the first time we'd been here when it wasn't raining. The men of the expedition had groaned about the rain. We could imagine how slowly the dreary months passed for them. The journals don't indicate that Sacajawea ever complained, but it must have been a rugged winter here with her little boy.

This was the end. We wandered among the fir trees feeling somewhat elated, somewhat lost. I think, as we viewed Fort Clatsop, we all traveled back mentally over that long trail we had come. Although we still had a few areas to cover in later trips, the main part of our westward expedition was over.

HOW TO GET THERE NOW . . . See map 8.

FORT CLATSOP. From Astoria, Oregon, go west on U.S. 101, 6.5 miles to junction with airport road. Take gravel road .6 miles to where woodland road cuts off to the right up a little hill. Take this road .2 mile to top of hill. The site of Fort Clatsop is marked in the clearing to the left.

SALT CAIRN. Markers indicate direction in town of Seaside, Oregon, one block from the beach.

Tillamook Head, which Clark climbed on the way to see a whale, can be seen from the beach. It extends out in the ocean about 4 miles from Seaside.

PACIFIC TO THE BITTERROOT VALLEY

FORT CLATSOP was left sodden and desolate among the dripping ever-greens on the hilltop. The men looked back to the shore and saw Chief Comowool standing in the rain frowning over the certificate of good merit given him by the captains.

As the expedition glided down the river "the Old Bawd" and her six girls over-took them in her canoe. Although she long ago had given up the idea of selling the tarnished wares of her proteges, she still had something to offer. With dried fish, pointed Chinook basket hats and an otter skin she tried to part the men from the few trinkets that remained.

The party took the wrong channel as they canoed up the Columbia on the first lap of the long trip home. A Cathlamet Indian, noticing their mistake, overtook them with flailing paddle. The captains were grateful when he guided them back to the

155

main channel. Their thanks dissolved in extreme chagrin when the native caimly told them he was owner of the canoe they had stolen at Clatsop. Owning another canoe, he was happy to accept two elk skins the embarrassed Lewis and Clark offered as recompense.

On Wednesday, March 26, the captains gave a small medal to a chief of the Cathlamets. The honored chief reciprocated by presenting the party with a large sturgeon. The hungry men stopped to feast on Fanny's Island, named after Clark's younger sister Frances. After dinner the canoes shoved off again and Clark walked along the south shore of the river through an "eligant bottom" which he named Fanny's Bottom.

The captains sent hunters ahead to Deer Island to secure meat so the party could camp a while to repair the still-leaky canoes. Sergeant Ordway noticed "the game is pleanty about this place," his strong farmer instinct making him add "& soil rich &c." Pulling their canoes up on shore, the men spread out the baggage to dry and poured melted pitch into the leaks in their canoes.

When the hunters returned they testified that Deer Island was well named. They had seen more than 100 deer and had killed seven. Lewis was interested in a vulture one of the hunters shot and brought to camp. He was surprised later when the men sent to get the deer came back to report that vultures had eaten four of them.

Always alert to every aspect of nature, Lewis also commented on the innumerable garter snakes which were "seen entwined arround each other in large bundles of 40 or 50." That night they heard frogs croaking in the marshes along the river.

Moving upriver, the party met several groups of Indians coming downstream. The natives told them the salmon had not commenced the run. Food, they said, was very scarce among their people up the river. The captains, deciding to stop and stock up on food where it was plentiful, ordered camp set up on Wappato Island, 15 miles above Deer Island and about 107 miles from Fort Clatsop.

The hunters added a bear and several deer to the meat supply. Indians were as plentiful as game but not so cooperative. Sullen and bad-tempered, they "higgled" with Clark when he tried trading with them for wappatos. Clark, a resourceful diplomat, thought a little magic might give him the prestige he needed. While distracting the Indians with his compass and magnet, he surreptitiously threw a port fire match, or artillery fuse, into the campfire. As the startled natives watched the needle spin furiously in the magnetized compass the port fire match burst into a hot and brilliant flame. Terrorized, the Indians instantly gave Clark the wappatos he wanted and begged him to appease the wrath of the fire god. Clark was the man who could do it. He put his magnet away and the needle of the compass stopped turning. The port fire match burned itself out. The captain paid for the wappatos and left happily, his reputation as a demon secure.

MEMALOOSE ISLAND. Most of the islands along this section of the Columbia had been used as burial places by the Indians. On one of them Clark found vaults that contained bones for a "debth of 4 feet." Since Memaloose is the Indian word for dead, this is literally the island of the dead. Clark observed, "This must bee the burrying place for maney ages for the inhabitants of those rapids."

"WELL CALCULATED FOR DEFENSE," Clark said of Fort Rocks at The Dalles, Oregon. The natives above had warned the captains that the Indians in this vicinity were hostile. This was the expedition's campsite of October 25, 1805.

Wɪᴛʜ ᴛʜᴇ ʜᴜɴᴛᴇʀs in advance, the party started slowly up the river April 2. Stopping occasionally to jerk or dry the elk or deer the hunters had killed, it was six days before they passed Beacon Rock, which marked the end of the tidewater.

The canoes were unloaded at the Cascades. Some of the men carried the load over the portage while others pulled the canoes through the white water with ropes. One canoe broke away and was recovered for the party by Indians. When another craft broke loose in the brisk current it swept down the river and out of sight for good.

Whether they were sorry the white men came or sorry they were going, the Indians became increasingly unfriendly. Shields, stopping to buy a dog, became separated from the rest of the party. Two Indians, blocking his path, attempted to take the dog from him. He had no gun but before they could string their arrows he whipped out a long knife. As he charged with his knife they broke and fled into the woods.

When the natives stole Scannon, Lewis's dog, three men were sent out to recover it and ordered to shoot if there was resistance. "Our men seem disposed to kill a few of them," Lewis said; "We keep ourselves perfectly on guard." Lewis had to strike another unruly Indian and have him removed from camp. "So arrogant and intrusive have they become," the captain commented, "that nothing but our numbers we are convinced, saves us from attack."

After recovery of the dog and the physical punishment meted out by Lewis, the natives kept their distance but their dispositions didn't change.

Clark went on ahead to do some horsetrading. With no trinkets for barter he somehow got a few horses from the unfriendly Indians. As rapidly as horses were acquired the baggage was taken from the canoes and placed on the animals. The canoes seemed a solution to the firewood problem. As they got additional horses they started chopping up the boats.

The Indians didn't bother to trade for the canoes since they fully intended to merely take them over when the party started the land trek. Their interest changed to alarm when they saw Drewyer beginning to chop up the last of the boats. They offered a few strings of beads, then, which the captains accepted, knowing they would be good money later on.

On April 27 seven Walla Walla Indians joined the party. The warm hospitality of these Indians was a welcome change after the sullen hostility the expedition had received all the way up the river. They furnished fuel and four dogs. That evening the men danced to the the tune of Cruzatte's fiddle to entertain the Indians. The natives reciprocated by dancing to their own chanting.

158

"THE CLIFFS AGAIN APPROACH THE RIVER," observed Clark. The party climbed them at this point and marched ten miles across the high plain, coming back to the Columbia just above and across the river from where Wallula, Washington is now.

"MANEY LARGE BANKS OF PURE SAND," Clark said, "which appear to have been drifted up by the wind to the hight of 20 or 30 feet." Civilization has fastened down with vegetation most of the sand dunes that once roamed this section, but there are still a few like this one constantly moving and shifting with each change of the wind.

TWIN SISTERS. Just below the junction of the Walla Walla with the Columbia, these two landmarks looked down on Chief Yellept's village across the big river. Lewis and Clark saw them on both the westward passage and the return trip. Too bad they weren't named the Two Captains.

Chief Yellept, who had been friendly and had been given a medal on the way down the river the year before, presented Clark with a beautiful white horse. He wished a kettle in return, but kettles were scarce; there was only one for each eight men. Lewis gave the chief his sword.

The captains' fairly steady medical practice further endeared them to the natives. To a woman with a "coald" Clark "gave such medesene as would keep her body open and raped her in flannel." Really, Clark's morals were on a higher level than his spelling.

The Walla Walla's sociability became almost irksome. Camped on the north bank of the Columbia opposite the mouth of the Walla Walla River, the captains decided to cross over on the 28th. There was an overland route to the Clearwater, the Indians had told them, that would save 80 miles. But Chief Yellept would not hear of their leaving. He had invited another tribe over to see the strange white men dance. The best Lewis and Clark could do was take advantage of the pleasant day to ferry their horses and baggage to the other side, returning for Yellept's dance.

In the evening the Walla Wallas, now numbering over 100, were joined by about as many of their friends, the Chimnapoos. As the men of the expedition prepared their evening meal, several hundred Indians, including a few women, formed a half circle around them.

The party finished their dinner in spite of the disconcerting audience, then danced for an hour. The Indians, taking over the entertainment, lined up in a solid column forming a square. Some of the more energetic natives cavorted around the inside of the square to the chanting of the whole assemblage. Those forming the square jumped up at intervals in time to the music. When some of the white men joined in, the Indians were thoroughly pleased. "The exercise was not indeed very violent nor very graceful" the captains agreed thoughtfully. But Yellept's dance was the social event of the season.

The following morning when the Indians ferried Lewis and Clark across the river they rapturously promised to dance day and night until the captains returned.

Tʜᴇ ᴘᴀʀᴛʏ with their newly-acquired horses left the camp at the mouth of the Walla Walla River, on the south side of the Columbia, and headed overland for the Lewis, or Snake River. A Nez Perce Indian was their guide and he brought his family along.

The next day they crossed a large sand plain broken here and there by dunes fifteen or twenty feet high which were beautifully streamlined by the prevailing winds. After going about 14 miles the party came to the Touchet River where they chose a campsite. Cottonwood grew heavily along the banks and there was plenty of firewood. Soon the men and the tireless Sacajawea were enjoying a beaver Drewyer killed and two pheasants shot by Clark. The Indian guide and his family feasted on an otter Drewyer had brought in with the beaver. It was one of their favorite foods.

Moving up the Pataha Valley on May 1 they found the country not unlike the plains of the Missouri except that here there were no vast herds of buffalo, elk, deer and antelope.

The party had just pitched camp that night when three young Indians pounded in on horseback. They apparently had been riding furiously from the camp on the Walla Walla River. When packing, the expedition had overlooked a steel trap and the three Indians had gone to all this trouble to return it. Lewis and Clark had previously commented, ". . . of all the Indians we have met since leaving the United States the Wolla Wollas were the most hospitable honest and sincere." These three natives joined the party.

When preparing to break camp the next morning, they found one of the horses missing. It was afternoon before he was captured and the party could go on.

As they moved into higher country game became even scarcer. They were "agreeably surprised" on May 3 "by the appearance of Weahkoonut or the Indian whom we called the Bighorn from the circumstance of his having a horn of that animal suspended from his left arm." He was an influential chief among the Nez Perce who, the year before on the journey down the Snake, had been of great service to the expedition.

Weahkoonut came with ten of his people, saying he intended to help the party to the Snake. Perhaps the Walla Wallas, only three in number, and the guide thought he had other motives. They left abruptly without even waiting for thanks.

The night of May 3 the party camped in a grove of cottonwoods on Pataha Creek. While they sat eating the last of their dogs, a cold wind changed the rain to snow.

After a miserable night, the expedition went down a creek toward the Snake. Eagerly the men kept watch for an Indian encampment where Weahkoonut had said they would find food. When they finally reached the encampment they found

"IT RAINED HAILED SNOWED & BLOWED" when the expedition camped in this grove of "cotton trees," on Pataha Creek near Pomeroy, Washington. Here they gloomily ate their last dog.

"A REVINE WHICH FORMS the source of a small creek." Down this stream the party traveled seven and one-half miles to the Snake River.

"CLEAR AND RAPID WITH SHOALS or swift places." The Clearwater River just below the forks. It is thought that the packsaddle cache was made in the timbered bend of the river. Canoe Camp of October, 1805, was just around the corner.

only six very poor families. All the natives had to offer were two lean dogs and "a few large cakes of half cured bread made from a root resembling the sweet potato." It was pretty scanty nourishment for 30 hungry men.

Rapidly they went three miles up the Snake, where they were met by more of the Nez Perce tribe who ferried them across the river in canoes. When the party made camp that night, on the north side, the Nez Perce were not only friendly but "crouded about our fire in great numbers insomuch that we could scarcely cook or keep ourselves warm."

PRACTICING AT MEDICINE

THE YEAR BEFORE, when they had gone down the Clearwater by canoe, the party had stopped long enough for Clark to establish himself as an eminent physician. Tinkering with medicine because of Lewis's illness, Clark had prescribed a liniment for an Indian's lame knee and thigh. The treatment could have worked no better had a doctor ordered it. Stories of the captain's powers traveled fast from lodge to lodge among the Nez Perce winter camps along the river.

Returning upriver by land — on the north side, at the suggestion of the Nez Perce — the party found Clark had accumulated a fine practice in *absentia*. The lame, the halt and the blind flocked to the expedition's camp at the junction of the Clearwater and Potlatch rivers where the party spent the night of May 5.

Since their supply of trade goods was almost gone, the captains decided to take advantage of Clark's reputation as a medicine man. For a horse, Clark opened an abcess on a woman's back. Doses of flour of sulphur and cream of tartar he traded for some dogs. In return for bundles of roots the captain passed out vials of eyewater. "After administering to them for several hours," Clark said happily, "we found ourselves in possession of a plentiful meal." Nothing they had prescribed, the captains assured themselves, was harmful — and in some cases it even might do some good.

Among the Nez Perce only Twisted Hair, the chief with whom they had left their horses the year before, did not seem glad to see the party. He and Cut Nose and Broken Arm had quarreled almost immediately after the expedition left over who was the most capable custodian for the horses. Perhaps each wished the use of the animals during the winter; perhaps they coveted the two guns and ammunition promised as a reward for the care of the horses. Whatever the reason, the argument resulted in the horses being scattered among Indians all the way up the Clearwater.

On May 6 they moved up to camp four miles below the mouth of Bed Rock Creek. Next day, noticing the river was rising rapidly, they borrowed an Indian canoe to cross to the south side. Swimming the horses and making repeated trips with the canoe for men and baggage, it took the party four hours to make the crossing. They found their cache near Canoe Camp had become exposed. Several

165

saddles were lost but Twisted Hair had recached most of them. Although an Indian's dog had dug up the hidden ammunition, his master had faithfully cared for the powder and shot, and returned it to the party.

After dining they went on up the south side of the river and climbed a high hill. "We saw the Rockey Mountains covred with snow," Ordway said. Finding it rough going along the river bank, they cut south up Little Canyon Creek.

The party recovered more of their horses at each Indian camp they passed. Now that their own horses were coming to hand, they got rid of several unruly "Stonehorses" the Yakimas had given them. The recalcitrant stallions, they found, were better in the cook pot than on the trail.

Leaving the Columbia didn't mean leaving the rain. On the cold night of May 9 the rain turned to snow. They rode about 20 miles the next morning through the six-inch fall, their horses slipping and sliding as the wet snow balled up under their hoofs. Toward evening they descended a steep hill to the encampment of Chief Broken Arm and his tribe on Lawyer's Creek. Riding into camp they noticed the stars and stripes the captains had given the chief the previous fall proudly flying over the village.

Received with dignity by the Nez Perce chief, the party was escorted to a camp. Dinner was horsemeat and roots provided by the Indians. The men were pleased, Lewis commented, to "have their stomachs once more well filled with horsebeef and mush of the bread of cows."

After eating, the captains smoked and counciled with the Indians.

Feeling good now, the men played the fiddle and danced. Indians from neighboring villages assembled to watch these frolicking white men.

The following morning they learned some of the visitors were chiefs and decided to remain another day in council.

A MONTH'S DELAY

The Indians would not soon forget the party's stay in the camp on Lawyer's Creek May 10, 11 and 12. While Clark impressed the Nez Perce with his luck at healing the sick, the men of the expedition danced themselves to eternal renown to the tune of Cruzatte's fiddle. Their zest was rewarded with plenty of good food and the return of all but two of their horses. Although some of the animals showed evidence of hard riding, most of them were in good shape. Chief Broken Arm told the captains the two missing horses were taken by Old Toby, the Shoshone guide of the year before. Remembering that Old Toby and his son had left without their back pay, Lewis and Clark did not begrudge the loss.

On the clear frosty morning of May 13, the party gathered their 60 horses and moved four miles down to the Clearwater. Next day, swimming their horses across the river, they traveled a short distance to the site of a Nez Perce winter camp.

166

"WE DECENDED THE HILLS to Commearp Creek." The village of Broken Arm was about 80 paces from this "little run," and over it floated the American flag the captains had given the chief the year before. The expedition camped on the flat just beyond the creek.

"EXTENSIVE OPEN BOTTOM of the Koos Kooske." The expedition crossed the Clearwater at about the center of the picture, and made their Kamiah camp about where the sawmill is now located at the extreme left. When they left for Lolo a month later they went over the hills in the center. They found it ". . . thinly timbered . . . hills to the E. and north of us high broken and but partially timbered."

Lolo Trail was ahead of them. The Indians had told them there would be no feed for the horses on Lolo until the first of July. They decided to stay at this bend in the river until the snows melted from the high ridges.

They built a good camp for themselves and, Ordway said, "a bowery for the officers to write in." It was an easy life with enough food. Several stud horses, still too unruly to ride, were added to the larder. Nez Perce dogs were thin but plentiful. Pheasant, some deer, black bear and those of the "white kind" were brought in by the hunters. Lewis noticed the men "who are not hunters are geting reather lazy and slouthfull."

On the Kamiah prairie masses of wild flowers bloomed. Cock ruffed grouse drummed in the alder thickets. Lewis appreciated these things but commented that "the honey bee is not here."

Only Private Bratton, who had become seriously ill at the saltworks, failed to enjoy late spring at Kamiah. Troubled with a mystifying lumbar ailment, he had had to ride prone in the canoe, be carried over portages and carefully helped on horseback the entire way. Although his appetite was good, he had no strength. Lewis's medical knowledge was no help, and the man grew weaker. Even Clark, whose healings among the Indians had put the native medicine men into disrepute, had no suggestions to offer.

One day Bratton feebly told the captains that an Indian had recommended the sweathouse treatment. It was the universal cure-all for Indians from the mouth of the Missouri to the Pacific Ocean. The captains had wasted no admiration on this drastic, primitive cure nor on the medicine men who prescribed it. But they were desperate about Bratton, for they thought he would die on the hard trip over Lolo. Reluctantly they permitted him to try the remedy they had laughed at.

Hot stones from a campfire were placed in a small circular lodge covered with skins, then water was thrown over the stones until the lodge was filled with steam. Bratton crawled into the sweathouse when the interior was almost suffocatingly hot. After steaming as long as he could stand it, he left the lodge and jumped into the icy stream. The next day Bratton started to get well.

Sacajawea's baby was teething and "unwell." Early in June little Baptiste developed a high fever and serious swelling in the throat. It seemed the infant might die. But the baby improved when the captains put a poultice of wild onions on the swelling, and also a salve of bear oil, resin and beeswax which Clark made.

The party had hoped salmon would soon appear in the Clearwater, but there was not a sign of them. Melting snows in the mountains made such a roaring torrent of the river they probably could not have caught the big fish if they had been available.

The expedition hadn't forgotten the hungers of Lolo Trail and were determined to have a good food supply before starting back over it. Ordway, Frazier and Wiser

"GREAT SNOWEY BARRIERS." The expedition twice crossed the Bitter Root Mountains which are still almost a trackless wilderness. "We were intirely Serounded by those mountains . . . to one unacquainted with them it would have seemed impossible to have ever escaped."

INDIAN POST OFFICE. Down through the generations the Indians paused to smoke a pipe here. Warriors, returning from their raids on the plains Indians, left messages about their success or failure and probably about the condition of the trail.

were sent to the Snake for fish. Most of the fish they caught spoiled before the men reached Kamiah.

When the Indians tried to cross the river with a raftload of camas root their craft floated downstream in the swift current and smashed against a rock. The Indians swam ashore but the food sank. The captains dispatched Charbonneau and Lepage on a trading mission with the Indians. Their horse fell in the river and the few remaining trade goods were lost. The ingenious men cut the buttons off their clothing to replenish their trade goods. Potts, Collins and Shannon made another try at the river. Potts was nearly drowned and all three lost their blankets. Blankets were precious; there was hardly more than one left to each man.

The captains decided to move camp farther into the mountains where they hoped game might be more plentiful. Private Bratton and little Baptiste, well again, were able to travel. On June 10, 1806 each man riding a horse and leading one loaded with provisions and baggage, the party started up over the "riverhills which are very high and 3 miles in extent."

FIRST ATTEMPT TO CROSS LOLO

Weippe Prairie, Ordway said, consists of "2,000 ackers of level smooth prarie on which is not a single tree or shrub but the lowest parts is covrd with commass which is now in bloom."

The expedition camped in pine woods bordering the prairie near a small cold stream. When they awoke next morning their first impression was that they were camped on the shores of a beautiful lake. The prairie was solid with blue camas blossoms and the air heavy with their chocolate fragrance.

The prairie was so frequently hunted by the Nez Perce Indians that game, although a little more plentiful, was exceptionally wild. It was four days before the hunters had accumulated enough meat to satisfy the captains that all was in readiness for the trip over Lolo Trail.

Snow still lay deep on the ridges, the Indians had told them, and the horses would be without grass during the trip. But 150 miles of snow and windswept trail was not too forbidding to these hardened men of the wilderness. On the rainy morning of June 15 the party started their journey.

After crossing the creek, they traveled through "high broken country." The first day, over slippery ground and fallen timber, they made 22 miles.

Next morning they collected their horses and started out at six o'clock over "handsome meadows of fine grass." The air was perfumed with the fragrance of dogtooth violets, columbine, wild roses of two kinds, bluebells and yellow flowering pea, but the cold nights reminded them that winter still gripped the ridges of Lolo Trail.

170

"OVER DEEP SNOWS" the party followed this "dividing ridge" over Lolo Pass June 28, 1806. "We find the travelling on the Snow not worse than without it as, the easy passage it givs us over rocks and fallen timber fully compensates for the Sliping." The snow sank two or three inches under the horses feet.

BULL MOOSE. Several times on the expedition Lewis and Clark encountered "moose deer" as they called North America's largest animal, but their journals make no note of their having killed any.

The streams were high. As the party moved farther into the Rockies they found snow 12 to 15 feet deep even on the south side of the ridges. "Winter now presented itself to us in all its rigours," Lewis worried.

Two days later Colter's horse fell while crossing a creek. Although Colter was dashed against the rocks by the swift current and lost his blanket, the accident only "hurt him a little," Ordway said. The same day Potts fell on his big knife, cutting an artery. The expedition stopped a few minutes while Captain Lewis "sowed him up."

Their experience crossing the pass the previous fall was no help now with all traces of the trail buried deep beneath the snow. They had no guide because no Indian was willing to undertake the trip so early in the year. The horses had good footing in the heavily-crusted snow, but the captains knew that without food the animals would soon weaken. They decided to go back to the lower levels and wait until they could get some Indians to guide them. Placing the baggage on scaffolds and carefully covering the food and instruments, the party set out at 1 o'clock. Drewyer, Shannon and Whitehouse were sent on ahead of the retreating men to try to secure some Indian guides. "The mortification of being obliged to retrace our steps," Lewis said disconsolately, "rendered still more tedious a route everywhere so obstructed by brush and fallen timber."

They stubbornly camped on Collins Creek for two days. There was food for the horses but none for the men, so on June 21st they moved farther down. About 7 in the evening their dejection lifted when they came to the old camp on Weippe and found a deer the hunters had killed for supper.

UP AND OVER LOLO PASS

The captains, anxiously awaiting the return of Drewyer, Shannon and Whitehouse, were relieved when they showed up two days later with three Indian guides.

As they left the prairie camp the men were again buoyed up although Ordway, a farmer at heart, remarked regretfully, "The strawburys are pleanty in this place."

Although the snow had melted some at the lower altitude, it became deeper as they moved up the ridges. "The fog rose up thick from the hollers" but the Indian guides knew the country well.

A few days later when one of the guides became sick, the captains were not surprised as "such complaints with an indian is generally the prelude to his abandoning any enterprise with which he is not well pleased." The native and his two companions dropped behind. Lewis and Clark were amazed when the guides rejoined them later in the day, and even more astonished to find the man was really ill. Noticing he was trudging through the snow clad only in moccasins and an elk hide, the captains gave him a buffalo robe.

172

"WATER NEARLY BOILING HOT as it spouted from the rocks," Clark said. "I tasted this water and found it hot and not bad tasted." At Lolo Hot Springs the Indians had scooped a hole in the sand under the rocks. Here the men on their return trip had their first hot bath in nearly two years.

The cache they had made eight days before was in good shape. After eating, they spent two hours repacking their horses to include the supplies of the cache, while the Indians urged them to move onward rapidly. It was still a long way to grass for the horses.

The steep trail through the mountains between the Clearwater and the Choppunish was slippery with hard-crusted snow. As the path wound along the edge of precipices, the men knew that if the horses stumbled they would roll down hundreds of feet into the canyon. Marks the Indians had made on the trees to locate the trail were far apart. "But our guides traverse this trackless region with a kind of instinctive sagacity," Lewis marveled, "never hesitate . . . never embarrassed; yet so undeviating is their step that where ever the snow has dissappared for even a few hundred paces, we find the summer road."

About noon the fourth day, the party came to an eight-foot stone mound the Indians had raised on top of the ridge. At the request of their Nez Perce guides the men paused to smoke a pipe in deference to an ancient Indian custom. As they smoked the captains viewed the mountains which completely surrounded them, and were grateful for their "admireable pilots," the Indian guides.

Food was getting low for the men and there was still none for the horses. The few deer and "white buffalo," as the Indians called the Rocky Mountain goat, were too elusive to be shot. The horses skidded and plodded twenty-eight miles that day in the race against hunger.

The horses looked "extreemly gant" the next morning. Heartened by the Indians' promise of grass by noon, the party breakfasted early and started out again over the deep snow. At noon the next day after passing Packers Meadows, they descended Lolo Creek. The terrible summer-winter of the Bitter Root Mountains lay behind them.

The men had their first hot bath in two years at Lolo Hot Springs, soaking off the dust of the plains, the fleas of Clatsop and the snows of Lolo. Lewis luxuriated in the steaming warm springs for 19 minutes.

That evening, warm and clean, they feasted on fresh venison. Although the Continental Divide was ahead of them, the Columbia, Snake, and Clearwater rivers and the ridges of Lolo were a part of the past. Now, they felt, they really were on their way home.

PLAN MADE AT TRAVELERS REST

On the morning of July 3 the tough, lean men of the expedition, their sun- and wind-burned faces blending with their soiled buckskin clothing, worked about the camp adjusting packs and tightening cinches. Probably the two captains, while keeping a watchful eye on the final packing, further discussed their plans for the rest of the trip.

174

A GROUND SQUIRREL. Lewis described it as something larger than "those of the U States," adding, "this is a much handsomer anamal . . . an inhabitant of the open plain altogether wher it burrows and resides . . . their burrows sometimes . . . run horizontally near the surface for a considerable distance . . . but those in which they reside or take refuge strike much deeper in the earth." They "usually sit erect on their mounds and make a shrill whistling noise something like tweet tweet tweet &c &c."

Lewis with Sergeant Gass and eight others was to go directly to the Missouri River. There three of the men, including the invalids, were to prepare carriages for moving the baggage over the portage of the Great Falls. Lewis, with the remaining six, was to explore up the Marias River to "ascertain whether any branch of that river lies as far north as Latd. 50."

Captain Clark, Sergeant Ordway and the rest, they decided, would go up the Bitter Root Valley and over the Continental Divide. When they reached the Forks of the Beaverhead, they were to pick up the canoes and supplies cached the year before and go down the river to Three Forks. There the party would subdivide; Ordway and nine men would take the canoes and continue down the Missouri to rejoin Lewis. Clark, his servant York, Sacajawea and the five others were to go with the horses up the Gallatin Valley and across the pass to the Yellowstone River. They were to build canoes on the Yellowstone and float down the river to its junction with the Missouri. Here Clark was to wait for Lewis to rejoin him.

By now the men were regular army soldiers, toughened by two-and-a-half years of hardship. But back of the rough jokes they made while preparing to separate was a tension and sadness. They had paddled endless miles together and divided their last wolf meat and rotten fish. Together they had suffered the snows of the Rockies and the rains of the Pacific. Now they were parting. Each knew he might not see the others again. Perhaps the vast wilderness would simply swallow them up. This was the only time during the whole expedition that all its members felt depressed.

TRAVELOGUE . . . Although our trip from St. Louis to the Pacific covered most of the Lewis and Clark trail, there were sections we visited later — because Al does have to earn a living, and couldn't stay away forever on one journey.

Driving east on a trip from Missoula to Cutbank we turned at Bonner to go up the crystal clear Blackfoot River. We almost had to hold Bert in the car each time we passed one of the trout pools below the riffles.

Decades ago there was an old Indian trail right where the road is now. In imagination we saw the Flatheads, the Nez Perce, the Shoshones and the Pend O'Reilles trekking eastward to their yearly buffalo hunt, and hoping they would not meet the Blackfeet, which they all too often did. They called the stream Cokahlerisk kit, or River of the Road to Buffalo.

We came out of the wilderness to a town of log cabins and buildings. Al stopped the car and for a minute we just looked at each other. Why, this was frontier stuff — a real log-cabin city. What had we stumbled onto? Then we saw that the log houses were beer parlors and super gas stations. Well, it was cute anyway, and its name — Lincoln — most appropriate.

Since the road doesn't cross the continental divide by way of Lewis and Clark Pass, we went through Rogers Pass just south of the route the explorers took. On the east side Al stopped the car. Here was a fine view of Lewis and Clark Pass — and a ridge surrounded with barbed wire. When Al leads us through barbed wire into some rattlesnake-infested, rocky, windblown ridge I'm never sure if he's after a high spot to take a good picture, as he claims, or if he's on the prowl for artifacts. Anyway, as we picked our way among the cactus plants Al let out a yip and picked up a fine large arrowhead. As usual we all started combing the ground but with no luck. "Think how many people have passed this up," Al gloated. "Well," we all replied at once, "they just didn't realize what it was." There was a time when we wouldn't have either, but now we scrutinized each unusual rock. We probably will be permanently round-shouldered because we simply can't afford to stand up straight anymore; might miss something.

A little further on we saw an Indian rock fort on a hilltop. How long had it been there? How many Blackfoot had stood watch on this windy mound? Overlooking both Rogers and Lewis and Clark passes, it was a wonderful vantage point. We wanted to stand right where the Blackfeet stood, so we did. To climb to such a fort a traveler should have strong legs and stout shoes. It is no place for toeless sandals even if the Indians did negotiate it in moccasins. As we stood by the fort we thought that probably a Blackfoot crouched here watching Lewis and his party as they wound their way down onto the plains from the continental divide.

The next day we went north from Great Falls to Marias River to follow Lewis's route into the Blackfoot country. Al has learned to dream right past the modern buildings we see along the road, and instead he sees teepees and old buffalo trails. I think he was a bit angry when I pulled him out of his dream by pointing out the sign at Shelby marking the spot where the arena seating 45,000 persons was built for the Dempsey Gibbons fight.

Maybe that's why he drove so fast, although he says he just wanted to reach the monument 22 miles beyond Cutbank marking the northernmost point of the Lewis and Clark explorations before sunset. Anyway we drove like crazy but Al was crestfallen — we reached it too late to get pictures.

HOW TO GET THERE NOW . . . See maps 7 and 6.

THE BLACKFOOT RIVER. From Missoula go west through Hellgate Canyon on U.S. 10 to Bonner. Here turn left up Blackfoot River. Lewis and his party followed the left side of the river. It is 44.2 miles to Ovando. Just before entering Ovando the "Prairie of the Knobs" described by Lewis can be seen to the left.

177

MOUNTAIN GOAT. The Indians called them "white buffalo" and the captains called them "mountain sheep." "The Indians inform us . . . they inhabit the most rocky and inaccessible parts, and run but badly that they kill them with great ease with their arrows when they can find them." These shaggy white fellows still are abundant in the cliffs and crags of the Bitter Root Mountains.

BETWEEN GRASSHOPPER CREEK AND THE CACHE. Clark's men thought only of the tobacco in the cache ahead—their moccasined feet rushed unheedingly over the millions of dollars worth of gold dust that lay along Grasshopper Creek. Bannack, one of the richest placer diggings of all time, is on Grasshopper Creek at the foot of the high mountain in the center.

CLARK'S RETURN TO THREE FORKS

FED BY SNOWS melting in the early July sun, the streams came roaring and tumbling out of the mountains which hem the Bitter Root Valley. On the first day Clark and his party crossed 10 of the creeks which ". . . came roleing their currents with Velocity into the river."

The small, open plains were covered with varieties of sweet-scented wild flowers, while white clover and rich grass for the horses grew at the stream's edge. Rising early each day the party pounded so rapidly up the valley that John Potts became ill from the jolting of his hard-trotting horse. Clark gave him "a pill of Opiom which soon releve him."

They halted early and "selebrated" the Fourth of July, their third in the wilderness, with a "Sumptious Dinner of fat saddle of Venison and mush" made of cow roots.

The party had trouble fording some of the larger creeks; several horses were swept down and their loads soaked. Crossing the west fork of the Bitter Root, they camped in Rosses' Hole the night of July 5, near their last-year's camp among the Flatheads. The horses scattered over the grassy valley. They worked several hours the next morning rounding up the animals before they could go on.

179

Nothing, Clark felt, could be worse than the route they'd followed into the valley the year before. Noticing several buffalo roads going in one direction, he also observed that Indian trails went the same way. Buffalo usually followed the easiest route. That the Indians also went that way was proof enough to Clark that it was the best path. They followed the buffalo road.

Late in the afternoon such a furious rain and windstorm blew up that Clark had to form the men in "a solid column to protect ourselves from the Violency of the gust." After the storm they moved on about five miles and found dry timber on a small creek. Making camp for the night, they dried their drenched clothing before the fires.

Sacajawea recognized the country as one of the places where her people dug camas roots. Coming to a hot springs on July 7, Clark observed it "actually blubbers with heat for 20 paces below where it rises." Sergeant Pryor and John Shields cooked meat in the bubbling springs. One piece was done in 25 minutes and the other, slightly larger, in 32 minutes.

After a "remarkable cold night" Clark said regretfully, "I now take leave of this butifull extensive vally which I call hot spring Vally."

The next day, almost a year after they had cached the canoes and supplies, the party reached the junction of Trail Creek and Beaverhead River.

Longing for the tobacco they had left in the cache, the men rode hard nine miles after dinner to reach it. When they arrived the "Chewers of Tobacco become so impatient to be chewing it that they scarcely gave themselves time to take their saddles off their horses before they were off to the deposits," Clark said with amusement.

All the canoes but one were in good condition, as were the contents of the cache. They did fail to find a special pack of tobacco Lewis had buried where their lodge stood the previous summer.

180

"A LOW GAP IN THE MOUNTAIN." Bozeman Pass, the route from the Gallatin Valley to Yellowstone, followed by Clark early in the morning of July 15, 1805. "Over a low dividing ridge to the head of the watercourse which runs into the Rochejhone."

"A BOLD MOUNTAIN WHICH BEARS EAST." Clark noticed the Crazy Mountains from Bozeman Pass. "I can see no timber large enough for a canoe," he grumbled.

"THE LODGE WHERE ALL DANCE," was the name the Indians gave a nearby river, perhaps because this rock resembled a huge lodge. All of these high rocks along the Yellowstone were used by the Indians as signal towers from which their smoke signals communicated warnings to other Indians along the river.

This was familiar country to Sacajawea, and "The Squar" brought Clark a plant, the root of which resembled a carrot. As always, Clark immediately familiarized himself with the plant, finding it similar to the carrot in all respects and the "taste not unlike."

The morning of July 10 was "white with frost and the grass stiff frozend." Clark directed Sergeant Pryor, with six men, to take the horses overland and move along moderately. The captain, with Sergeant Ordway and the rest, started down the Beaverhead river in the loaded canoes.

The Beaverhead was high. Where the year before they had toiled so strenuously up the rapids, they now floated quickly downstream. In one day they passed six campsites of the preceding year. On July 11, passing Rattlesnake Cliff and Beaverhead Rocks, they camped on their old site at the junction of the Beaverhead and Big Hole rivers. During the night they were kept awake by beavers whacking their tails in the river in front of the camp.

When Clark and his party arrived at Three Forks Sunday, July 13, they found Sergeant Pryor, his men and the horses waiting for them. They had stopped to hunt along the way, killing six deer and a bear, and had beat Clark's group by only one hour.

THE GALLATIN VALLEY

July 13 was just two weeks short of a year since the expedition had camped at Three Forks on their way west. The "Musqueters" were still there, "more troublesome than we have ever seen them before," Ordway said. "My face and eyes are swelled by the poison of these insects which bite verry severe indeed."

Sergeant Pryor and his party had killed 6 deer and a grizzly. There was a fine dinner at Three Forks, but no rest for men who were on their way home. Immediately after eating they loaded the baggage into six canoes. Then Ordway and nine men started down the Missouri to join Lewis.

Clark had the horses driven across the Madison and Gallatin rivers where they could get a good feed. Next morning at 5 o'clock the herd, now numbering 49 horses and a colt, were rounded up and the overland trek to the Yellowstone begun. Clark's party now consisted of Sergeant Pryor, Shields, Shannon, Bratton, Labiche, Windsor, Hall, Gibson, Charbonneau, Sacajawea and her baby, and Clark's man York.

Although the horses' feet were sore from miles of travel over rocky ground, the party moved rapidly up the Gallatin Valley. They followed an Indian road which appeared to lead to a gap in the mountains 18 or 20 miles away until Sacajawea told them the best pass was a few miles to the south.

The river meandered in the level valley and many large springs were dammed and made into ponds by beaver. Clark, following along the river bottoms "after being swamped as I may say in this bottom of beaver," was forced to cut to the right and get on higher ground.

"RIVERS ACROSS." The stream entering from the left is Big Timber River. The "river across" of Clark's description enters a little below this spot, although the Yellowstone passing an island creates the illusion of a third river at this point. Said Clark, "Crossed a large creek which heads in a high Snow toped Mountain to the N.W. . . . opposit to the enterance of the creek one something larger falls in . . . those Creeks I call rivers across."

DOWN THE YELLOWSTONE. Clark said, "I proceeded on Down the Rochejhone passing over a low ridge . . . Buffalow is getting much more plenty." Clark did not camp at Rivers Across as the monument indicates. He merely noted the spot as he passed.

The next night they camped at the edge of the valley. In the morning, after an early breakfast, they followed an old buffalo road through the low gap recommended by Sacajawea, descending to the Yellowstone River on the other side. Here they hoped to build canoes in which to complete the trip.

DOWN THE YELLOWSTONE

Aʟᴛʜᴏᴜɢʜ ᴛʜᴇ Yellowstone River was wide and easily navigable, there was no timber large enough to build canoes. The party's disappointment was allayed somewhat by the prospect of good food, for there were many buffalo. The men feasted on a fat bull and made "Mockersons" of the tough green hide for the horses' sore feet.

It rained hard the night of July 16. All the men were soaked but they collected the horses early next morning and started off again. Coming to a spot where two creeks entered the Yellowstone directly across from one another Clark said, "Those creeks I call Rivers Across."

"The high lands . . . on either side . . . are partially covered with low pine & cedar none of which are sufficiently large for Canoes," Clark worried. "Nor have I seen a Cotton tree in the low bottoms sufficiently large for that purpose."

In the evening they investigated an Indian fort built the year before in the river bottom. This fort, one of many built by plains Indians when pursued by larger war parties, was circular in form and about 50 feet in diameter. It was built of logs lapped closely over each other and covered with pieces of bark. They noticed that the entrance, facing the river, was barricaded on each side.

Seeing Indian smoke signals in the distance, two days later, Clark optimistically said, "I think it most probable that they . . . takeing us to be Shoshones &c . . . have made this Smoke to Shew where they are." Doubt entered his mind and he added "or otherwise takeing us to be their Enemy made this signal for other bands to be on their guard."

Charbonneau's horse, chasing a buffalo, stepped in a badger hole throwing Charbonneau over his head. Clark said the man was "a good deel brused on his hip sholder & face."

That evening Gibson, trying to mount a skittish horse after shooting a deer, fell on a sharp, burned snag about an inch in diameter. It went "nearly two inches into the Muskeler part of his thy."

Clark dressed the wound but Gibson slept little that night, complaining of pain in his knee and hip as well as his thigh. He couldn't ride but since the party wanted to reach "the U states this season" Clark decided to make a litter to carry him until they could find trees large enough for canoes. Clark placed skins and blankets on the back of his strongest and gentlest horse in such a position that Gibson was as comfortable mounted as lying down. Shields was sent ahead to search for large trees and to get wild ginger for poulticing the wound.

INDIAN ROCK WRITING on the wall of a cave near Billings, Montana. Each picture tells a story; of a deer shot in the heart with an arrow; two soldiers with guns, killed; plenty of beaver and buffalo. The pictures are painted with black or red paint. This campsite apparently was a winter camp of the Indians for many generations before and after the coming of Lewis and Clark.

It was slow traveling that day. Gibson's leg became numb and they had to stop frequently to let him rest. Shields rejoined the party bearing the bad news that he had found no trees and no ginger. He was welcomed back, however, because he had killed two fat bucks, and it was dinnertime.

When Gibson's thigh became so painful he couldn't continue, Clark made him comfortable in the shade of a tree and left Sergeant Pryor and another man with him. Going on down the river four miles, the captain found trees large enough for small canoes. He camped in a thick grove of cottonwoods where the grass was "tolerably good." Later Sergeant Pryor brought the injured man in.

Clark, after such a day, said, "It may be proper to observe . . . the emence Sworms of Grasshoppers . . ."

TANDEM CANOES

July 20 was a Sunday but it was no day of rest for the men of Clark's party. Sergeant Pryor and Shields, both good judges of timber, were sent down river to look for better trees for the canoes. Two others were dispatched to find chokecherry wood for axe handles. Labiche, Charbonneau and Hall left to bring in the skin and flesh of an elk Labiche had killed the night before. Clark dressed Gibson's wound.

Pryor and Shields, returning at 11:30 in the morning, reported that they had been 12 miles down the river and had found nothing but cottonwood trees that were no larger than those at camp. When the other two came back with chokecherry wood the axes were sharpened with a file and the new handles inserted. Then the men started to make their canoes. The valley of the Yellowstone rang with the sound of axes until dark.

The next day Clark learned all too well the meaning of the Indian smoke signals he had seen up the river. In the morning, 24 of their horses were gone. Three days' search revealed nothing but the tracks of Indians who had returned the next night to try to filch the remaining 25.

The canoes were finished by noon of the 23rd. Although 28 feet long, they were only 16 or 18 inches deep and 16 to 24 inches wide. Clark had them lashed together to steady them. When oars and paddles were made the party was ready to set off again.

The morning of the 24th, Sergeant Pryor, Shannon and Windsor were ordered to take the remaining horses overland to Fort Mandan. As Clark and the rest pushed off in the loaded canoes, Pryor and his men rode away, driving the extra horses ahead of them.

The swift waters of the Yellowstone carried the party in their double canoes into camp that night ahead of Pryor.

Pryor, when he showed up with Shannon and Windsor, was red-faced and exasperated. The pesky Indian ponies had persisted in chasing every buffalo herd

187

they saw. The faster horses would head off the buffaloes while the slower animals zealously rounded them up just as if their erstwhile Indian owners were astride them. Pryor, his men and their mounts were worn out trying to keep the ponies in line. Pryor finally decided to take a man along the next day who could go ahead and scare off the buffalo before the ponies spied them. Hall, who could not swim and was justifiably nervous about the double canoes, was assigned to the Pryor party.

Nakedness was no novelty among men whose clothing was as limited as it was ragged. When Hall pointed out that he was nude, Clark gave him one of his "two remaining Shirts a par of leather Legins and 2 pr of mockersons which equipt him completely." Hall left with Pryor, apparently sans trousers.

WHERE IS LEWIS?

Paddling down the Yellowstone July 25 Clark and his party noticed a huge, remarkable rock several hundred paces from the river. About 4 p.m. they stopped to investigate. Climbing to the top, Clark viewed the valley and distant mountains and saw "Emence herds of Buffalows, Elk and wolves." He added his name and the date to the many Indian pictographs he found carved in the soft sandstone. As he left the towering rock Clark decided to call it Pompey's Pillar, probably after Sacajawea's son Baptiste, whom he affectionately had dubbed Little Pomp or Little Chief.

Moving on, the party camped the next evening at the mouth of the Big Horn River. Often the men were kept awake by the continuous bellowing of the buffalo bulls. Not even the raucous distraction of the buffalo could keep Clark from his work. By the light of the campfire the captain wrote his records of courses and distances and painstakingly prepared his maps.

They set out early again on July 27, Clark saying pensively, "I take my leave of the View of the tremendous chain of Rocky Mountains white with Snow in View of which I have been since the 1st of May last."

As the party drifted downstream two days later they ran into some rapids where they "let the canoes down by hand for fear of their Striking a rock under water and splitting." Battling six miles of the rapids, Clark was still not too busy to name them. "From the circumstance of a bear's being on a rock in the Middle of this rapid," he called one Bear Rapid. Another he named for a buffalo standing in the stream. Twice when traveling they were forced to land while vast herds of buffalo swam the river downstream from them.

At the mouth of Powder River the party killed two fat buffalo cows. Loading the meat into their canoes they crossed to camp "under a large Spredding cotton tree" by a brook. Next day Clark saw the largest grizzly he had ever seen, feeding on a buffalo carcass on a sandbar. The men shot the bear twice. "I landed and fired 2 more shots into this tremendious animal without killing him," Clark marveled.

188

CLARK'S SIGNATURE ON POMPEY'S PILLAR. All sides of this sandstone rock are covered with names, dates, messages and Indian pictographs, but the most distinguished signature is Clark's for which the Northern Pacific Railroad has provided an iron grill to guard against vandalism.

POMPEY'S PILLAR. "This rock I ascended and from its top had a most extensive view in every direction," Clark said, adding that the Indians had made two piles of stone on top of this tower. "The nativs have ingraved on the face of this rock the figures of animals &c near which I marked my name and the day of the month & year," which was Friday, July 25, 1806.

The huge beast, although bleeding profusely, escaped in the twilight shadows. The men dared not pursue him.

Gliding down the river about 8 the next morning, they were startled when a bear of "the large vicious species" jumped into the water and swam toward the canoes. Three musket balls prompted the animal to turn back to shore.

"Last night the Musquetors was so troublesom that no one of the party Slept half the night. For my part I did not sleep one hour," Clark lamented on August 3. Arriving at the junction of the Yellowstone and Missouri rivers that day they unloaded the canoes and spread out the baggage to dry. Although they intended to wait here for Lewis, the mosquitoes were too much for them. The baby Baptiste was so terribly bitten that, in spite of being conditioned by hundreds of previous bites, his little face was painfully "puffed & Swelled." Clark decided to move to a "more eligeable spot . . . at which place the Musquetors will be less troublesom and Buffalow more plenty."

Leaving a note for Lewis, they started slowly downriver, hoping the other captain and his party would catch up with them.

On August 8 Clark was alarmed to see Sergeant Pryor and his men paddling furiously down the river toward them in a buffalo-skin canoe. Where were the horses?

Indians, Pryor told the captain, had surrounded his camp the first night and stolen the remainder of the horses. Not only that, but Pryor stupidly had picked up the note left for Lewis at the junction. There would be no rendezvous with Lewis at that place, and no note of explanation.

TRAVELOGUE . . . As we swung up the Gallatin River we looked for the willow thickets and beaver dams that troubled Clark and his party. Most of them were gone, but the meandering sloughs of the river as it works its way down through the farms prove they were once there. I remembered something I'd been told as a child — one of those things that sticks in the mind when more important things are forgotten. "If you just dig a little hole in your back yard," a man told me, "you change the face of the earth." I suppose it made me feel powerful. Anyway, the beavers had certainly influenced the face of this country, with the irrigation project they carried on decades ago.

At Bozeman Al looked up his friend Louis True, Director of Publications at Montana State College. Louis is not only a photographer, but can pilot a plane. He volunteered to fly Al over the three forks. While they were gone I visited with photographer Chris Schlecten, who gave me a wonderful picture of Helena. Cities have personalities like people do, and Chris certainly captured the personality of Helena.

When Al and Louis returned an hour later they had covered territory that Lewis and Clark had labored weeks to cover. Al was delighted because Louis knew exactly how to maneuver the plane for good camera shots of the country. And Louis had even showed him a few tricks about his camera that Al didn't know.

The next morning we drove through the rocky gorges of Bozeman Pass. Although Lewis and Clark climbed a less precipitous grade until they got to the pass, their route followed the old buffalo road we were on going down to Livingston.

First called Clark City, Livingston is a railroad center. Great locomotives slowly move up and down the tracks as though restless to be about their work, which is to help the regular engines over Bozeman Pass.

As we drove on through Big Timber we stopped at a monument designating Rivers Across Camp. "Nice marker, " he said, "but it has an error. Clark only mentioned Rivers Across — their camp for that night was ten or fifteen miles below here, so this isn't actually a campsite." A monument maker would alternately love and hate Al; he admires monuments so, yet he's always finding mistakes on them. Perhaps the monument maker sometimes realizes he's made a boner, too, but how's he going to erase something he's chiseled into a half ton of granite?

After crossing the Yellowstone River we walked through a grove of cottonwood to where the Big Timber joins the Yellowstone. Al pointed to a limb of one huge, gnarly tree and said, "A man was hanged there. This used to be a stage station on the old Bozeman Road. The man murdered a school teacher and headed for here. The vigilantes caught him and up he went."

Near Columbus we tried to locate the place where Clark and his party made their canoes. But Clark's maps and his description, usually so meticulous, are confusing at this spot and we could only guess.

When we reached Billings it was hard to decide where to go first. At the Place of Skulls there is a cliff under which the first white men to explore the area discovered hundreds of skeletons. The people in Billings call it Sacrifice Cliff, saying Indians were killed here as a part of a religious rite. Some think, however, that it is a place where the Crow Indians, terror-stricken by a smallpox epidemic, committed mass suicide.

About five miles east and a little south of Billings we went to Indian caves where Al had, on another trip, found so many artifacts that he could hardly wait to get back. While I kept an eye out for rattlesnakes, he plunged into his favorite occupation and soon had a perfect flint knife and several broken arrow heads. This was an Indian winter camp. At such places most of the artifacts are broken; often they were broken a century or so ago and discarded by the Indians themselves.

It was a terrible temptation to Al to drive 50 miles out of the way to Custer battlefield at Hardin. But since he has visited it about twenty times and we had many miles to go we went on down the Yellowstone instead.

Pompey's Pillar loomed up across a wheatfield; a great sandstone rock which Clark climbed and named. In our entire travels on the Lewis and Clark trail we were able to see only two physical traces of the expedition. The salt-cairn at Seaside was one. Here, at Pompey's Pillar, was the other — Clark's name which he carved in the stone.

Al's mind was still on Custer when we passed the little community of Rosebud. He pointed out the junction of the Rosebud River with the Yellowstone. "This," he said, "is where Custer and his officers planned what developed into the Battle of the Little Big Horn. Custer and his Seventh Cavalry followed the Sioux trail up this river."

We drove on through Miles City, in the center of the cattle country. The children admired the cowboys with their ten gallon hats and hoped, I'm sure, they'd see a rousing gunfight such as enlivened the town decades ago. But this was 1949 and there were no stray bullets to puncture our tires.

In this area Clark and his men were making good time floating down the river in their tandem canoes. But we slowed down. We'd covered all the trail now.

HOW TO GET THERE NOW . . . See maps 6 and 5.

BOZEMAN PASS. From Bozeman, Montana, go east on U.S. 10, 12.6 miles to summit of pass.

RIVERS ACROSS. From Big Timber, on the east side of town, take Montana 19, cutting north from U.S. 10 at about the city limits. Cross Yellowstone bridge at .5 miles, then turn right .6 mile to bridge crossing Big Timber Creek. Walk down stream through field .3 mile to junction with Yellowstone.

POMPEY'S PILLAR. From Billings, Montana, take U.S. 10, 29.8 miles east. The rock is on the north side of the road across an open field. The Montana Highway Dept. has erected a sign identifying it and telling some of its story.

LEWIS TO THE MOUTH OF THE YELLOWSTONE

"I took leave of my worthy friend and companion Capt. Clark and the party that accompanyed him. I could not avoid feeling much concern on this occasion," brooded Lewis on July 3, as he moved down the Bitter Root River to a place recommended by the Indians for crossing.

The Indians swam their horses over, pulling their baggage after them in little deerskin basins which it took them only a few minutes to construct. Lewis's men drove their horses across but it took them from 11 in the morning to 3 in the afternoon to make rafts for the baggage. With each crossing the rafts drifted farther down the river. When Lewis's turn to cross came, he and two men got on a raft just above a rapids. The rushing river carried the raft a mile and a half before it approached the other shore. Just as it reached shore the raft sank. Lewis was scraped off by

193

"PRARIE OF THE KNOBS," Lewis called the Blackfoot Prairie. Here the worried men observed that a Blackfoot war party had camped and concealed their fires.

"DIVIDING RIDGE BETWEEN THE WATERS of the Columbia and Missouri River." Lewis and his party crossed the Continental Divide July 7, 1806, and saw on the rolling hills, shown in the foreground of this view, vast "gangues" of buffalo. The low gap in the center is now called Lewis and Clark Pass.

brush and had to swim for it. The raft, lighter now, rose and drifted downstream a bit and the other two men, who were poor swimmers, climbed ashore.

The Indian guides called the Blackfoot River "Cokahlarishkit," the river of the road to buffalo. It would take him to the Missouri, they told Lewis, but they weren't going along. The warlike Blackfeet lived on the upper Missouri, and the Nez Perce Indians wanted nothing to do with them. Lewis gave the guides a good supply of meat, smoked a pipe with them and regretfully said good-by.

The party saw a number of wild horses as they followed the well-worn trail up the Blackfoot. With plenty of food, beautiful scenery and no mosquitoes the men enjoyed their travel.

On July 6 they passed through what Lewis called "the prarie of the knobs from a number of knobs being scattered irregularly thru it." Entering the mountains again they saw fresh tracks on the trail ahead, which Lewis took to be those of a Blackfoot war party. Lewis warned his men to be constantly alert so they would not overtake the Indians.

The next morning Reuben Fields wounded a large moose to the consternation of Lewis's dog, Scannon. Experienced as Scannon was, this new kind of animal puzzled him.

They passed the "dividing ridge between the waters of the Columbia and Missouri" at 2 p.m. that day. The men were "much rejoiced," Lewis said, "at finding themselves on the plains of the Missouri." As an added treat they enjoyed hump roast from a fat buffalo bull Joseph Fields killed.

Moving down the valley they saw tremendous herds of buffalo. Lewis thought there were 10,000 of them within two miles. It was mating time. The massive bulls pawed and bellowed in every direction, keeping up a continual swelling roar all day and all night. Their rumbling frightened the horses but, typically, Lewis remarked that "a vast assemblage of little birds which croud to the groves on the river sung most enchantingly."

THE CACHE RE-OPENED

Lewis and his men reached White Bear Island at the upper end of the Great Falls of the Missouri on July 12. They were anxious to see what the year had done to the cache just across the river.

The captain found the river had risen so high during the winter that his bear-skins were "entirely destroyed by the water," his plant specimens lost and many papers dampened. A phial of laudanum had spilled into and ruined many of the medicines. But "the Chart of the Missouri fortunately escaped." Lewis philosophically opened his trunks and boxes to let the sun and breezes dry out the contents.

The men could not be philosophical about the great swarms of mosquitoes that were so thick they breathed them into their throats. Lewis escaped some of the

INDIAN LOOKOUT. Ever watchful, Indians often built these rock outposts on high points overlooking routes that were usually traveled by their enemies. This lookout, from which Lewis and Clark Pass and Rogers Pass may be scrutinized, may have been occupied by a Blackfoot brave as Lewis and his party filed through the pass into the buffalo country. A second lookout can be seen on the higher hill in the background.

BUFFALO COW. The buffalo played a very important part in the economy of the Indians and also of Lewis and Clark. They furnished not only rich and tender meat for food but also hides for clothing and shelter since their skins were commonly used for making teepees. Further, the skins, when left with the hair on, served as bed covers to protect against the icy winter weather of the western plains.

time by simply staying in a bed covered with mosquito netting. Even his great Newfoundland Scannon howled with pain.

By now the bellowing buffalo had drifted away but they left many wolves "of the large kind" in their wake. The men could see the animals just a few hundred yards from camp, snarling over the carcasses of old and weak buffalo they had managed to pull down from the herd.

Blackfoot Indians didn't help the situation any when they stole seven of the party's 17 horses one night. Several searchers failed to find them. Lewis worried about bears and when Drewyer returned after scouting two days the captain was "so perfectly satisfyed that he had returned in safety that I thought but little of the horses although they were seven of the best I had."

On the 15th McNeal was sent to inspect the cache at the lower end of the portage. As he rode along dreaming, a great grizzly lumbered out of the thick brush. His terror-stricken horse reared up, throwing McNeal to the bear, and galloped away over the horizon. McNeal, landing at the very feet of the grizzly, was no more surprised than the bear at this sudden meeting. As the huge animal rose on his hind legs to attack, McNeal, too close to shoot, whacked him over the head with his rifle. While the beast rubbed his aching head with his paws, McNeal scrambled up the nearest tree. The angry animal waited two hours at the foot of the tree before giving up. McNeal, venturing down, had to chase his horse two miles before he could catch it and return to camp.

"There seems to be a certain fatality attached to the neighbourhood of these falls," Lewis commented that night, "for there is always a chapter of accedents prepared for us during our residence at them."

LEWIS UP MARIAS RIVER

Lewis was uneasy when he started to explore Marias River with Drewyer, Joe Fields and Reuben Fields on July 16. This was Blackfoot country. The Blackfoot Indians already had stolen some of their horses, for which Lewis condemned them as a "vicious lawless and reather abandoned set of wretches."

Sergeant Gass and five men stayed on the river to portage the supplies beyond the falls. They were to wait for Ordway who had left Clark at Three Forks and was coming down the river.

The captain planned to meet Gass at the mouth of Marias River August 5. Apparently having a premonition of trouble, Lewis told Gass to wait no longer than September 1 for his return.

The four set out across the blue clay soil of the prairie toward the Marias. Churned during the rains by myriads of cloven buffalo hoofs, the ground was now sun-baked to a solid mass of sharp raised points, painful to the already footsore horses.

On July 17, they saw the trail of a freshly wounded and bleeding buffalo. It could mean only one thing: Blackfoot Indians. The captain, who wanted to "avoid

WESTERN CHICKADEE. Lewis at all times watched for wild life, observing at one moment the vast herds of the mighty buffalo and the next moment intently studying the tiniest of birds.

an interview with them if possible," sent the Fields brothers ahead to scout. Drewyer was told to kill the wounded buffalo while Lewis reconnoitred. An hour later when all returned to camp they reported there were no further signs of Indians, and the wounded animal had disappeared.

The party continued up the river until they saw its entrance into the mountains. Lewis decided it didn't extend to N. latitude 50 degrees, but they camped for two days while the captain did his arithmetic with latitude and longitude to be sure. The horses were allowed to graze although it was risky in Blackfoot territory. Lewis did his work, come what may.

LEWIS'S FIGHT WITH THE BLACKFOOT INDIANS

WHEN LEWIS'S PARTY started back toward the Missouri on July 26, Drewyer moved down the river valley while the captain and the Fields brothers kept to higher ground where they could see more.

Riding along more sharply alert than ever, Lewis glimpsed "a very unpleasant sight." There was a group of about 30 horses a mile in the distance. With his spyglass Lewis saw that a number were saddled and then noticed that on a hill just above the horses, eight Indians stood staring into the valley. They were watching Drewyer. Lewis suspected more Indians were nearby because he thought there were more than eight saddled horses.

Lewis's horses were too worn to run; there were too many Indians to fight; besides something had to be done about Drewyer. Therefore the captain "resolved . . . to approach them in a friendly manner." With Joe Fields waving a flag, the men rode forward apprehensively.

At first the Indians were too intent on Drewyer to notice the other three white men. When they caught sight of Lewis and his companions they milled about in consternation. Some dashed wildly off the hill and back on again; one rode swiftly toward Lewis, halted a hundred paces away, whirled his horse about and galloped back to his comrades. Perhaps he told them there were only three white men to contend with, for they all mounted their horses and rode directly toward the party.

Lewis, not comforted by the sight of their bows and arrows and tomahawks, was alarmed when he saw they had two guns. He told his men these were probably Blackfeet, and Blackfeet with or without guns meant trouble.

When the parties were within 100 yards of one another all the Indians but one halted. Lewis went on alone and shook hands with the advancing native. Then the others came up. With tentative friendliness the Fields brothers, Lewis and the Indians shook hands all around. Wanting to know the worst at once, Lewis talked to them in sign language. Were they Blackfeet? They were.

The captain asked for the chiefs. Although he was doubtful about the three who were pointed out, he gave one a medal, another a flag and the third a handkerchief. When the Indians suggested a smoke, Lewis told them Drewyer who had the only pipe was still in the river bottoms. The Blackfeet, who were "extremely fond of smoking," sent one of their youths along with Reuben Fields to find Drewyer.

The captain nervously kept expecting more Indians to appear. When none arrived he was relieved, because he was confident that he and his three companions could handle eight.

In the evening when, at Lewis's suggestion, they all rode toward the river to make camp, Drewyer, Reuben Fields and the young Indian showed up. Making a shelter of dressed buffalo skins, the natives invited the little white party to be their guests. The Fields brothers preferred hugging the campfire but Lewis and Drewyer went into the hut. Thomas Jefferson had asked some questions about these people and Lewis was going to take back the answers, trouble or no trouble. With Drewyer interpreting, the captain talked of his peaceful intentions. The Indians with their fingers crossed voiced their same intent. They were silent when Lewis offered them 10 horses and some tobacco if they would return with him to his men camped on the Missouri. The Indians knew a simpler way to get the horses and tobacco.

It wasn't a night for easy sleeping. Lewis took the first watch and Reuben Fields the second. By daybreak all were asleep except Joe Fields who was standing third watch.

"Damn you, let go my gun." It was Drewyer. Lewis and Reuben Fields, instantly awake, grabbed for their guns which were gone. Joe Fields' gun, which he had carelessly laid on the ground behind him, was gone.

Quick as a cougar, Drewyer, the man of the woods, twisted his gun from the hands of the Indian. Reuben Fields, slashing with his long knife, leaped on an Indian who had two of their weapons. As he stabbed viciously, the native released the guns, staggered a few steps and fell dead.

Lewis, pistol in hand, rushed the native who was making off with his gun. As the Indian lay the gun down, the Fields brothers drew a bead on him. No sooner had Lewis forbidden their shooting him than Drewyer aimed his gun. Again Lewis said no.

The undiscouraged Blackfeet started driving off the party's horses. When Lewis and his men swung out after them, one of the Indians turned to fight. The captain shot him in the stomach. Although the Indian fell to the ground, before he died he managed to send a shot whistling through Lewis's hair.

The captain who, in his haste to rescue the horses, had left his powder pouch in camp, now was out of ammunition. Further chase was useless. Joined by Drewyer, he returned to camp.

The Indians, they found, had made away with five horses but had, in their haste left 12 of their own. Catching several of the windfall, Lewis and Drewyer

200

MARIAS RIVER JUNCTION WITH THE MISSOURI. The Marias River was in the heart of the Blackfoot country. Lewis's exploration up this river resulted in the only difficulty with the Indians that ended in bloodshed. Even civilization later didn't tame the Blackfeet. The stone in front of the clump of trees in the center of the picture marks the common grave of the luckless Friends party, massacred by the Blackfeet.

quickly began saddling and packing. The Fields brothers returned triumphantly driving four of the five stolen horses.

Shields, bows, quivers of arrows and "sundry other articles" were strewn about the camp. Lewis burned the Indian weapons but retrieved the flag he had given away the evening before. The medal he had presented at the same time because he "thought it best to please them" was on the body of the Indian Fields had knifed. Lewis left it "that they might be informed who we were."

LEWIS'S FLIGHT FROM THE BLACKFEET

THE LITTLE GROUP felt almost certain the Indians would return, to avenge their fallen comrades. Lewis even had told the Blackfeet which way they were going, when he had so earnestly tried to get guidance for the trip to the junction of the Marias and Missouri rivers. Not only was there danger to them at the camp and all along the trail, but also to the other party on the Missouri whom the Indians might attack without warning, unless Lewis's party reached the junction first.

The men rode hard 63 miles before 3 o'clock that day, when they stopped for an hour and a half on the Tansy River to let the horses graze. Before dark they pressed on 17 miles farther. They killed a buffalo for dinner, ate and rested while the horses grazed some more, then mounted and rode off again. The moon shone eerily through slits in the black thunderclouds overhead. The riders passed through great herds of buffalo, huge black blots looming up in the darkness.

By two in the morning the four had ridden about 100 miles almost continuously. They dismounted and men and horses lay down together to sleep the sleep of exhaustion. The next morning, so stiff and sore from riding that they could scarcely stand, the men mounted again. Their lives and those of their friends on the Missouri depended on it. The men suggested that they cross the Missouri at its closest point, thus putting the river between them and the Indians. It might be safer but it would mean delay in reaching the others, so Lewis decided to go straight to the intended meeting place. "I told them that we owed much for the safety of our friends and that we must wrisk our lives on this occasion," the captain said.

As they rode, the four plotted a defense for the expected attack. They would tie the bridles of their horses together, and then stand and defend them, selling their lives as dearly as possible.

When pushing close to the Missouri, they suddenly heard rifle shots echoing against the bluffs along the river. Their hearts sank. Were they too late? Speeding to a point where they could overlook the river they fearfully scanned its banks. White hunters were doing the firing! "We had the unspeakable satisfaction to see our canoes coming down," Lewis said.

The hunters were Sergeant Ordway and his nine men who had joined Gass and the others on the 19th, after having made a quick and uneventful trip down the river from Three Forks.

The two parties saluted each other with gunfire. The canoeists paddled to shore. "Capt. Lewis took us by the hand," said Ordway.

LEWIS GETS SHOT

THE PARTY FOUND all but one of the caches at the mouth of the Marias in good shape. Still fearing an Indian attack, they quickly loaded the five canoes and the white pirogue, slapped their horses on the rump and turned them loose, and swept on down the river.

The men must have mumbled under their breath as the methodical and painstaking Lewis halted them from time to time to collect specimens of bighorn sheep or some other animal for Thomas Jefferson. Going down stream and rowing with a will, they made about seven miles an hour, almost as much as they made on some whole days on the way up.

"About 11 a.m. we entered the high clay broken country" said Ordway on July 29, "and the white walls resembling ancient towns & buildings &c."

Once Ordway and Willard, who had stayed behind to hunt, got in trouble when their canoe was swept by the swift "boald" current into a stretch of water full of "sawyers." When the canoe rammed into one, Willard was swept overboard by an outstretched limb. Ordway managed to maneuver the boat through the rest of the snags and to shore about half a mile below. Racing back up the bank he found Willard had clung to the sawyer and, though still in the middle of the river, was more concerned about the contents of the canoe than his own plight. The water was too treacherous for Ordway to reach him. Willard calmly tied two sticks together, piled his clothes on them and, hanging onto his miniature raft, swam and drifted down stream. Ordway rushed back to the canoe and picked up his floating comrade a half mile farther down the river.

On August 7 the main party came to the mouth of the Yellowstone where Lewis planned to meet Clark. They found only his abandoned camp, a pole to which was tied a piece of paper with Lewis's name in Clark's handwriting, and a fragment of paper fastened to a piece of elk horn. No instructions and no Clark.

Thinking his partner couldn't be far ahead, Lewis traveled rapidly the rest of that day and the next. Not overtaking Clark and not even knowing where he was, the captain decided to camp and take advantage of the good hunting to lay in a food supply. They took one day off to kill game and dress skins. Then they moved down the river, hunting leisurely as they went.

Just before noon of the 11th they saw a large herd of elk on the shore. Lewis and Peter Cruzatte went after them, killing one elk and wounding another. Reloading their guns they split up and worked their way through the thick willows, pursuing the wounded animal. Lewis jumped the elk. Just as he drew a bead on it, a rifle roared and he felt the impact of the bullet. "Damn you, you have shot me," the captain yelled as he fell. The wound was through both buttocks. The captain called to Cruzatte several times. Since the shot had come from close by and Cruzatte did not answer, Lewis decided it was an Indian who had wounded him. Shouting a warning to Cruzatte, he made his way to the canoes and called the men to arms.

Led by Sergeant Gass, the men charged into the thicket to save Cruzatte. Lewis, who had tried to lead them but was too weak from shock, dragged himself back to the boats where he prepared to "sell my life as dearly as possible." The party returned in 20 minutes with Peter Cruzatte. There were no Indians, they said. The near-sighted Cruzatte had mistaken the elkskin-clad Lewis for an elk. "Peter knew that it must have been him tho an exidant," said Ordway.

Sergeant Gass helped Lewis remove his clothes and dressed the wound which the captain modestly said was thru "the hinder part of my thye." The men made a comfortable place for him to lie in the pirogue. He had no broken bones but bled profusely and was in great pain.

As the boats moved down the river they passed one of Clark's encampments. This time they found a note from Clark explaining that Sergeant Pryor by mistake had removed the message left at the Yellowstone, and that the main party was not far ahead.

That night the suffering and feverish Lewis slept in the pirogue rather than attempt to go ashore with the party.

DOWN THE MISSOURI TO ST. LOUIS

MEANWHILE CLARK and his party, gliding swiftly down the Missouri, were elated to see a white man's camp on the river's edge. Swinging the canoes sharply into shore, they stopped to talk to the first white men they had seen in nearly two years. The men, Forest Hancock and Joseph Dickson, greeted the travelers but had no news to offer for they had been hunting and trapping so long they were as out of touch with the outside world as the party itself. Dickson and Hancock accepted Clark's invitation to travel with the party.

They moved along, Clark scanning the river above and wondering if he would ever again see or hear of the companions he had parted from at Traveler's Rest. At noon, August 12, as he anxiously watched upriver he suddenly saw the familiar white pirogue slide around a bend, followed by the five dugout canoes. Even before Lewis's party caught up with them, Clark eagerly searched the bronzed faces. Where was Meriwether Lewis? His friend was not there.

As the canoes came closer his anxiety increased, and was not much relieved when he saw Lewis lying wounded in the bottom of the pirogue. Carefully Clark examined and dressed the gaping wound. That evening the two captains talked late of their individual experiences.

The next day, aided by a stiff breeze, they made 86 miles. On the 14th, the party came to an encampment of Gros Ventres whom they recognized as Indians they had met on their trip up the river. They "directed the Blunderbuses fired several times" as a greeting. The Indians were pleased to see them. When one chief "cried most imoderately," Clark was flattered until he inquired the cause. The chief was not crying with joy at sight of the white men but with grief at the loss of his son who had been killed by Blackfeet.

Moving down the river the explorers came to the village of the Mandans. As they talked over the past months with the natives they were disgusted to learn there had been war as usual between the Mandans and the Cheyennes, the Arickaras and the Sioux. The promises of peace the Indians had made the captains that winter of 1804 and 1805 had proved too irksome to keep. Clark upbraided them for their fickleness but the Mandans blamed the Sioux, saying they were the aggressors.

The night of the 14th they camped at a place convenient to the two Indian villages. Dickson and Hancock were still with them. All the men but Lewis were in good spirits and fine health. The captain was in such extreme pain he fainted when Clark dressed his wound.

The captains planned to take some Indians back to Thomas Jefferson, along with their other specimens. They suggested that the Mandan chiefs "Pitch on some man on which they could rely on and send him to see the Great Father."

The Indians looked around at one another and apparently mutually agreed it would be fine to rid the camp of its blacksheep. This was a man who had so recently stolen Gibson's knife that he still had it on him.

Clark scolded the chiefs for wishing to send so poor a "charackter." The Indian leaders "hung their heads" and appointed a second chief of the tribe to take his place. The chosen one thought it over, decided it was a doubtful honor and declined. Finally She-he-ke, a chief with prematurely white hair the captains had known during their stay at Fort Mandan, volunteered to go if he could take his wife, another man's wife and all their children. Lewis and Clark accepted with some hesitation.

Like anyone else, Clark was curious about what once had been his home, so he visited the site of Fort Mandan. He found the buildings had been burned and nothing remained but ruins.

Most of the men had no thought but to get home as quickly as possible. But John Colter, who for some days had had a quizzical look in his eyes, asked permission to leave the party and join Dickson and Hancock on a two-year trapping expedition. The captains, who didn't want a general exodus from the expedition, granted Colter permission to leave on the condition that no other man of the party make the same

ARROWHEAD MAKING. Top, left to right: the raw material, a beautiful agate; the preliminary break to determine the proper fracture angles; chips broken away as the stone is shaped. Bottom row, left to right: the stone starts to take shape; nearly finished it looks like an arrowhead; a flaw makes the point useless and the Indian starts again; after the arrowhead is practically completed the delicate stone point breaks off and the workman must start over again; a finished point, clumsily made; lastly, a beautiful gem point perfectly shaped by a real artist.

ARROW POINTS. Top, left to right: An Arickara Indian clear agate war point; a Shoshone hunting point of agatized wood; a Crow hunting point of clear yellow agate; a Flathead crude buffalo hunting point of yellow jasper; a Blackfoot hunting point of gray chert. Lower row, left to right: a Blackfoot gray chert hunting point; a Mandan hunting point of pink agate; a Blackfoot gray chert hunting point; a Shoshone white opal bird point; a Crow clear agate hunting point.

ARROWHEAD-MAKERS' TOOLS. Left to right: an arrowhead-maker's chisel; an arrow shaft straightener; a crude plane for shaping the bow or arrow shaft; another arrowhead-maker's chisel over 1,000 years old. All tools are of buffalo bone, in this picture.

DOMESTIC TOOLS. Top row, left to right: a banded agate end scraper; a gray chert side scraper; a thumb nail scraper of agate; an end scraper of jade; a beautifully made end scraper of yellow jasper. These were used in removing the flesh from hides and in the tanning process. Lower row, left to right: a small knife blade; a thumbnail scraper of gray chert; a red agate awl or needle; a clear agate awl; another gray chert scraper. These are mostly Sioux and Crow.

request. "They are determined to stay," Ordway said, "untill they make a fortune &c &c."

Clark observed, "The example of this man shows how easily men may be weaned from the habits of civilized life to the ruder but scarcely less fascinating manners of the woods. This hunter . . . might naturally be presumed to have some anxiety or some curiosity at least to return to his friends and to his country yet just at the moment he is approaching the frontiers he is tempted by a hunting scheme to give up these delightful prospects and go back . . . to the solitude of the woods."

The Mandan country was the home of Charbonneau and Sacajawea. The leaders felt it was time to discharge the erratic Frenchman and the competent Indian woman. Clark, feeling reluctant to just turn them loose, offered to take them to St. Louis and get Charbonneau a job. The squaw man thought he would be out of his element in the big city and refused.

Clark hated to leave Little Pomp who had come to mean so much to him, and suggested that he take the baby and raise him as he would his own son. But the Indian child, who was 16 months old by now, was not weaned and Sacajawea thought she should not let him go. Later, she promised, she would bring the child to St. Louis.

The captains paid Charbonneau $500.33⅓, and Sacajawea nothing.

DOWN THE MISSOURI

A MID MUCH WEEPING and wailing on the part of She-he-ke's friends, the party of explorers fired a salute and set off down the Missouri. They had lashed the smaller canoes together to make them safer, although not quite so speedy, in the deep water.

On the morning of the 18th their start was delayed until 8 o'clock by strong winds. At 9 they saw an Indian running along the shoreline excitedly. Pulling to shore the party found it was She-he-ke's brother come to say good-by. "The chief gave him a par of Legins and took affectionate leave," Clark said. Most of the day as they glided along the river, the chief entertained Clark with the legends and history of the Mandan tribe.

On August 20 they made 81 miles in spite of a violent wind that splashed waves into the small canoes so frequently that one man in each boat spent the day bailing.

It rained hard for two nights. The heavy downpour together with the winds on the river must have reminded the captains of their hardships as they approached the Pacific the year before.

On August 21 the two leaders visited a camp of Arickaras where Clark made a speech telling them the same things he had told the Mandans. The story did not go over any better than it had the first time and the captain got no Arickara to show to Thomas Jefferson. He then took the chiefs to task for their aggression against the

Mandans. The Arickaras solemnly said the Sioux had been a bad influence and their young men had just gone along on the war party.

Chiefs came in from a Cheyenne camp on a hilltop nearby. Again Clark tried to get another specimen for the President. But the Cheyennes were a wild people and afraid to go. There were several chiefs who would like to go, but first they wanted to see the chief who went down return. Chief Grey Eyes said he would be glad to go but he thought he should stay in the village and see that the young men did no more wrong to the Mandans. The only satisfaction Clark could get was their promise to have nothing more to do with the Sioux. Nothing more, that is, after just one trading trip on which they expected to get guns and powder from the Sioux in exchange for their surplus horses.

The frustrated captains got into their canoes and fired a two-gun farewell as they swung out into the river.

"My Frend Cap. Lewis is recovering fast the hole in his thy where the Ball passed out is closed and appears nearly well. the one where the ball entered discharges very well," Clark said on the 23rd. Three days later Lewis told his partner he was "fully convinced that the wound is sufficiently heeled for the tents to be discontinued." But on the 27th Lewis took too long a walk and had a relapse. He had no rest that night and the healing wounds were painful the next day.

The party stopped several times on the 28th to replenish their dwindling meat supply. At noon they killed an elk. In the evening as they glided through a gorge they heard the bellowing of buffalo bulls on an island. They stopped to kill one and camped at the lower end of the island on a sandbar.

Two days later the party encountered 80 or 90 Teton Sioux, the Indians whom the other tribes had blamed for all the warfare. Since they had mistreated the captains on the way up the Missouri the summer of 1804, Clark kept the river between them, although the Indians made gestures of friendliness. "These fellows requested to be allowed to come accross the river and make cumerads." But the captains would have nothing to do with them. When three Indians swam across, Clark told them to stay "away from the river or we Should kill every one of them &c &c." Whereupon seven of the Indians stood on top of a hill "and blackguarded us told us to come across and they would kill us all &c of which we took no notice."

That night the party camped on a bleak sandbar six miles down the river. Here there was less danger of the Sioux creeping up on them and attacking at night, and the winds swept the mosquitoes away, but it was an uncomfortable place at best. About 11 p.m. they heard the crash of thunder. Heavy rains poured down on them and the wind became so violent they had to try to keep the canoes from being blown off the sandbar. Two of the boats broke away, blowing clear across the river. It was nearly 2 in the morning before the party was reassembled on the sandbar, to wait shivering in the downpour for daylight.

IMPLEMENTS. Right, a stone axe. Top center, a tomahawk blade. Lower center, a broken blade of a tomahawk. Right top, a Sioux peace pipe. Lower right, a Mandan gambling token—Indian version of a poker chip.

STONE KNIVES. Upper row: knives of gray chert, usually held in the hand without handles. Lower row, left to right: stone knife blade that had a wooden or horn handle fastened to the extension at the bottom; the next two articles are small knife blades, very sharp, which were fastened to the ends of sticks for delicate cutting; a beautifully-fashioned hand knife with ends and sides shaped for different purposes; lastly, a splinter of agate that shows no workmanship but displays some evidence of use as a knife.

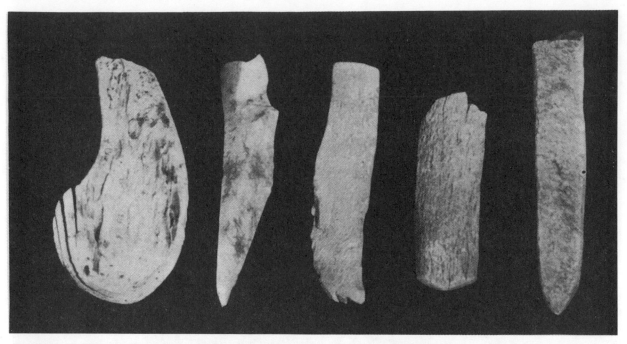

BONE TOOLS. Left to right: a buffalo bone spoon; a bone awl; a bone knife blade; a bone knife handle; a bone dagger. All Mandan.

COOKING AND MEALS. Top row, left to right: a pot rock heated and dropped into the kettles to boil the food; a buffalo marrow bone—the Indians cracked the bones and sucked out the marrow, usually raw. Lower row, left to right: a pot handle and fragment; a fragment of Mandan pottery showing their art and design; Kansas pottery fragments of much cruder design; charcoals from a campfire built in the Crow country over 1,000 years ago.

THE PARTY SET OUT as usual September 1 but the morning fog on the river became so thick they landed and waited half an hour for it to blow away. When the fog lifted, the leaders sent Joe and Reuben Fields and young Shannon after some deer they had spotted on Ponceras Island. The main party, after moving down the river a few miles, saw nine Indians signaling them to come ashore. The captains took these men to be a Teton Sioux war party. The Corps of Discovery stayed in the middle of the river until they rounded a bend out of sight of the Indians. Then, remembering the Fields brothers and Shannon, they pulled ashore to wait for the hunters.

Fifteen minutes later Clark was shocked to hear gunfire up the river. Certain the hunters were being attacked, he and 15 men grabbed their rifles and ran up the shore. Lewis hobbled up on the bank and formed the remaining men in a situation "well calculated to defend themselves and the canoes &c."

When Clark rounded the point he was relieved to see the hunters' canoe still up the river, and the Indians where he had seen them last. It turned out that these Indians were friendly Yankton Sioux, who were merely enjoying target practice at a floating keg the party earlier had thrown from one of the canoes. "We were glad to see and take them by the hand as faithfull Children who had opened their ears to our Councils," Clark said. The party tied ribbons in the Indians' hair and the Mandan chief gave a "par of elegant Legins" to the head man of the Yankton Sioux.

The two long years of travel telescoped that night when the expedition camped on Bonhommie Island, their campsite of Sept. 1, 1804. The flag staff they had planted that morning, seemingly so far in the past, still stood.

The captains, always keeping Jefferson's request for specimens in mind, paused frequently to collect skeletons and skins of barking squirrels, mule deer and other wild life. But the men wanted to get home. After one such day of searching Clark remarked wonderingly, "Our party appears extreamly anxious to get on, every day appears to produce new anxieties to get them to their country and friends."

Chief She-he-ke, on the other hand, bowed his white head in gloom as the miles piled up between him and his home. He and the squaws and the children were "aweary of their journey. Children cry &c," Clark said.

NEWS OF THE WORLD

USUALLY THE MEMBERS of the party were "Routed at an early hour by Musquetoes," against which their dwindling supply of clothing was not much protection. The sandbars crowding the river made good campsites because here they "could get as much out of the musquetoes as possible," but the same sandbars made the Missouri more difficult to navigate. Yet, in spite of sandbars and a headwind, the party made 60 miles on September 3.

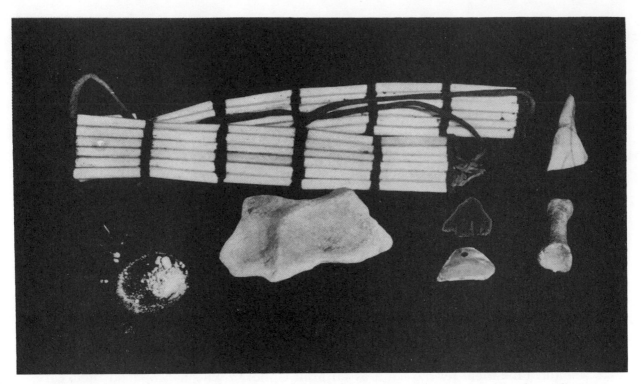

ORNAMENTS. Top row: a Crow porcupine-quill necklace; an elk's tooth. Lower row: powdered vermillion war paint; a stone of yellow ochre used for paint; a sharp agate used for cutting and extracting whiskers; a shell ornament; a human thumb bone, worn by a chief as a trophy of battle.

MISCELLANEOUS. An elk's hoof, the shells of which were pulled off and used as rattles; a grinding stone used for sharpening bone tools; another that is more worn; one more item, not ancient but sooner or later added to any artifact hunter's collection—rattlesnake rattles.

About four in the afternoon they saw two boats on shore and near them a group of men preparing to make camp. News of the world, at last? The men pulled hard on the oars, swung in and landed. James Aird, a Scotch-American trader, greeted them. Accompanied by 18 men in two boats he was on his way to trade with the Sioux.

Aird was sick. Clark said he had "chill of the agu," perhaps contracted when one of his boats met with misfortune in a windstorm downriver. But Aird received the captains with courtesy and offered them what little hospitality he could. It wasn't much but it seemed good to Lewis and Clark. When a violent rainstorm struck they sat dry in a tent!

Far into the night the captains listened to the pleasant Scottish burr of James Aird relate what had been happening in the civilized world while they had been exploring the uncivilized. Two British ships had fired on an American ship in New York harbor, Aird told them. Aaron Burr had killed Alexander Hamilton in a duel. General Wilkinson had been appointed governor of Louisiana. The Spaniards had taken two U.S. frigates in the Mediterranean. There was talk of war with Spain.

The party moved on the next day, more anxious than ever to reach civilization. However, they paused at Floyd's Bluff. Lewis, now able to get around fairly well, climbed the hill with several men. Sergeant Floyd's lonely grave had been opened by Indians. The men covered it again and stood a moment in silent tribute looking out over the broad and no-longer mysterious Missouri. When they left "they ply'd thier orers very well," and made 36 miles that day and 33 the next.

Two days later the Corps of Discovery met a boat owned by Auguste Choteaux manned by Henry Delorn and 12 Frenchmen. Delorn had spread his cargo out to dry while several of his men hunted. After the successful hunters returned, Delorn gave the men of the expedition a gallon of whiskey. It was only a dram for each man, but the drink was good and the only one they had had since their little 4th of July celebration at Great Falls in 1805. Now that they were pushing closer to a city they were eager for better clothing. Delorn's party gave them linen shirts in exchange for elk and deerskins, and "corse hats" for beaver pelts.

Each successive meeting with travelers on the river brought a louder cheer and a greater salvo of guns to announce the return of Lewis and Clark. On Sept. 12 they met Robert M'Clellan, an old army friend of Clark's. With M'Clellan's party were Pierre Dorion and Gravelines, the interpreter the captains had sent with the Arickara chief to see Thomas Jefferson the summer of 1804. The chief had died in Washington; Dorion and Gravelines were on their way to explain to the Arickaras why the Great White Father couldn't save their chief. M'Clellan passed out a dram of whiskey to each of the men of the expedition.

On the 14th at 2 p.m. the party met three large boats under the command of LaCroy, Aiten and Coutau. These agreeable young men pressed all the whiskey the men of the expedition could drink on them. The Corps "only" made 53 miles that day but in camp they laughed and "Sung Songs untill 11 o'Clock at night in the greatest harmoney," Clark said with pride.

The party met Captain John McClallon on September 17, 1806. He was astonished to see the captains alive. Everyone thought they were lost, he said, or that they had been killed, or that Spaniards had taken them to the mines. By now, he added, they had been almost forgotten. If this news was a letdown, the party soon buoyed up again when McClallon poured whiskey generously for the men and treated the two captains to wine.

THE LAST LONG MILES

Only the last long miles separated the travel-weary Corps of Discovery from the United States. "We intend to return to our homes to see our parents once more as we have been so long from them," said the homesick Ordway, who two and a half years before nonchalantly had told his parents he would write next winter if he had a chance. The two captains were anxious, too, and no longer tormented the men by stopping to collect specimens. Nothing was permitted to delay them now. Although there were only a few biscuits to eat, the fat wild turkeys they saw here and there in the thickets along the river bottoms didn't interest the men. They were hungry for home.

By September 18, the men, hatless day after day under the merciless glare of the sun on the water, began to get sore eyes. Potts and young Shannon were particularly affected. Their eyelids, even their eyeballs, were scorched. When they and another member no longer could see to use the oars, the three were placed in other boats. The double canoe — the boat made on the distant Yellowstone — was abandoned to float aimlessly away.

"The party being extreemly anxious to get down ply their ores very well," Clark said.

On the morning of the 20th when the men who had eaten horse heads, ravens, rotten fish, and who had manfully professed a liking for dog meat, saw cattle — live beef — on the riverbank they wept, then raised a mighty cheer and pulled even harder on their oars.

As the setting sun reddened the river the hard-rowing men came in sight of the little French village of La Charette. The resounding cheers of the happy boatmen echoed over the riverbanks. The crews of five trading boats anchored opposite the village enthusiastically returned the salute. Lewis and Clark's men cheered again and "Sprung to their ores."

The astonished people of the village rushed from their dinner tables to the riverbank. It just couldn't be the expedition of explorers that had gone up the river two years before. They hadn't been heard from since they left Fort Mandan eight months later. The party had been given up for dead, yet here they were.

216

SANDBAR ISLANDS OF THE MISSOURI. The "long river" down through the ages constantly has been changing. The sandbar islands move downriver or disappear entirely; others form in their places. Dangerous as they sometimes were, these places were favorite camping spots for the expedition. The winds blowing up and down the channel abated the mosquitoes, and the water was often a welcome barrier between the party and Indians on shore.

"DEEMED ENDLESS." Here near Mobridge, South Dakota most of the labors of the journey were over. The wide, deep channel of the Missouri carried the boats swiftly and comparatively safely on its bosom.

The villagers, gathering around as the men beached their canoes, pressed invitations on these men from the wilderness. As the members of the party made the rounds in celebration, the townspeople gave them "pork Beef and flour &c and the French people got us some milk &c &c." The men were thirsty and a profiteering citizen sold the captains two gallons of whiskey at four dollars a gallon — an "Exortinatable price," the thrifty Ordway complained.

Clark collected his men early on the morning after. They were soon revived by the realization they were almost home. Two years, four months and eight days of hardship and over 8,000 miles of travel were behind them. Moving along, they "Plyed thear ores with great dexterity."

It was a quiet Sunday afternoon at the little town of St. Charles on the Missouri. Young ladies and men strolling along the river in the autumn sun were startled when, suddenly, volley upon volley of rifle fire echoed along the water. The townspeople looked out in the channel and saw seven dugout canoes filled with 32 furiously rowing Robinson Crusoes. The bearded men in the boats gave cheer after wild cheer.

Quiet St. Charles became a bedlam. These people had worried about the Lewis and Clark expedition at first, then given it up for lost and forgotten about it.

When the flotilla landed just below the village the whole population gave them a hero's welcome. Mr. Proulx, Mr. Taboe, Mr. Duquette, Mr. Quarie and Mr. Tice Dejonah pressed invitations to their homes on the captains. The villagers vied with one another for the honor of entertaining the men. The captains and the men, too, visited from house to house telling modestly of their tremendous adventure.

Even the heavens saluted them about ten that night with chain lightning and rolling peals of thunder.

Clark rose early the next morning but had not the heart to shorten the first night of complete comfort the party had had in over two years. He and Lewis waited until the rain ceased about 10 o'clock before rousing their men. It was nearly noon before they moved down the river again.

The 17-star flag snapped briskly in the breeze over Fort Bellefontaine as a thunderous salute from the field pieces roared its welcome. The soldiers of the garrison turned out to honor the forgotten men who were now entering America's hall of immortal fame.

Staying that night at Fort Bellefontaine the excited men rose early the next morning. Clark bought the bewildered Chief She-he-ke his first store-clothes so he could be presented to society. After an early breakfast the party went down to the end of the "heretofore deemed endless Missouri" where it joined the Mississippi.

Ammunition no longer was irreplaceable. The men wasted it freely as they approached St. Louis.

When they reached their journey's end the cheering, rollicking explorers of the wilderness were greeted with a frenzied celebration in their honor. These were not piles of white bones in some distant mountain pass. These men were real, bearded, bronzed, lean and in ragged clothes but conquerors of the great unknown west of the Missouri.

Peter Choteau invited the partner-captains to his home. The men visited from house to house during the afternoon and evening and were given the run of the town. Lewis wrote a note to the postmaster at Cahokia suggesting he delay the mail, which was due to leave, until the captains had time the following day to write letters.

Old friends greeted them. They visited Clark's friend, Major Christy, a tavern keeper. "I sleped but little last night," the captain said ruefully the next day.

Yet both partners rose early and wrote letters — Lewis to Thomas Jefferson and Clark to William Henry Harrison. Anxious to shed their worn and shiny buckskins, they bought cloth and ordered a "tayler" to make them clothes.

Some few people in St. Charles and St. Louis mixed their ink powder with water and wrote letters to friends in other parts of the nation telling of the return of Lewis and Clark. These letters, carried in the mailsacks of river boatmen and by men on horseback traveling the forest trails, scattered the news over the nation.

Ten or twelve days after the captains' return, items began to appear in some of the papers closer to St. Louis.

Often the newspapers would pick up the story verbatim from the columns of a neighboring editor. Typical is the excerpt from "a letter from a gentlemen at St. Charles" dated Sept. 23, 1806. Run first in the Frankfort, Kentucky, Palladium Oct. 9, 1806, it appeared next in Washington, D.C., November 3; in Philadelphia, Pennsylvania, November 7; next in Burlington, Vermont; and finally in the Hart-

219

ford, Connecticut, Courant of November 19, under the bizarre headline "More Wonders. Rocky Mountain Sheep beats the horned frog all hollow." The excerpt was:

> I have the pleasure to inform you of the arrival of Captains Lewis and Clark.

> They were the first white people that ever visited that country. By the best accounts they could get there are about ninety or one hundred thousand inhabitants, [Indians] on the west side of the Rocky mountains; horses without number. It is thought to be a very poor Indian that did not own 300 horses. Not an iron tool among them. — They erected a fort on the sea shore and engraved their names. They have a number of curiosities; among which is a wild sheep; its head and horns weigh about 80 or 90 pounds. He was caught on the Rocky Mountains.

Most of the newspaper men of the day were printer-editors; sensational news reporting had not yet come into its own.

Even President Jefferson, who at last had seen his dream come true, concisely reported to congress December 2, 1806, "The Expedition of Messrs. Lewis and Clarke, for exploring the river Missouri, and the best communication from that to the Pacific Ocean, has had all the success which could have been expected, they have traced the Missouri nearly to its source, descended the Columbia to the Pacific Ocean, ascertained with accuracy the geography of that interesting communication across our continent, learned the character of the country, of its commerce and inhabitants: and it is but justice to say that Messrs. Lewis and Clarke and their brave companions have by this arduous service deserved well of their country."

Thomas Jefferson's primary purpose of strengthening the American claim to the vast territory between Spanish California and the Columbia had been accomplished. His secondary purpose, the study of the life and customs of the Western American Indian tribes was done so well that the Lewis and Clark journals are still a must for student anthropologists.

Three decades later, when the great migration to the west began over the Oregon Trail, the covered wagons followed the route of Lewis and Clark along the Missouri. When the wagon trains struck west overland along the Platte River, they used information secured by the two captains as their guide; and they picked up the actual route of Lewis and Clark on the Columbia River again. The Missouri River route explored and mapped by the captains was the one followed by the early fur traders and gold seekers, who played such an important part in the development of the west.

All the members of the expedition eventually were given land grants, but few settled on them.

SIXTEEN STAR RELIC. This old powder horn was found in 1922 on a Lewis and Clark campsite near Hamilton, Montana. The stars on the flag indicate it was made between 1796 and 1803. It might well have been lost by a member of the expedition.

Bratton fought in the War of 1812, married, fathered ten children. He died at Waynetown, Indiana, in 1841.

Shannon lost a leg in a fight with Indians while trying to return Chief She-he-ke to his tribe. In later years he became a circuit court judge and died at Palmyra, Missouri, while holding court.

Alexander Willard had seven sons, one of whom he named Lewis and another Clark. He crossed the plains by covered wagon and settled in the Sacramento Valley where he died in 1865.

John Colter returned to the wilderness as a trapper and trader. During his travels he discovered Yellowstone Park, which for a time was called Colter's Hell.

George Drewyer and John Potts also returned to the mountain country and both were killed by Blackfeet.

Little is known about the later lives of the other enlisted men.

Sacajawea and Charbonneau lived for a time among the Mandans. Later they separated. Sacajawea wandered here and there and finally died on the Wyoming Shoshone Indian Reservation in 1884. She is buried there beside her adopted son Basil.

Charbonneau spent the remainder of his life in the wild country, serving the fur traders from time to time as an interpreter. He died among the Indians.

Little Baptiste served as a member of several fur-trading expeditions. The name Charbonneau is mentioned in several early journals of trappers, but it is not certain whether it refers to Baptiste or to Toussaint Jr., his half brother.

Sergeant Pryor was leader of the party which unsuccessfully attempted to return Chief She-he-ke to his village in 1807. She-he-ke eventually got home.

Sergeant Ordway married and settled on a farm in Missouri.

Sergeant Gass was wounded in the War of 1812. He married at 60 years of age and had seven children. He died at 90, the last survivor of the expedition.

Both the captains became governors, Clark of Missouri Territory and Lewis of Louisiana Territory. Clark lived comfortably in St. Louis and died there. Lewis became mentally unbalanced. Some historians think he was a suicide. Others claim he was murdered for his money by a Kentucky backwoodsman while on a trip to Washington.

But this was the future. When they celebrated at St. Louis, the explorers only knew that they were safely back in the "U. States."

Most of the men had over two years' pay coming to them. It amounted to $166.00 on the average — a tidy fortune. The captains made arrangements to pay off and discharge their men.

The great American adventure ended September 25, 1806. "A fine morning," Clark said; "We commenced wrightin &c."

222

SALUTE!

A Journal Commenced at River Dubois — monday 14th 1804

may 14th 1804 Showerey day Capt Clark Set out at 3 oclock P m for the western expidition the party Consisted of 3 Serguntes and 38 working hands which maned the Battow and two Progues we Sailed up the missouria 6 miles and incamped on the N. side of the River

Tuseday may 15th 1804 Rainey morning fair wind the later part of the day Sailed 5om and incamped on the N. side some Land Cleared the Soil verry rich

Wensday may 16th 1804 Set out eriley this morning pleasent arrived at St Charles at 2 oclock. P m one Gung fired a Great number of French people Came to See the Boat &c this place is an old French village &c oman

First Page of Floyd's Journal.

Junction of Columbia and Lewis's Rivers,
sketch-map by Clark.

Heads of Clatsop Indians, by Clark—an old man, a young man,
and a woman; and a child in process of having
its head flattened.

Great Falls of the Columbia River,
sketch-map by Clark.

ACKNOWLEDGMENTS

MANY PEOPLE have contributed to the making of this book, but none more than our partners, Albert T. and Genevieve Johnson. Both read the manuscript and made shrewd criticisms which helped us avoid several pitfalls that would have marred the book. Their most valuable contribution, however, was less tangible: it was their great patience with partners who were off somewhere on the Lewis and Clark trail, mentally or physically, when work needed to be done at the business where we make our living.

Mr. Louis True of Montana State College helped with his willingness to take me in a plane over the upper reaches of the Missouri.

John Nelson of Bozeman, Montana, took us to the buffalo jump.

Rush Jordan, president of the State Teachers College at Dillon, Montana, took time off to give me directions on the Lewis and Clark trail over Lemhi.

R. G. Bailey, author, of Lewiston, Idaho, helped us locate landmarks on the upper Clearwater.

Ed McKay of Darby, Montana, helped clear up questions about the Lolo Trail.

Elers Koch, with his infinite knowledge of the Lewis and Clark Expedition aided us as much as his father, Peter Koch, helped Coues and Wheeler nearly 50 years ago.

Mr. Wade Wilson at Kamiah, Idaho, pointed out the Kamiah and Lawyers Canyon campsites.

Mr. Leonard Nelson of Billings, Montana, showed us Indian rock writings, and helped us become amateur archeologists.

Mr. Ronald Todd at the University of Washington library, Northwest section, provided some of our most valuable source material.

Dr. Paul C. Philips at the University of Montana helped locate local areas of the trail.

The Fathers of St. Benedict's College, Atchison, Kansas, aided in locating campsites.

Dr. Mel Jacobsen, anthropologist at the University of Washington, helped us interpret Lewis and Clark's studies of Indian life.

Mr. W. S. Sams and his brother of North Bonneville, Washington, allowed us to prowl over their property to locate the site of an Indian village described by the two captains.

Mike and Laura Lee Greeley of Great Falls, Montana, helped us get information in that area. Bill and Marcia Brown of the same city located White Bear Camp for us.

Al McVay of the Walla Walla, Washington, Chamber of Commerce put us in touch with people who helped us locate the sand dunes mentioned by Lewis and Clark.

Dr. George Savage of the University of Washington, and the members of his class which we attend, gave us constant suggestions, encouragement and helpful criticisms in the development of the manuscript.

Ted and Esther Simpson edited the final draft.

Harry Higman, Seattle author and student of Lewis and Clark, read and criticised the manuscript in its early stages.

The American Philosophical Society generously gave us full permission to quote from the original Lewis and Clark journals and to reproduce the old maps of the expedition.

The Wisconsin Historical Society permitted us to quote from the *Journals of Lewis and Ordway.*

We are grateful to the following for pictures:

Forest Service: deer, page 12; antelope, page 35; beaver dam, page 56; grizzly bear, page 65; bighorn sheep, page 77; Indian postoffice, page 169; moose, page 171.

Fish and Wildlife Service: geese, page 51.

Washington State Game Department: beaver, page 56; cougar, page 93; salmon, page 130; geese, page 135; ducks, page 136; goat, page 178.

Verne Peterson of Hamilton, Montana: rattlesnake, page 72; ground squirrel, page 175.

Linfield Studio, Bozeman, Montana: elk, page 144.

Bob and Ira Spring, of Seattle, Washington: Mount St. Helens, page 136.

Harleth Steinke, Seattle, Washington: lightening, page 222.

Fred Milkie, Seattle, Washington: photographs of artifacts and powder horn.

Kurt Willanetz colored the photograph on the jacket.

Northwest Mapping Service prepared the maps.

Carter Lucas, of Seattle, did the fine art work depicting the incidents of the expedition.

ALBERT AND JANE SALISBURY

INDEX

Abraham Lincoln, Fort, 57, 58
Ahsakka, Idaho, 140
Aird, James, 213
Aitken, 215
Amahte Arzza, 68
American Philosophical Society, 4
Antelope, 35, 55, 62, 112
Arickara Indians, 41, 50, 209
Armstead, Montana, 97, 112, 114
Armstrong, John, 4
Arrow Creek, 65
Arrow heads, 207, 208
Arrow Rock, 22, 46
Astoria, Oregon, 147, 153, 154
Atchison, Kansas, 24, 26, 44
Badlands, 54
Bad River, 38, 45
Bannack, Montana, 178
Baptiste, 55, 58, 76, 133, 168, 170, 183, 188, 190, 222
Beacon Rock, 133, 134, 158
Beaver, 56, 57, 59, 62, 183
Beaverhead River, 91, 92, 102, 104, 112, 114, 176, 180, 183
Beaverhead Rock, 92, 112, 114, 183
Bellefontaine, Fort, 218
Benton, Fort, 79
Beuffe de Medicine, Chief, 38
Bighole River, 91, 92, 114, 183
Big Horn River, 188
Bighorn Sheep, 76, 87, 89
Big Sandy, 79, 80
Big Timber River, 184
Billings, Montana, 186, 191, 192
Bismark, North Dakota, 57, 58
Bitter Root Mountains, 114, 139, 169, 174, 178
Bitter Root Valley, 113, 115, 116, 117, 137, 176, 179, 193
Black Bear, 61
Blackfoot Indians, 79, 100, 110, 177, 194, 195, 197, 199, 200, 201, 202, 203
Blackfoot Prairie, 194
Blackfoot River, 176, 195
Blowing Fly Creek, 62
Boleye, John, 11
Bonhommie Island, 213
Bonner, Montana, 176
Bonneville, Capt. B. L. E., 140
Bonneville Dam, 140
Boone, Daniel, 21, 44
Borgne, Chief, 50
Bozeman, Montana, 191, 192

Bozeman Pass, 85, 181, 182, 191
Bratton, William, 11, 28, 32, 55, 60, 149, 152, 168, 170, 183, 222
Broken Arm, Chief, 165, 166, 167
Buffalo, 53, 55, 63, 74, 88, 114, 180, 195, 196, 210
Burr, Aaron, 213
Butte, Montana, 138
Cactus, 77
Camas Flower, 118, 119, 120, 138
Camas, Washington, 140
Cameahwait, Chief, 105, 106, 110
Cannon Beach, Oregon, 151
Canoe Camp, 121
Canoes, 122, 140, 164, 165, 185
Cascades, 133, 138
Cape Disappointment, 153
Catherine, Queen of Russia, 4
Cathlamet Indians, 155, 156
Celilo Falls, 131, 132, 140
Charbonneau, 47, 48, 53, 55, 58, 60, 62, 73, 76, 83, 89, 104, 108, 170, 183, 185, 187, 209, 222
Carbonneau River, 55
Chickadee, 198
Chinook Canoes, 142, 146
Chinook Indians, 146, 150
Choteaux, Auguste, 215
Christy, Major, 219
Clark, William—
  description of, 5
  carbuncle on ankle, 89
  on Lemhi, 108
  explores Yakima River, 124
  Governor, 222
Clark, George Rogers, 4, 5
Clarks Canyon, 102, 114
Clarkston, Washington, 139
Clatsop, Fort, 145, 147, 153, 154, 155, 156, 174
Clatsop Indians, 146
Clearwater River, 120, 121, 122, 125, 127, 139, 164, 165, 166
Cloudburst, 76
Collins, John, 11, 18, 23, 55, 170
Colter, John, 11, 23, 34, 36, 55, 74, 110, 116, 172, 206, 222
Colt Killed Camp, 138
Columbia River—
  headwaters of, 83, 86, 99
  junction with Snake, 127, 128, 140
  expedition down mouth of, 129, 130, 141, 143

Columbus, Montana, 191
Comowool, Chief, 155
Continental Divide, 96, 99, 100, 101, 106, 176, 194
Cook, Captain, 4, 55
Copperhead snakes, 44
Courant, Hartford, Connecticut, 220
Coutau, 215
Crazy Mountains, 182
Crow Indians, 191
Cruzatte, Peter (Pierre), 27, 31, 55, 62, 70, 78, 131, 158, 166, 204
Culbertson, Alexander, 79
Custer, General George A., 57, 191
Cutbank, Montana, 176, 177
Cut Nose, Chief, 165
Deer, 12, 59, 143, 156
Deer Island, 156
Dejonah, Tice, 218
DeLorn, Henry, 215
Devils Raceground, 20
Dickson, Joseph, 205, 206
Dillon, Montana, 94, 112
Doniphan, Kansas, 44, 46
Dorion, 21, 34, 38, 215
Double Ditch historic site, 57, 58
Drewyer, George, 11, 23, 27, 28, 31, 32, 55, 60, 63, 68, 89, 90, 94, 95, 96, 102, 150, 158, 162, 172, 197, 200, 202, 222
Duquette, 18, 20, 218
Durfee, Commander E. H., 79
Ecola State Park, Oregon, 153
Elk, 143, 144, 150
Experiment, The, 78
Fields, Joseph, 11, 23, 25, 32, 55, 68, 83, 149, 195, 197, 198, 200, 202
Fields, Reuben, 11, 18, 28, 55, 83, 90, 195, 197, 198, 200, 202, 213
Flathead Indians, 115, 116, 120, 177, 179
Floyd, Sergeant Charles, 11, 20, 23, 25, 27, 28, 29, 30, 31, 44, 46, 215
Floyds River, 31
Fort Rocks, 131, 157
Fortunate Camp, 112
Fourth of July Creek, 23
Fraser River, 4
Frazier, Robert, 11, 55, 83, 168
Friends Massacre, 79, 201
Gallatin, Albert, 86
Gallatin River, 86, 87, 112, 114, 190
Gallatin Valley, 85, 176, 181

INDEX

Gasconade River, 21

Gass, Sergeant Patrick, 11, 15, 18, 21, 23, 32, 36, 49, 55, 64, 78, 89, 108, 111, 116, 118, 120, 124, 131, 133, 137, 141, 148, 176, 197, 203, 204, 222

Gates of the Mountains, 114

Geese, 51, 59, 124, 133, 135

Giant Springs, 72, 73, 80

Gibson, George, 11, 32, 55, 68, 149, 183, 185, 187

Goodrich, Silas, 11, 55, 68

Grand River, 46

Grasshopper Creek, 178

Gravelines, 41, 61, 215

Gray, Robert, 5

Great Falls, Montana, 79, 80, 176, 177, 195, 215

Grey Eyes, Chief, 210

Grizzly bear, 42, 59, 68, 78, 188, 197

Gros Ventre Indians, 47, 48, 69, 86, 106, 206

Ground Squirrel, 175

Hall, Hugh, 11, 18, 23, 55, 183, 187, 188

Hamilton, Alexander, 215

Hamilton, Montana, 221

Hancock, Forest, 205, 206

Harrison, William Henry, 219

Hauser Lake, 112

Heart River, 42

Helena, Montana, 82, 112, 114, 138, 191

Hellgate Canyon, 177

Hill, Captain, 146

Horse Prairie Creek, 90, 96, 102, 104

Horses, 95, 97, 100, 105, 110, 187

Houston, Sam, 44

Howard, Thomas P., 11, 55

Independence Creek, 23, 26, 44, 46

Independence, Missouri, 43

Indian gambling, 145

Indian implements, 207, 208, 211, 212, 214

Jefferson River, 87, 89, 90, 91, 99, 114

Jefferson, Thomas, 3, 4, 5, 36, 53, 86, 152, 203, 209, 213, 220

Jessaume, Rene, 43

John Day River, 131

Jordon, President Rush, 112

Joseph, Chief, 138

Judith River, 88

Kamiah, Idaho, 140, 167, 168, 170

Kansas City, Missouri, 44

Kansas Indians, 44

Kansas River, 21

Kickapoo Indians, 20

La Biche, 28, 55, 106, 183, 187

La Charette, 21, 42, 216

La Clede, 13

La Croy, 215

La Hontan, Baron, 3

La Liberte, 28

Last Chance Gulch, 112

Lawyers Creek, 166

Ledyard, John, 4

Lemhi Pass, 96, 98, 99, 101, 108, 110, 114

Lemhi River, 106, 108

Le Page, 55, 170

Lewis and Clark Pass, 177, 194, 196

Lewis and Clark River, 143, 147

Lewis, Meriwether—
  description of, 5
  meets Shoshones, 95
  at Lemhi, 106
  31st birthday, 108
  ill, 118
  fight with Blackfeet, 197
  wounded, 202
  death of, 222

Lewiston, Idaho, 139

Lisa, Manuel, 9, 13

Little Missouri, 55

Livingston, Montana, 191

Logan, Montana, 88

Lolo Hot Springs, 114, 173, 174

Lolo, Montana, 114

Lolo Pass, 114, 116, 117, 138, 167, 168, 170, 171, 174

Loma, Montana, 79, 80

Lost Trail Pass, 114

Louisiana Purchase, 5, 9, 13, 44

Lovejoy, Elijah, 43

Lower Brule Indian Reservation, 45

Mackenzie, Alexander, 4

Madison, James, 86

Madison River, 86, 87, 112, 114

Maha Indians, 28, 40

Mandan, Fort, 47, 48, 52, 55, 58, 206

Mandan Indians, 42, 43, 48, 50, 53, 57, 58, 206, 209

Mandan, North Dakota, 41, 48

Marias River, 64, 65, 69, 70, 80, 176, 177, 197, 201, 202

Maria Wood, 69

Marthasville, Missouri, 44

Megler, Washington, 142, 153

Memaloose Island, 133, 157

Meriwether Camp, 82

Michaux, Andre, 4

Miles City, Montana, 192

Missoula, Montana, 114, 138, 176

Missouri River, junction with—
  Mississippi, 13, 14, 16
  Big Bend of, 38
  Grand Detour, 45, 46
  Great Falls of, 68, 71, 80
  three forks of, 83, 84, 86, 87
  headwaters of, 112

Mobridge, South Dakota, 45, 46, 217

Moncacht-Ape, 4

Mosquitoes, 83

Mussellshell River, 62

McClallon, Captain John, 216

M'Clellan, Robert, 215

McCracken, Hugh, 43

McNeal, Hugh, 11, 55, 90, 95, 96, 98, 148, 197

Nemaha River, 25

Newman, John, 11, 23, 41

Nez Perce Indians, 108, 118, 120, 162, 165, 166, 170, 174, 177, 195

Niobrara River, 45

North Bonneville, Washington, 140

Northwest Company, 43

Old Bawd, 150, 152, 155

Old Toby, 107, 111, 124, 166

Otoe Indians, 27, 28

Ordway, Sergeant John, 11, 17, 18, 21, 25, 28, 32, 34, 49, 55, 57, 64, 74, 78, 89, 104, 110, 115, 116, 118, 127, 133, 145, 156, 166, 168, 172, 183, 197, 203, 209, 216, 218, 222

Oregon Trail, 220

Orofino, Idaho, 140

Ovando, Montana, 177

Owen, Fort, 138

Pacific Ocean—
  arrival at, 137
  winter on, 141
  views of, 151

Packers Meadow, 114, 119, 138, 174

Palladium, Frankfort, Kentucky, 219

Panther, 70, 93

Partizan, Chief, 38

Pasco, Washington, 128, 139

Pataha Valley, 162, 163

Peck, Campbell K., 79

Peck, Fort, 79

Pierre, South Dakota, 39, 45, 46

Pirogues, 15, 41, 55, 60, 62, 63, 64

Platte River, 27

Pomeroy, Washington, 163

Pompey's Pillar, 153, 188, 189, 191, 192

Portage Camp, 73

Portage Creek, 73

Portland, Oregon, 153

Potlatch River, 165

INDEX

Potts, John, 11, 18, 55, 83, 170, 172, 179, 216, 222
Powder River, 188
Powell Ranger Station, 114, 138
Prairie dog, 37
Proulx, Mr., 218
Pryor, Sergeant Nathaniel, 11, 34, 53, 55, 64, 143, 180, 183, 187, 188, 190, 204
Rainier, Mount, 136
Rattlesnake, 62, 72, 73, 79, 94
Rattlesnake Cliffs, 94, 104, 114, 183
Red Rock Creek, 102
Reed, Moses B., 11, 28, 31
Riparia, Washington, 139
Robertson, John, 11
Rocky Mountains—
    first sight of, 63
    Gates of, 81, 82
    from the west, 166
    description of, 172, 174
    last view of, 188
Rocky Mountain Goat, 174, 178
Rogers Pass, 177, 196
Rosebud River, 191
Rosses Hole, 113, 114, 179
Rush, Dr. Benjamin, 86
Rush's Pills, 86, 104, 118
Sacajawea, 45, 47, 48, 53, 55, 58, 62, 70, 73, 76, 79, 83, 86, 90, 95, 102, 104, 108, 112, 129, 133, 142, 143, 145, 148, 149, 168, 176, 180, 183, 185, 209, 221
Sacajawea Park, 128, 139
Sacrifice Cliff, 191
St. Charles, Missouri, 18, 19, 20, 43, 46, 218
St. Helens, Mount, 136
St. Joseph, Missouri, 44
St. Louis, Missouri, 7, 13, 218, 222
St. Mary's Mission, 138
Salmon, 120, 127, 130, 132, 153, 156, 168
Salmon, Idaho, 109, 114
Salt making, 148, 149, 153, 154
Sams, Will, 140

Sauvies Island, 133
Sawyers, 29
Scannon, 8, 11, 23, 27, 32, 62, 63, 158, 195, 197
Seaside, Oregon, 149, 153, 154
Seattle, Washington, 15
Serviceberry Valley, 104
Shannon, George, 8, 32, 34, 36, 55, 90, 172, 183, 187, 213, 216, 222
She-he-ke, 49, 206, 209, 213, 218, 222
Shields, John, 11, 32, 34, 55, 90, 95, 96, 102, 123, 158, 180, 183, 185, 187
Shelby, Montana, 177
Shoshone Cove, 108, 110
Shoshone (Snake) Indians, 48, 73, 83, 86, 89, 95, 100, 102, 106, 108, 110, 116, 124, 177
Sioux City, Iowa, 30, 44
Sioux Indians, 50, 53
Snake River, 100, 124, 126, 127, 128, 139, 162
Spirit Mound, 33, 44, 46
Sugar Lake, 24, 46
Sweathouse treatment, 168
Tabeau (Taboe), 41, 218
Tayon, Charles, 7, 8, 20
Teton River, 39
Teton Sioux Indians, 38, 39, 40, 210
Texas Rapids, 139
The Dalles, Oregon, 157
Thompson, Robert B., 11, 55
Three Forks, 81, 83, 86, 106, 113, 114, 176, 179, 183
Tillamook Head, 149, 154
Tillamook Indians, 146
Trail Creek, 96, 98, 180
Travellers Rest Camp, 114, 116, 138, 174
Twin Bridges, Montana, 93, 114
Twin Sisters Rocks, 140, 160
Twisted Hair, Chief, 165, 166
Umatilla River, 131
Union, Fort, 58
Vancouver, Fort, 140

Verendrye, 44
Vermilion River, 32
Vermilion, South Dakota, 44
Vigilante Road, 112, 114
Vultures, 156
Wahkiakum Indians, 146
Walla Walla Indians, 158, 160, 161
Walla Walla River, 160, 161, 162
Walla Walla, Washington, 161
Wallula, 140, 159
Warvington, Richard, 11, 55
Washburn, North Dakota, 51, 58
Washington, George, 5
Washtucna, Washington, 139
Wayne, Anthony, 5, 8
Weippe Prairie, 118, 119, 170, 172
Werner, William, 11, 18, 55, 143
Wheeler, Olin D., 139
White Cliffs, 65, 66, 67, 80
White Bear Camp, 74, 75, 78, 80
White Bear Islands, 74, 75, 195
Whitehall, Montana, 87
Whitehouse, George, 11, 17, 18, 21, 25, 50, 55, 78, 86, 90, 111, 120
Wilkinson, General, 215
Willard, Alexander, 11, 25, 55, 203, 222
Williston, North Dakota, 57, 58, 79
Willow Run Camp, 74
Windsor, Richard, 11, 18, 55, 183, 187
Wiser, Peter, 11, 55, 110, 168
Wishram, Washington, 132
Wood River, 8, 10, 13, 18
Worrell, Lieutenant Stephen, 8
Yakima Indians, 127, 129, 166
Yakima River, 131
Yankton Sioux Indians, 34, 35
Yankton, South Dakota, 35, 45, 213
Yellept, Chief, 160, 161
Yellowstone River—
    mouth of, 57, 58
    Clark on, 176
    Rivers Across, 184
York, 11, 23, 40, 41, 76, 83, 106, 176, 183